AAT

Qualifications and Credit Framework (QCF)

AQ2013

LEVEL 2 CERTIFICATE IN ACCOUNTING

COMBINED TEXT AND QUESTION BANK

Work Effectively in
Accounting and
Finance

2015 Edition

For assessments from September 2015

Third edition June 2015
ISBN 9781 4727 2178 5

Previous edition
ISBN 9781 4727 0912 7

British Library Cataloguing-in-Publication Data
A catalogue record for this book is available from the British
Library

Published by
BPP Learning Media Ltd
BPP House
Aldine Place
London
W12 8AA

www.bpp.com/learningmedia

Printed in the United Kingdom by Page Bros
Mile Cross Lane
Norwich
NR6 6SA

Your learning materials, published by BPP Learning Media Ltd,
are printed on paper sourced from traceable sustainable sources.

CONTENTS

A NOTE ABOUT COPYRIGHT

Dear Customer

What does the little © mean and why does it matter?

Your market-leading BPP books, course materials and e-learning materials do not write and update themselves. People write them on their own behalf or as employees of an organisation that invests in this activity. Copyright law protects their livelihoods. It does so by creating rights over the use of the content.

Breach of copyright is a form of theft – as well being a criminal offence in some jurisdictions, it is potentially a serious breach of professional ethics.

With current technology, things might seem a bit hazy but, basically, without the express permission of BPP Learning Media:

- Photocopying our materials is a breach of copyright

- Scanning, ripcasting or conversion of our digital materials into different file formats, uploading them to facebook or emailing them to your friends is a breach of copyright

You can, of course, sell your books, in the form in which you have bought them – once you have finished with them. (Is this fair to your fellow students? We update for a reason). Please note the e-products are sold on a single user licence basis: we do not supply 'unlock' codes to people who have bought them secondhand.

And what about outside the UK? BPP Learning Media strives to make our materials available at prices students can afford by local printing arrangements, pricing policies and partnerships which are clearly listed on our website. A tiny minority ignore this and indulge in criminal activity by illegally photocopying our material or supporting organisations that do. If they act illegally and unethically in one area, can you really trust them?

BPP LEARNING MEDIA'S AAT MATERIALS

The AAT's assessments fall within the **Qualifications and Credit Framework** and most papers are assessed by way of an on demand **computer based assessment**. BPP Learning Media has invested heavily to ensure our materials are as relevant as possible for this method of assessment. In particular, our **suite of online resources** ensures that you are prepared for online testing by allowing you to practise numerous online tasks that are similar to the tasks you will encounter in the AAT's assessments.

Resources

The BPP range of resources comprises:

- **Texts**, covering all the knowledge and understanding needed by students, with numerous illustrations of 'how it works', practical examples and tasks for you to use to consolidate your learning. The majority of tasks within the texts have been written in an interactive style that reflects the style of the online tasks we anticipate the AAT will set. When you purchase a Text you are also granted free access to your Text content online.

- **Question Banks**, including additional learning questions plus the AAT's sample assessment(s) and a number of BPP full practice assessments. Full answers to all questions and assessments, prepared by BPP Learning Media Ltd, are included. Our question banks are provided free of charge online. (Note that for this unit the Text and Question Bank have been combined into one book.)

- **Passcards**, which are handy pocket-sized revision tools designed to fit in a handbag or briefcase to enable you to revise anywhere at anytime. All major points are covered in the Passcards which have been designed to assist you in consolidating knowledge.

- **Workbooks**, which have been designed to cover the units that are assessed by way of computer based project/case study. The workbooks contain many practical tasks to assist in the learning process and also a sample assessment or project to work through.

- **Lecturers' resources**, for units assessed by computer based assessments. These provide a further bank of tasks, answers and full practice assessments for classroom use, available separately only to lecturers whose colleges adopt BPP Learning Media material.

This Combined Text and Question Bank for *Work Effectively in Accounting and Finance* has been written specifically to ensure comprehensive yet concise coverage of the AAT's **AQ2013** learning outcomes and assessment criteria.

Each chapter in the Text at the front contains:

- Clear, step by step explanation of the topic

- Logical progression and linking from one chapter to the next

- Numerous illustrations of 'how it works'

- Interactive tasks within the text of the chapter itself, with answers at the back of the book. In general, these tasks have been written in the interactive form that students can expect to see in their real assessments

- Test your learning questions of varying complexity, again with answers supplied at the back of the book. In general these test questions have been written in the interactive form that students can expect to see in their real assessments

The Question Bank at the back contains these key features:

- tasks corresponding to each chapter of the Text. Some tasks are designed for learning purposes, others are of assessment standard

- the AAT's practice assessments and answers for and further BPP practice assessments

The emphasis in all tasks and test questions is on the practical application of the skills acquired.

Supplements

From time to time we may need to publish supplementary materials to one of our titles. This can be for a variety of reasons, from a small change in the AAT unit guidance to new legislation coming into effect between editions.

You should check our supplements page regularly for anything that may affect your learning materials. All supplements are available free of charge on our supplements page on our website at:

http://www.bpp.com/about-bpp/aboutBPP/StudentInfo#q4

Customer feedback

If you have any comments about this book, please email nisarahmed@bpp.com or write Nisar Ahmed, AAT Head of Programme, BPP Learning Media Ltd, BPP House, Aldine Place, London W12 8AA.

Any feedback we receive is taken into consideration when we periodically update our materials, including comments on style, depth and coverage of AAT standards.

In addition, although our products pass through strict technical checking and quality control processes, unfortunately errors may occasionally slip through when producing material to tight deadlines.

When we learn of an error in a batch of our printed materials, either from internal review processes or from customers using our materials, we want to make sure customers are made aware of this as soon as possible and the appropriate action is taken to minimise the impact on student learning.

As a result, when we become aware of any such errors we will:

1) Include details of the error and, if necessary, PDF prints of any revised pages under the related subject heading on our 'supplements' page at: www.bpp.com/about-bpp/aboutBPP/StudentInfo#q4

2) Update the source files ahead of any further printing of the materials

3) Investigate the reason for the error and take appropriate action to minimise the risk of reoccurrence.

A NOTE ON TERMINOLOGY

The AAT AQ2013 standards and assessments use international terminology based on International Financial Reporting Standards (IFRSs). Although you may be familiar with UK terminology, you need to now know the equivalent international terminology for your assessments.

The following information is taken from an article on the AAT's website and compares IFRS terminology with UK GAAP terminology. It then goes on to describe the impact of IFRS terminology on students studying for each level of the AAT QCF qualification.

Note that since the article containing the information below was published, there have been changes made to some IFRSs. Therefore BPP Learning Media have updated the table and other information below to reflect these changes.

In particular, the primary performance statement under IFRSs which was formerly known as the 'income statement' or the 'statement of comprehensive income' is now called the 'statement of profit or loss' or the 'statement of profit or loss and other comprehensive income'.

What is the impact of IFRS terms on AAT assessments?
The list shown in the table that follows gives the 'translation' between UK GAAP and IFRS.

UK GAAP	IFRS
Final accounts	Financial statements
Trading and profit and loss account	**Statement of profit or loss (or statement of profit or loss and other comprehensive income)**
Turnover or Sales	Revenue or Sales Revenue
Sundry income	Other operating income
Interest payable	Finance costs
Sundry expenses	Other operating costs
Operating profit	Profit from operations
Net profit/loss	Profit/Loss for the year/period
Balance sheet	**Statement of financial position**
Fixed assets	Non-current assets
Net book value	Carrying amount
Tangible assets	Property, plant and equipment

UK GAAP	IFRS
Reducing balance depreciation	Diminishing balance depreciation
Depreciation/Depreciation expense(s)	Depreciation charge(s)
Stocks	Inventories
Trade debtors or Debtors	Trade receivables
Prepayments	Other receivables
Debtors and prepayments	Trade and other receivables
Cash at bank and in hand	Cash and cash equivalents
Trade creditors or Creditors	Trade payables
Accruals	Other payables
Creditors and accruals	Trade and other payables
Long-term liabilities	Non-current liabilities
Capital and reserves	Equity (limited companies)
Profit and loss balance	Retained earnings
Minority interest	Non-controlling interest
Cash flow statement	**Statement of cash flows**

This is certainly not a comprehensive list, which would run to several pages, but it does cover the main terms that you will come across in your studies and assessments. However, you won't need to know all of these in the early stages of your studies – some of the terms will not be used until you reach Level 4. For each level of the AAT qualification, the points to bear in mind are as follows:

Level 2 Certificate in Accounting

The IFRS terms do not impact greatly at this level. Make sure you are familiar with 'receivables' (also referred to as 'trade receivables'), 'payables' (also referred to as 'trade payables'), and 'inventories'. The terms sales ledger and purchases ledger – together with their control accounts – will continue to be used. Sometimes the control accounts might be called 'trade receivables control account' and 'trade payables control account'. The other term to be aware of is 'non-current asset' – this may be used in some assessments.

Level 3 Diploma in Accounting

At this level you need to be familiar with the term 'financial statements'. The financial statements comprise a 'statement of profit or loss' (previously known as an income statement), and a 'statement of financial position'. In the statement of profit or loss the term 'revenue' or 'sales revenue' takes the place of 'sales', and 'profit for the year' replaces 'net profit'. Other terms may be used in the statement of financial position – eg 'non-current assets' and 'carrying amount'. However, specialist limited company terms are not required at this level.

Level 4 Diploma in Accounting

At Level 4 a wider range of IFRS terms is needed, and in the case of Financial statements, are already in use – particularly those relating to limited companies. Note especially that a statement of profit or loss becomes a 'statement of profit or loss and other comprehensive income'.

Note: The information above was taken from an AAT article from the 'assessment news' area of the AAT website (www.aat.org.uk). However, it has been adapted by BPP Learning Media for changes in international terminology since the article was published.

ASSESSMENT STRATEGY

Work Effectively in Accounting and Finance (WKAF) is a skills unit where students are required to demonstrate they have the skills to be able to work effectively in an organisation. Working practices will vary between organisations and as such students will be required to demonstrate that these skills are transferable to all organisations.

The assessment is divided into eleven standalone tasks, which cover all of the learning outcomes and assessment criteria within the unit standards. All eleven tasks will be computer marked. Assessment duration is 2 hours.

Workplace evidence

With guidance and support from training providers, students can provide workplace evidence to be assessed locally by their training provider. The local assessor (training provider) will be required to ensure that all assessment criteria are covered.

Competency

For the purpose of assessment the competency level for AAT assessment is set at 70 per cent. The level descriptor in the table that follows describes the ability and skills students at this level must successfully demonstrate to achieve competence.

QCF Level descriptor	Summary
	Achievement at Level 2 reflects the ability to select and use relevant knowledge, ideas, skills and procedures to complete well-defined tasks and address straightforward problems. It includes taking responsibility for completing tasks and procedures and exercising autonomy and judgement subject to overall direction or guidance.
	Knowledge and understanding
	■ Use understanding of facts, procedures and ideas to complete well-defined tasks and address straightforward problems
	■ Interpret relevant information and ideas
	■ Be aware of the types of information that are relevant to the area of study or work
	Application and action
	■ Complete well-defined, generally routine tasks and address straightforward problems
	■ Select and use relevant skills and procedures
	■ Identify, gather and use relevant information to inform actions
	■ Identify how effective actions have been
	Autonomy and accountability
	■ Take responsibility for completing tasks and procedures
	■ Exercise autonomy and judgement subject to overall direction or guidance

AAT UNIT GUIDE

Work Effectively in Accounting and Finance (WKAF)

Introduction

This unit is about students developing the generic work skills which they can transfer into any working environment. The fundamentals of working as an accounting technician, such as ethical behaviours, numeracy, literacy and communication skills are also covered. The unit does not presume any prior knowledge of accounting. The skills learnt in this unit will be invaluable for all areas of further study.

The purpose of the unit

This unit is about gaining a range of transferable knowledge and skills which will enable the student to work effectively within an accounting environment. Students will be able to work independently or as part of a team. It aims to prove a good standard of literacy and numeracy skills which is essential for the workplace. This unit also develops the student's understanding and awareness of ethical and sustainable values within an organisational context.

Learning objectives

Students will develop an understanding of how to work within the accounting/payroll environment and of what is expected of them at this level. The role of the accountancy or payroll functions (referred to as the 'accounting department' in these guidance notes) must be fully understood. They will develop an insight into how their role interacts with others and how they are expected to communicate with effective results. Students will develop an awareness of the need for ethical and sustainable values within organisations and how these are practically applied in an organisational or departmental context.

Learning outcomes

The unit consists of six learning outcomes.

QCF unit	Learning outcome	Assessment criteria	Covered in Chapter
Work Effectively in Accounting and Finance	Understand the accounting or payroll function within an organisation	Policies, procedures The accounting department Reporting lines Contributions of people and functions	**2, 3**

QCF unit	Learning outcome	Assessment criteria	Covered in Chapter
	Be able to use a range of communication skills	Literacy and communication skills Numeracy	**4, 5**
	Work independently or as part of a team	Time management and prioritisation of work Impact of work on others Dissatisfaction within your working environment	**6, 7**
	Develop skills and knowledge to meet personal and organisational needs		**8**
	Understand ethical values and principles		**9**
	Understand sustainable values		**9**

Delivery guidance: *Work Effectively in Accounting and Finance*

Topics and procedures that can be tested:

1a Policies, procedures

Organisational policies and procedures influence most aspects of working practices and students should understand the importance of adhering to organisational requirements in order to ensure efficiency and effectiveness.

Students should be familiar with a range of policies and procedures, which are appropriate to the work of the accounting department including both accounting function specific policies and procedures and organisation wide policies and procedures. In addition students should be able to explain how these policies and procedures affect them, their colleagues and the organisation as a whole.

Students may be required to identify policies and procedures which would and which would not be applicable to an employee working in an accounting department. They may also have to understand how specific policies and procedures are applied in the working environment for an accounting department employee.

1b The accounting department (including payroll function)

One of the roles of the accounting department is to provide a service to other departments within the organisation. In order to fulfil this role the accounting department will both provide information to and receive information from other departments. Therefore, students should be familiar with a range of different departments/functions within an organisation and the types of information each may provide to, or receive from, the accounting department.

The wider aspects of providing a service to others within and outside of the organisation should also be considered such as checking expense and petty cash claims, providing budgetary information, paying suppliers, providing an internal audit function, payment of wages, conducting reference checks on new customers and advising others within the organisation of the financial implications of actions.

The accounting department will also provide information to external stakeholders for example banks, debtors, creditors, trade associations, auditors, regulators, government departments etc. Students should be aware of the types of information that may be requested by stakeholders for example, forecast figures, profit figures, cash forecasts, sales and purchases ledger information, sales figures, wages and salary details, VAT figures.

Students should be aware that the primary role of the staff of the accounting department is to provide information to support the other functions within the organisation. Information provided should be complete, accurate, timely and fit for purpose. Students may be required to explain each of these qualities, why they are important and the implications to the accounting department, the organisation and the stakeholders if information is **not** complete, accurate, timely and fit for purpose. Students must understand that the role of an accounting department extends beyond the production of statutory financial statements. Therefore, good communication is very important in order to liaise effectively with other departments within the organisation and also with external stakeholders. Students may be assessed on the types of information provided by the accounting department or received by the accounting department.

1c Reporting lines

Different organisations will have different structures and varying practices in relation to reporting lines. Students will be expected to recognise the most likely reporting lines within a given scenario and to appreciate that some line managers may have multiple employees reporting to them and some employees may report to more than one person depending upon the nature of the work. To this end students will be expected to be familiar with reporting structures within the accounting department and within organisations, and the fact that these structures tend to operate in a hierarchical manner and within a functional chain of command, with job holders reporting to those fulfilling more senior roles in the organisation. Students will also be expected to understand that those in the most senior position in an accounting department are likely to report to the most senior officer heading up the organisation, and that job titles will vary from one organisation to another.

Students should be familiar with typical structures and reporting lines within an accountancy practice and also within the accounting department of an organisation.

Students may have to complete an organisation chart which focuses on the accounting department and the reporting lines within the department but which also includes some reporting lines beyond the accounting department. They may also have to identify to whom they would refer specific queries.

Students may be assessed on the consequences of not reporting to the appropriate person and the consequences to the organisation of not having determined reporting lines in place.

1d Contributions of people and functions

Students should be aware of a range of appropriate actions by those in the accounting department in order to contribute to the smooth running and efficiency of the accounting department and success of the organisation as a whole. These actions will range from something as simple as treating each other with respect to producing procedural information for accounting tasks.

Students may be assessed on how to achieve efficient practice both within the accounting department and across the organisation and how they may contribute to the smooth running and efficiency of both the accounting department and the organisation as a whole; for example ensuring everyone is trained to perform their job role, ensuring staff adhere to organisational standards of performance, ensuring sufficiency of staff at all times etc.

Students should have a basic understanding of how the accounting department manage working capital (daily funds) and ensure the organisation remains solvent. They should understand that the accounting department has a very important role in ensuring an organisation can meet its debts as they fall due (solvency) and so it will provide information about the cash flow implications the organisation's activities, details of when debts should be repaid, and of its activities, details of when debts should be repaid, and how to minimise the cost of finance and the long and short term sources of finance. Students may have to identify actions of those within the accounting department to manage working capital and ensure the organisation remains solvent.

In addition to providing information to all departments within an organisation, the accounting department will ensure that all regulatory requirements for the preparation and recording of financial and payroll information are adhered to. This will ensure future liabilities (fines and remedial work) are minimised. Accounting department staff are required to ensure their working practices comply with legislative requirements and hence should be aware of the appropriate actions they should take to contribute to the legal compliance of the organisation. Students may have to identify actions of those within the accounting department which assist in ensuring organisational compliance with legal and regulatory requirements and explain the consequences of deviation from legal and regulatory requirements. Students should understand that many areas of work and working practices are subject to legislation and regulation for example health and safety, data protection, presentation of financial information, employment law, working practices etc. Students are also required to understand that they must maintain confidentiality in both business and social situations.

Students will be required to have knowledge and understanding of working practices which do and which do not comply with legislation and regulatory frameworks. They will **not** be required to have an in depth knowledge of specific legislation.

2a Literacy and communication skills

Students will be able to communicate effectively using business communications, including informal business reports, letters, emails and memos, using literacy skills which would be expected at Level 2. Students will be required to ensure the communication is professionally presented, the content is technically correct and is clearly understandable and projects the appropriate corporate image.

Students must show they understand that business language is more formal than everyday language. Attention to detail is important with all communications and students should have the ability to identify errors, for example, spelling, grammar, and format, as well as to recognise when the language used is inappropriate for the communication. Students will be required to proof read information in order to identify errors and ascertain appropriate prose.

In the identification of errors learners should not identify as incorrect words which have a valid alternative spelling, for example if the word 'organisation' was used in a task this would **not** be classified as an error (even though learners may be more familiar with the spelling as 'organization') as it is a valid alternative spelling of the word. However, if the word has a different meaning e.g. 'right' and 'write', 'your' and 'you're' in the context of the communication then students would be required to identify that which is incorrect in that situation. When students are required to identify errors of spelling or technical nature, reference to identifying incorrect words includes any collection of letters or digits. For example invoice numbers such as 'SB1234' and '8730' would be considered a 'word' in the context of identifying an incorrect word.

Understanding the format and content of formal business reports, letters, emails and memos is an important skill for the student at this level and will not only help when progressing to other levels, but also in everyday life situations.

Students should recognise that an important part of communication is considering the requirements of the recipient. Students should understand that content, presentation and the clarity of communication will impact on business relationships.

The component parts/sections of formal business reports, letters, emails and memos are assessable both in terms of format and content. Students may be required to construct all or parts of a communication from a range of information and data or review a form of communication and draw conclusions. Where students are provided with a selection of data/information, they will be required to interpret the data/information and identify that which is relevant for inclusion in the communication. Students may also be required to match the given data/information to component parts of the communication. All communications will be expected to be presented professionally, include content which is technically correct and clearly understandable and project the correct image for the organisation.

Formal business reports

In addition to the general points above, students will be expected to understand the order, purpose and content of the following seven sections: title/title page, summary/executive summary, introduction, main body/findings, conclusions, recommendations and appendices. Students may be asked to select the most appropriate title, summary, introduction, findings, conclusions, recommendations or appendices for a given scenario, and hence to interpret given data/information. They will be assessed on the completion of one or more sections of a business report from given information.

Letters

In addition to the points above, students will be expected to know how to present a letter, use appropriate business language, include addresses of the sender and recipient, a date, subject heading, opening and closing paragraphs, and appropriate salutation and complementary close.

Email and memo

In addition to the general points above, students should recognise that the language used in emails and memos is usually less formal, but still courteous, and presentation is less dictated. Salutations and complementary closes are usually informal and varied, however still appropriate for use in business. Students will be expected to complete an email or memo from given information. As emails are less prescribed in structure where students are required to structure an email the house style will be provided.

2b Numeracy

Students will be required to demonstrate numeracy skills required at Level 2. They will be able to use relevant skills including (but not confined to) addition, subtraction, multiplication, division, percentages, proportions, ratios, averages, and fractions. Students will need to understand the rounding of numbers.

For example:

- 18.499 rounded to the nearest whole number would be 18 and the same number rounded to two decimal places would be 18.50.

- 18.500 rounded to the nearest whole number would be 19 and the same number rounded to one decimal place would be 18.5.

- 18.649 rounded to the nearest whole number would be 19 and the same number rounded to two decimal places would be 18.65.

Students will need to be able to convert numbers in the written form to those numbers presented numerically.

For example:

Two million, seven hundred thousand = 2.7 million = 2,700,000.

Students may be required to perform calculations which involve utilising a range of skills as detailed above; for example, students may be required to use both percentages and subtraction to answer a task.

3a Time management and prioritisation of work

Students will be required to demonstrate they have the necessary skills to work independently and manage their own workload effectively in order that outcomes are achieved in the most efficient manner. They must understand the importance of planning and prioritising work tasks, changing priorities as appropriate, meeting agreed deadlines, adhering to agreed working practices and respecting confidentiality.

Workload planning may include regular scheduled tasks, ad hoc tasks and urgent tasks to which students will be required to respond appropriately. To help achieve outcomes students should be able to select and use the most appropriate planning aid from a range including, schedules, diaries, calendars, electronic programmes, charts, to do lists and action plans. They may be assessed on selecting and prioritising and reprioritising set tasks for a prescribed period of time and using a given planning aid.

It is important that staff keep their colleagues and line managers informed of their progress against deadlines. If a deadline is not met, or is in danger of not being met, this will need to be communicated to the appropriate person at the earliest opportunity and in a correct manner. Students may have to explain the consequences for themselves, colleagues or the organisation as a whole of not completing a prescribed task on time. They may also be assessed on how and when to with others when meeting work deadlines can be difficult.

3b Impact of work on others

Students must understand that in any organisation staff do not work in isolation. There are consequences following the non-completion of work which will affect the whole team, their department or others within the organisation, or external customers and suppliers. Students should understand that when work is not completed, completed badly, or completed late, this will have a negative effect on colleagues and resources, and may damage internal and external business relationships. They must be able to identify what these consequences are and how they will affect their team, the department and possibly the organisation as a whole. They will understand the procedures to follow if unexpected problems are encountered.

They will understand the procedures to follow if unexpected problems are encountered.

Students may be assessed on the characteristics of an effective team such as having; good communication channels, shared values, a mix of complementary skills, clear leadership, common purpose and clearly defined roles and responsibilities. The student's contribution to the success of the team in achieving its objectives and the impact on the team, department or organisation of working or not working effectively as a team are also assessable. The skills, attributes and behaviours of team members which contribute to a high performing team should also be understood. Students should understand how the completion of work to an acceptable standard, and within agreed deadlines; will have a positive effect on colleagues and the team as a whole, and on organisational resources. They will understand that one small task within their own remit contributes to a much larger activity and so cannot be viewed in isolation.

3c Dissatisfaction

Dissatisfaction as a result of working conditions, management, working styles or personality can occur within any team and a basic understanding of the causes and the types of dissatisfaction which impact upon team performance is required. These may range from issues regarding the siting of desks, or the temperature in the office environment, to a belief that some staff are being treated less equally than others, or that some are putting in more effort than others. Students may be assessed on the circumstances in which they can resolve dissatisfaction themselves and when and to whom they should refer issues which are outside their authority.

Dissatisfaction has a damaging effect on individuals, teams and organisations as a whole. Effective management of dissatisfaction can contribute to better team work and more productive working relationships and outputs. Students should be able to recognise causes of dissatisfaction and to identify issues that they should resolve themselves and those which they should refer to their line manager. They should be able to suggest ways of resolving issues and, where this is not possible, they should know what procedure to follow to refer the issue.

4 Personal Development

Students should understand that continuing professional development (CPD) is an important requirement for every member of the accounting department. It is the responsibility of every individual to maintain CPD appropriate to their current job role and their career aspirations. The sources of CPD (including, but not limited to, qualifications, technical updates, training courses/seminars/webinars, research, internet, publications, job shadowing, secondment) available and the requirement to record CPD must be fully understood. Students should appreciate the benefits to every member of the accounting profession in maintaining and recording their own CPD.

Students should be able to explain why it is necessary for those working in the accounting department to complete adequate CPD on an on-going basis and the benefits to the organisation and the individual of maintaining adequate CPD. Students should be able to describe the consequences to the organisation and the individual of not maintaining appropriate and sufficient CPD.

The effect the development of staff has on improving organisational efficiency must be understood by the student in order to recognise that CPD is an investment and not a burden. Students should recognise the concept of assessing individual strengths and weaknesses in skills knowledge and experience and know how weaknesses can be addressed by setting developmental objectives. They should understand that strengths and weaknesses may be identified as a result of an employer performance review. Students should be aware that a Personal Development Plan (PDP) is commonly used to record the evaluation of current skills and the identification of personal development objectives. Students should be able to select appropriate development opportunities and define timescales for the completion of activities to match identified weaknesses or personal development targets. In addition to a focus on weaknesses students should understand that strengths may be built upon through undertaking appropriate development activities. Students must also be aware that staff development is a cost to the organisation but it must also produce benefits for the organisation.

Students should understand that it is important to be able to set clear SMART (specific, measurable, achievable, realistic, time bound) objectives which are agreed with the line manager. Students may be assessed on the importance of having SMART objectives. The selection of appropriate activities to meet developmental objectives may include, but is not confined to, formal training courses, online training, self-research, spending time with others within the organisation and achieving formal qualifications. Students should also understand how coaching, mentoring and job shadowing can improve performance and how these processes benefit both the individual and the organisation as a whole.

Students should understand that coaching is generally used in the short term, for example when an organisation is introducing a new system or when developing staff in specific areas/skills. Mentoring is generally used for longer term development of its employees for example when ensuring it has the workforce to meet future needs of the organisation.

5 Ethical behaviour

Students should be able to identify and explain the fundamental ethical principles of integrity, objectivity, equality, professional competence and due care, confidentiality, and professional behaviour. Students should be able to apply the fundamental principles of ethical behaviour to business situations. Subsumed within these fundamental principles is the concept of equality and whilst learners will not be expected to identify this as a fundamental principle they will be expected to understand equitable behaviour expected of those working in an accounting department and how equality translates into acceptable business practice.

Students should be able to explain how conflicts of interest may arise, the importance of declaring any potential conflicts of interest and how one can minimise the potential for conflicts of interest to arise. Students may have to identify situations when there is potential for conflict of interest to arise and they may be required to suggest appropriate course(s) of action.

Students will be assessed on the importance of maintaining confidentiality at all times and the consequences of not maintaining confidentiality of information. Understanding should extend to the requirement for observing confidentiality from a legal perspective but also in developing business relationships. Students must understand the need to respect client, supplier, colleague and wider departmental and organisational confidentiality. The consequences to the individual and the organisation of not observing confidentiality should be recognised. Students should be able to recognise situations when information may be disclosed and situations when disclosure of information should be prohibited.

6 Sustainability initiatives and the resultant benefits

Students should be able to understand Corporate Social Responsibility in its simplest form. In particular students should be able to explain the three pillars of sustainability and the types of policies and procedures an organisation may adopt which support sustainability from an environmental, social and economic perspective. Environmental areas of focus include the actions an organisation or those within the accounting department can take in respect of environmental care, recycling, energy, resource consumption and travel efficiencies. Social areas of focus include actions an organisation takes in respect of its charitable and local community work. Economic areas of focus include the need for the organisation to be financially stable to provide continued employment to its employees and meet shareholder expectations. Students should be aware of the need for organisations to use resources efficiently to enable the organisation to be profitable both now and in the future. Initiatives may include supporting staff in social initiatives to benefit the local community and the wider world. Students should also be aware of the need for organisations to not only monitor their own initiatives but also the policies and practices in organisations with which they have business dealings such as customers and suppliers.

Students should be able to explain the impact and benefits of sustainable initiatives on the environment, stakeholders and the organisation. Students should be able to identify and explain the financial implications and resulting savings/benefits of sustainable initiatives.

For example, if an organisation decides to ensure its packaging is recyclable this will have a positive effect on the environment however this may involve costs for the organisation in sourcing different suppliers and perhaps different costing for the packaging.

chapter 1:
INTRODUCTION

---

chapter coverage 📖

In this chapter, we look at the information you are likely to be provided with in the assessment and the tasks you may be expected to perform. We then set out the approach you should take in order to pass the assessment and the ways in which the Combined Text and Question Bank will help you.

The topics covered are:

✎ Your assessment

✎ Passing the assessment

✎ How this Combined Text and Question Bank will help you to pass

---

YOUR ASSESSMENT

Your computer based assessment set by the AAT will be for two hours and will consist of eleven tasks covering the learning outcomes for the unit (reproduced in the front of this Combined Text and Question Bank).

The assessment will normally be delivered online and will be computer marked. In order to pass you need to demonstrate competence in all parts of the assessment.

Each task in the assessment is independent and you will not need to refer to previous tasks in your answer. You should aim to complete every task.

The tasks

Detailed below is information (provide by the AAT) on the new format of the AAT assessment for *Work Effectively in Accounting and Finance* (WKAF) for assessments from the end of September 2013.

WKAF

Assessment	Computer based test
Time allocation	120 minutes (2hrs)
Result	Provisional result available the same day
Tasks	**Tasks names/topics**
1.1	Accounting function, policies and procedures
1.2	Reporting lines and contributions of people and functions
1.3	Literacy (email or memo)
1.4	Time management and prioritisation of work
1.5	Literacy (letter)
1.6	Numeracy
1.7	Personal Development
1.8	Literacy(report)
1.9	Impact of work on others and dissatisfaction
1.10	Ethical behaviour
1.11	Sustainability initiatives and the resultant benefits

The AAT practice assessment is included in this Combined Text and Question Bank – have a quick look at the sorts of questions it contains before you read the rest of this chapter.

PASSING THE ASSESSMENT

The assessment will require you to demonstrate that you have the skills necessary to work effectively in an organisation.

Before you sit the assessment

Before you sit the assessment you will need to:

- Read and understand the contents of this Combined Text and Question Bank

- Carry out the tasks within each chapter and answer the questions at the end of each chapter

- Develop your communication and numeracy skills where necessary

- Work through all the questions in the Question Bank

- Complete both the AAT and BPP practice assessments available at the end of this Combined Text and Question Bank so that you have practised the types of task you may be asked to carry out

You should also try the AAT assessment in the online environment by visiting the relevant page on the AAT website. More information on the assessment is given below.

Sitting the assessment

When you sit the assessment you will need to:

- Read each task carefully and ensure that you do precisely what is asked; just as you would in a real working environment

- Answer the tasks, ensuring you follow any Computer Based Test (CBT) related instructions very carefully

In the bullet point above, we referred to CBT instructions. These are instructions on how to enter numbers, how many options to choose, how to select options etc.

These instructions can appear in two places:

- At the start of the assessment, applying to the whole assessment
- Within an individual task, applying to only that task

The AAT practice assessment available on their website at the time of writing this Combined Text and Question Bank (reproduced later in this Combined Text and Question Bank) allows students to practise an assessment similar to the real assessment they will encounter.

It provides an example of the introductory instructions you may encounter in your assessment and we have included this below (taken from the AAT practice assessment on the AAT website).

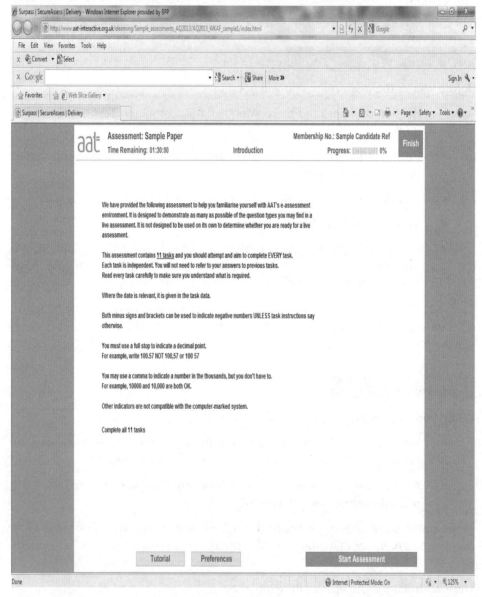

It is very important you read the instructions on the introductory screen and apply them in the assessment. You don't want to lose marks when you know the correct answer just because you have not entered it in the right format.

A full stop is needed to indicate a decimal point. We would recommend using minus signs to indicate negative numbers and leaving out the comma signs to indicate thousands, as this results in a lower number of key strokes and less margin for error when working under time pressure. Having said that, you can use whatever is easiest for you as long as you operate within the rules set out for your particular assessment.

You have to show competence in all sections of assessments and you should therefore complete all of the tasks. Don't leave questions unanswered.

When it comes to instructions within individual tasks, you must take note of any task specific instructions. For example you may be asked to enter a date in a certain format, to enter a number to a certain number of decimal places or to select a certain number of options from several options.

HOW THIS COMBINED TEXT AND QUESTION BANK WILL HELP YOU TO PASS

The purpose of this Combined Text and Question Bank is to help you to pass the assessment. Accordingly, it:

- Contains the technical information you need

- Explains the relevance of the information that may be provided to you in the assessment and how to interpret various documents that you are likely to see

- Explains the different documents you need to be familiar with to complete tasks in the assessment

- Sets out the skills you need to develop and suggests ways of improving your performance

- Contains tasks within each chapter, and 'test your learning' questions at the end of each chapter, which will provide you with the opportunity to test your understanding

- Contains additional tasks for each chapter in the Question Bank

- Contains both the AAT practice assessment and an additional BPP practice assessment which will give you a chance to practise tasks similar to those you will encounter in the real assessment

Tasks in this Combined Text and Question Bank

As you progress through the Chapters of this Combined Text and Question Bank, you will be asked to complete a number of tasks and tests. Many of the tasks will be similar to those you will encounter in the real assessment, however you will notice that some are more involved than those you will see in the AAT practice assessment. These tasks are there to aid your overall understanding of a topic area and to ensure you understand processes in their entirety.

For example, we may ask you to draft a business email in full even though, due the nature of a Computer Based Test that is marked only by the computer, you would not be asked to do so.

Instead you may, for example, be asked to select appropriate phrases/words for use in such an email. However, being tested on how to prepare business documents in full will help with your overall understanding, while still helping to prepare you for the tasks in the assessment. These tasks will also provide you with the everyday skills you need when working in an business accounting environment.

Don't forget, once you have progressed through the chapters, as well as the AAT assessment, you can practise tasks similar to those you will find in the real assessment using the Question Bank and the BPP practice assessment at the back of this Combined Text and Question Bank.

CHAPTER OVERVIEW

- The computer based assessment set by the AAT will consist of nine tasks covering the learning outcomes for the unit.

- Before you sit the assessment you will need to be familiar with the contents of this Combined Text and Question Bank and to have developed your skills.

- You should complete both the AAT and BPP practice assessment before the real assessment and try the AAT practice assessment provided on the AAT website in the online environment.

- When you sit the assessment you must take the same degree of care as you would in your real working environment.

- You must read any introductory instructions carefully and apply them throughout the assessment.

- You must follow any task specific instructions carefully, such as instructions to enter numbers to a specific number of decimal places or to select a particular number of options from several options.

chapter 2:
THE ROLE OF THE FINANCIAL FUNCTIONS

chapter coverage 📖

This chapter introduces the role of accounting, payroll and other financial functions within an organisation, and explores the various ways in which those individuals in financial roles contribute to business objectives.

It consists principally of information that you may need to refer to when carrying out the tasks in your assessment.

The topics covered are:

✍ Functions within an organisation

✍ The financial functions

✍ Contribution to business objectives

✍ The legal framework

FUNCTIONS WITHIN AN ORGANISATION

An organisation may perform a number of different activities in pursuit of its objectives, depending on what type of organisation it is. These activities may include:

- The research, design and development of products and services (R & D)

- Production (in a manufacturing organisation) or other operational activities (such as providing services)

- The marketing and selling of products or services to customers

- The development and use of information technology systems for the business (IT)

- The purchasing or procurement of materials and supplies used in the business

- The warehousing, transport and distribution of finished products (sometimes called 'logistics')

- The management of the organisation's staff or 'human resources' (HR) (sometimes referred to as personnel)

- Administrative and clerical activities supporting the running of the business

- The management of the organisation's finances and financial information (accounting and finance)

Some of these functions, known as LINE FUNCTIONS, are directly involved in the main service-delivering or revenue-earning activity of the business: they directly fulfil the organisation's primary purpose and objectives. Examples include the production, marketing, sales and distribution functions.

Other functions, known as STAFF FUNCTIONS, exist to support the line functions in fulfilling their objectives: providing them with the resources, systems and information they need to perform their activities efficiently and effectively. Examples include IT, HR (personnel), administration – and accounting and finance.

THE FINANCIAL FUNCTIONS

You may already have some grasp of the role and tasks of the accounting and payroll functions from your work, or studies for other Units. However, it may be helpful to have an overview here, with a particular focus on how accounting and payroll 'fit' within the organisation as a whole.

The accounting function

The role of the accounting function is to support the organisation's other functions by compiling, preparing and providing complete, accurate and timely information on all financial aspects of the business. Business accounting is the process of:

- Recording all financial transactions carried out by an organisation

- Summarising the transactions to present a financial picture which supports both:

    - Accountability to investors and other external interested parties (or 'stakeholders'), and

    - Internal management decision-making about the business

Financial accounting

FINANCIAL ACCOUNTING is mainly concerned with the processing and recording of transactions (bookkeeping), and the production of financial statements for users outside the business.

The financial accounts function firstly records transactions between the business and its customers, suppliers, employees and owners. These records then enable any business of any size, from a 'one man band' sole trader to a large professional partnership or company, to prepare its financial statements:

- A statement of financial position or SFP
- A statement of profit or loss or SPL and
- Other primary financial statements and notes if required

The law requires the financial statements of companies in particular:

- To be presented in compliance with detailed regulations;

- To be audited, where necessary (to ensure that they represent a true and fair picture of the financial position of the company); and

- To be lodged with a government official called the Registrar of Companies, so that they can be made available to suppliers, investors and other interested parties

Similarly, taxation records of all businesses must be compiled according to detailed rules, and submitted to HM Revenue & Customs.

Management accounting

MANAGEMENT ACCOUNTING is mainly concerned with the production of financial reports to assist managers in all the business's functions in

- Measuring performance
- Making decisions
- Generally running the business

Management accounts are not regulated by law: managers can ask for whatever records and reports they think will be helpful to them: unlike financial accounts, these are purely internal documents, and, for commercial reasons, are mostly kept strictly confidential.

Management accountants perform activities such as cost analysis, cost control, budget preparation and budgetary control (monitoring actual performance against budgeted performance).

Information flows to and from the accounting function

The accounts department needs to receive information from all the other departments of the organisation, in order to compile reports and records on the financial implications of their activities. Examples include: cost estimates; production schedules; expenses claim forms; records of staff work and overtime hours (eg timesheets or clock cards); changes to staff details (eg pay grades, leave arrangements, promotions); invoices to process and pay; purchase orders and goods received notes to check against invoices – and so on.

In return, the accounts department provides information to all the departments of the organisation on the financial implications of their activities: wage/salary costs; current costs against expected/budgeted costs; expenses; cash flow summaries; customer debts (for the sales or credit control department); revenue and profit forecasts; and so on.

Payroll

The payroll function may be a section of the accounting function. It is concerned solely with payroll processing, including tasks such as: the calculation of gross pay from salary data and timesheets etc; the calculation of tax, National Insurance and other deductions; preparing payslips; making appropriate returns to external agencies such as HM Revenue & Customs; making up wage packets with cash, or preparing data for direct credit of salaries to employees' bank accounts (BACS); distributing payslips to employees; preparing payroll statistics.

Task 1

From what we have just said about the tasks performed by the payroll function, see if you can determine from the following list :

(a) Information required by the payroll department from the HR department and other departments where people are employed

(b) Information provided by the payroll department to other internal and external parties.

Tick the appropriate box.

Information	Required by payroll from other departments	Provided by payroll to other parties
Total wage/salary and overtime costs		
Employees' National Insurance details		
Date of commencement of employment		
Information for individual employees about pay and deductions		
Statutory returns to external agencies		
Standard and overtime hours worked		
Wage/salary and overtime rates		

Other financial functions

An organisation may have separate sections for other (or more specific) aspects of finance, such as:

- Cash administration and money-handling tasks, such as cashiers, petty cash and banking

- Financing (eg managing loans and other sources of finance)

- Taxation

The financial functions as service and support providers

It is important to realise that people in finance do not work in isolation. Whatever their specific tasks, the financial functions as a whole provide a service to all the other functions in the organisation: supporting them in the fulfilment of their objectives – and through them, the objectives of the organisation as a whole. The 'customers' of the financial function include all of the other functions in the organisation.

Financial information

The main role of the accounting and payroll functions is to support managers and staff in other functions by preparing and providing complete, accurate and timely information on the financial implications of their activities.

The accounting function provides information about the financial implications of operational activities such as holding inventory, making sale and purchase transactions. The accounting function shows:

- What the activities cost (both immediately and over time);

- What revenues, returns or benefits they earn;

- What the balance is between cash coming into and cash going out of the business (CASH FLOW); and

- What the cash flow situation means for:

  - The availability of day-to-day finance to maintain organisational activity (this is the WORKING CAPITAL required by the business) and

  - The ability of the organisation to pay its debts when they fall due (its SOLVENCY)

For other functions of the organisation, this information highlights important decision factors such as:

- What they can afford to spend
- What they need to earn
- How profitable and efficient their activities are, and
- Where their profitability or efficiency may need to be improved

The payroll function similarly provides information about the financial implications of employing people:

- How much cash is needed to pay them

- How much it costs to keep the organisation staffed and operating, and

- Whether there is potential to increase – or a need to decrease – staffing or staff costs

Accounting information therefore supports managers in making sound decisions about the resources available to them. It equips managers for:

- PLANNING: helping them to understand the financial implications of their planned activities; what resources are or are not available to implement them (ie whether their planned activities are affordable); and their potential costs and benefits in financial terms (ie whether the planned activities are cost-effective and worthwhile).

- CONTROL: helping them to measure the results of their activities against their plans; whether they came in 'on budget' (in line with anticipated costs); whether they earned the expected revenues and profits; whether resources were efficiently used; and so on.

Complete, accurate and timely information

In fulfilling this service role, the important thing for the finance function is not the quantity of information but its quality. In order to be of maximum benefit to the organisation, the information provided must be complete, accurate and timely;

- **Complete**: including all data relevant to the purpose for which the information will be used

- **Accurate**: factually and numerically correct, and to an appropriate level of detail for the purpose for which the information will be used

- **Timely**: delivered at the right time for the information to be meaningful and used to support decision-making and action

CONTRIBUTION TO BUSINESS OBJECTIVES

We have looked at what the financial functions broadly 'do' within the business: that is, their role. But why is this important? What does it contribute to the fulfilment of business objectives and the success of the organisation as a whole?

By providing financial information to all functions and departments within an organisation, those in accounting, payroll and other financial roles make an important contribution in three key areas:

- The smooth running and efficiency of the business
- The working capital and solvency of the business
- The legal compliance of the business

Smooth running and efficiency

Information is the life blood of all business activity. The financial functions play an important role in the smooth running of the organisation, through supplying high-quality, timely information to support managers in their decision-making.

Organisational EFFICIENCY is about achieving objectives with the minimum use of resources (particularly, the minimum unnecessary expenditure or waste).

The financial functions support efficiency by providing information for planning (so that resources are not used thoughtlessly) and control (so that the use of resources is checked, and managers are held accountable for how they are used).

- In collaboration with other department managers, the accounting function produces annual budgets and long-term plans, which act as guidelines and benchmarks for measuring the performance of different departments, and the organisation as a whole.

- They periodically provide departments with information on how they are actually performing or progressing, for comparison against the benchmarks set out in plans and budgets.

- This enables departments to *measure* how effectively and efficiently they are operating, and to identify areas where performance and efficiency can be improved – or where forecasts and plans may need to be adjusted to be more realistic.

Working capital and solvency

The accounting function has a very important role in managing WORKING CAPITAL: the day-to-day finance which is used to keep the business running. Working capital basically comprises:

Inventory		Payables
Receivables	LESS	Overdrafts
Cash		

The accounting function provides information to other departments about the CASH FLOW implications of their activities: what money is flowing into the organisation and when (in income) and what money is flowing out of the organisation and when (in expenditure), and the balance between these two flows at any given time. The organisation and its various functions can then:

- Know what working capital is available for use at any given time

- Ensure there is an adequate cash balance at any given time by managing:

    - The level of inventory, by ensuring that no more is held than is necessary

    - The collection of receipts from receivables, by operating a strict credit control policy

    - The making of payments to payables, by negotiating favourable credit terms

- Plan to earn extra revenue, or to raise finance (eg by taking out a loan or selling assets), if required to maintain adequate reserves of working capital

By closely monitoring the cash balances of the business, the accounting function also has a very important role in ensuring the SOLVENCY of the organisation: that is, its ability to meet its short-term and long-term debts as they fall due.

The accounting function provides information to the organisation about:

- Debts that are owed to the organisation and when they are due to be paid by customers (receivables)

- The availability of cash to cover payables when they fall due

- The cost of raising finance (eg through share capital, loans and other means) to keep the organisation solvent

Legal compliance

The preparation of financial and payroll information and records is subject to complex legal and regulatory requirements.

It is yet another important role of the accounting and payroll functions to ensure that all legal and regulatory requirements are met. This helps the organisation:

- To benefit from a positive reputation and track record of financial integrity and legal compliance (which may, in turn, enable the organisation to attract and retain investors, customers, suppliers and high quality staff)

- To avoid or minimise liabilities arising from non-compliance, including: financial penalties (in the form of fines) or even imprisonment; the cost of remedial work to bring records and returns into compliance; the loss of shareholder, share market and regulator confidence; and the burden of more onerous scrutiny in future

For your assessment, you won't be required to demonstrate knowledge of specific legislation. However, you will be expected to demonstrate an awareness that payroll and accounting staff are always required to follow the rules and procedures laid down by their organisation to ensure that working practices comply with legislative and regulatory requirements.

In order to ensure compliance, the organisation should:

- Make all employees aware of the importance of compliance

- Brief all employees on their roles and responsibilities under the law (and up date the briefings as the law changes), from the induction of new recruits onwards

- Base organisational policies and procedures (and related employee training) on legal requirements

- Put in place checks and controls, to monitor and ensure compliance

HOW IT WORKS

Southfield Electronics is a supplier of a wide range of consumer electronics appliances to specialist retailers and department stores.

The accounting function regularly supplies the Sales department with information including:

- Breakdowns of sales revenue by region – so that plans can be made to increase sales effort in under-performing regions (and reward the best-performing sales teams)

- Reports on the value of the inventory of goods held in the warehouse

- Reports on sales revenue to date (compared with budget) and cost of sales activity to date (compared with budget)

- Reports on the amounts owing by each retail customer, and when they fall due, highlighting overdue amounts

The accounting function supplies the Purchasing department with:

- Reports on expenditure to date (compared with budget) on bought-in materials and services for the organisation

- A list of discrepancies between supplier invoices and purchase orders – so that Purchasing can query this with suppliers

Recent information has highlighted two issues of concern.

First, there is too much inventory of some product lines in the warehouse. The value of this inventory is falling due to deterioration and developments in consumer electronics. The Sales and Production managers have been alerted to the need either to 'push' the slow-moving product lines harder to customers *or* to adjust production plans to produce fewer items.

Meanwhile, cash flow summaries have highlighted another problem. The Purchasing department accepts 30-day credit terms from suppliers, and insists that they be paid strictly on time. However, the Sales department is giving customers 60 days' credit, and is reluctant to press them for payment. Southfield Electronics is giving money out more readily than it is getting money in – reducing its working capital and creating a threat to its solvency, since its cash reserves are small. The Accounts manager decides to call a meeting to discuss the need for longer credit terms with suppliers *and* stricter credit control with customers.

Task 2

As an accounts clerk at Southfield Electronics, you have been asked by the Chief Accountant to send a brief email to the Sales Manager, Hailey Skommett, notifying her of the cash flow situation, explaining its relevance to the Sales department. Today's date is 13/06/X2.

The partially completed email is shown below.

EMAIL

To: hskommett@southfield.co.uk

From: yourname@southfield.co.uk

Date: 13/06/X2

Subject: Cash flow and credit control issues

I'm sure you know how important it is to maintain [▼] cash flow, so that the organisation has sufficient day-to-day funds to maintain its operations and pay its [▼]. Recently, however, Southfield has been paying out money to suppliers [▼] than it has been collecting money from customers. The Sales department obviously has a key role in this, through its credit control policies. The Chief Accountant is keen to review this issue with you and the [▼].

Kind regards

YN

Complete the email using words from the picklist below.

Picklist
receivables
negative
positive
payables
faster
slower
Purchasing Manager
Production Manager

THE LEGAL FRAMEWORK

Organisations operate within a framework of laws which is very broad in scope, and deals with a range of specific issues. While you don't have to know about specific legislation in detail for this Unit, you are expected to appreciate the *importance* of an organisation's compliance with the law of the land or region in which it operates.

Compliance with all areas of the law is important because:

- The law is there to protect people from loss and suffering, and ensure minimum acceptable standards of management.

- There may be financial penalties (eg fines, compensation) and operational penalties (eg loss of licence) for non-compliance.

- Non-compliance can damage the reputation of the organisation, and its ability to attract investors, customers and staff.

- Non-compliance can lead to burdens and costs of corrective action, closer scrutiny in future and so on.

For an organisation in the UK, the main sources of law are UK statutes (or Acts of Parliament), EU Directives issued by the European Union, and regulations made under those laws.

It is the responsibility of every member of an organisation to comply with legislation (where you could reasonably be expected to be aware of provisions, as relevant to your job role) – and to monitor and ensure compliance within the area of your responsibility. For example, you have a personal duty not to discriminate against others; not to misuse personal data held on file; not to break health and safety rules; not to engage in criminal activities such as theft or assault at work – and to take appropriate steps if you see anyone else doing so.

As a member of an accounting or payroll function, you also have a shared duty to support the organisation's compliance with requirements for financial controls, records and reports.

The following are some examples of areas regulated under UK and EU law – many of which will have their equivalents in the legal regimes of other parts of the world.

Area of the law	Examples
How the organisation does business	*Contract law*: what constitutes a valid contract, and how rights and obligations under a contract can be enforced
	Data protection and confidentiality: what personal data organisations can legitimately hold and use, to protect the privacy of individuals
	Intellectual property: protecting the rights of the originators of product designs, written texts and artistic works, by preventing their copying and exploitation by others
How the organisation treats its employees	*Employment protection*: protecting employees from unfair dismissal and redundancy practices
	Health and safety: protection of employees and visitors in the workplace
	Working conditions, pay and benefits: minimum standards for remuneration, working hours and so on
	Diversity and equal opportunity: protection against harassment and discrimination at work on the grounds of sex, sexual orientation, race, religion, age or disability
Responsibilities to shareholders/stakeholders (Company law and corporate governance)	Duties of directors of the company
	Keeping accounts and registers
	Preparing and auditing financial statements
	Preparing and circulating annual reports and accounts
Responsibilities to the State	Collection and payment of taxes including VAT to HM Revenue & Customs (HMRC)
	Compilation and provision of reports and returns

Regulatory control

In addition to legislation, there has been an increase in the guidance, monitoring and control of organisational practices through 'watchdog' bodies, voluntary Codes of Practice and industry standards.

- Regulatory bodies oversee the activities of businesses in various areas: examples include the Accounting Standards Board (ASB) and the Health and Safety Executive.

- Codes of Practice may be agreed by industry representative or advisory bodies. For example, there are standards covering the reporting of financial performance (International Financial Reporting Standards) and the verification of reports by auditors (International Standards on Auditing).

- Professional bodies (like the chartered accountancy bodies and the AAT) develop and enforce standards of competence, ethical conduct and continuing professional education in their members.

CHAPTER OVERVIEW

- An organisation pursues a wide range of activities in pursuit of its objectives, and these activities are generally grouped as specialist 'functions'.

- Line functions (such as production and sales) directly further the primary activities of the business, while staff functions (such as accounting and finance) support them by providing resources, policies and information.

- The financial functions in an organisation include financial accounting, management accounting and payroll.

- Their main role is to support managers and staff in other functions by preparing and providing complete, accurate and timely information on the financial implications of their activities (including employing people).

- By providing this information, people in financial roles make an important contribution to the smooth running and efficiency of the business (by supporting planning, control and decision-making); the solvency of the business (by managing working capital, highlighting the cash flow implications of activity, and providing information about debts and the availability of funds to cover them); and the legal compliance of the business (in areas such as financial controls, records and statements).

- Accounting and payroll staff are always required to follow the rules and procedures laid down by their organisation to ensure that legislative and regulatory requirements are complied with.

- Legal compliance embraces not just accounting and payroll practices, but the conduct of the organisation and its employees, in areas such as data protection, health and safety at work, employment protection, equal opportunities and corporate governance.

Keywords

Line functions – activities or departments, such as production and sales, which directly further organisational objectives

Staff functions – activities or departments, such as accounting and finance, HR (Personnel) and IT, which support line functions in their objectives

Financial accounting – activities mainly concerned with the processing and recording of transactions and the production of financial statements for users outside the business

Management accounting – providing financial information to support management decision-making

Cash flow – amounts of cash flowing into and out of the organisation

Working capital – day-to-day finance required for operational activities

Solvency – the ability of the organisation to pay its debts when they fall due

Planning – using information about availability, costs and benefits of resources in order to make decisions about what will be done to achieve the organisation's objectives

Control – using information about activities that have taken place in order to hold managers accountable for those activities and to make decisions about how future activities should take place

Efficiency – achieving objectives with the minimum amount (and minimum waste) of resources

TEST YOUR LEARNING

Test 1

Which THREE of the following would be a staff function within an organisation?

Human resources ☐

Manufacturing ☐

Stores control ☐

Accounting and finance ☐

Information technology ☐

Test 2

Match the elements of accounting (on the right) to either financial accounting or management accounting.

Production of financial statements

Financial accounting

Prepares information for internal use

Processing and recording transactions

Management accounting

Prepares information for external use

Information for managers to make decisions

Test 3

Which of the following might be typical tasks involved in payroll?

The calculation of gross pay ☐

Purchasing supplies ☐

The calculation of tax, National Insurance and other deductions ☐

Preparing payslips ☐

Bank reconciliations ☐

Paying cash into the bank ☐

Making up wages, or preparing data for direct credit (BACS) ☐

Writing cheques ☐

Distributing payslips to employees ☐

Test 4

Which two of the following are elements of efficiency?

Providing a service at the least possible cost	☐
Minimum wastage	☐
Paying the minimum wage to employees	☐
Achieving objectives with minimum use of resources	☐

Test 5

Which TWO of the following laws, regulations or standards are likely to be most relevant to staff working in the financial accounts department of a UK retail business selling clothes in the UK?

Health and safety regulation	☐
Pollution emission regulations	☐
HMRC VAT rules	☐
Regulations over the export of goods	☐

chapter 3:
THE ORGANISATIONAL FRAMEWORK

---

chapter coverage 📖

This chapter looks at the organisational framework for working effectively in accounting and finance roles, including reporting structures and various organisational policies and procedures that may apply to your work. It also explains how to use an organisation chart.

The topics covered are:

- ✎ Organisation structure
- ✎ Identifying reporting lines
- ✎ Organisational policies and procedures

ORGANISATION STRUCTURE

ORGANISATION STRUCTURE is the 'shape' of an organisation, which reflects a number of decisions about how it will function most efficiently, including:

- How the organisation's tasks are grouped and divided to form different units, such as functions, departments and sections. This may be done on the basis of function (marketing, production, finance), geography (eg countries or sales territories) or product types.

- How power, authority and responsibility are allocated to different levels and positions in the organisation. This creates a hierarchy or CHAIN OF COMMAND, whereby authority flows 'down the line' from senior management to each level of the organisation – and accountability and reports flow back up.

- How different units, tiers and positions in the organisation are linked by lines of communication and co-operation – so that their plans and activities can be co-ordinated towards the achievement of overall objectives, and so that individuals and teams receive the information and resources they require to play their part.

Organisation charts

ORGANISATION CHARTS are often used to illustrate the formal structure of an organisation or function. In their most basic form, they use boxed or unboxed *captions* to indicate particular units (eg the Accounting Function) or positions (eg Accounts Manager) and linking lines to indicate the relationships and communication between them.

Vertical lines link different tiers or levels, illustrating chains of command (downwards) and reporting lines (upwards).

- Instructions, orders and work requests flow down the chain of command from people with more authority (superiors) to those with less authority (subordinates).

- Reports flow back up the line – because subordinates are ACCOUNTABLE to superiors for the tasks they have been given. Queries may also flow back up the line, if subordinates need to seek or confirm instructions. Certain decisions may have to be 'referred' back up the line if subordinates lack the authority to handle them themselves.

- Your LINE MANAGER is your immediate superior, following the vertical line of command: this is the person directly responsible for requesting work from you and to whom you report directly.

Horizontal lines link units/positions at the same level of the organisation, which are grouped together under the 'umbrella' of the next level up. Units/positions linked in this way need to communicate and co-ordinate their work to meet their shared objectives. They may occasionally be required to work together in CROSS-FUNCTIONAL TEAMS for projects requiring special co-ordination.

A horizontal line joining a vertical line from the side is often used to show 'staff' relationships, where a unit or position doesn't have direct authority 'over' the next tier down – but exercises influence by giving expert advice, or developing and enforcing policies or procedures, in relevant areas of work.

An IT department may exercise influence over other departments' IT systems development and data security procedures, say – while an accounts department may impose policies for budgeting, invoicing, payment authorisations, expenses claims and so on.

HOW IT WORKS

The organisation chart for Southfield Electrical is as follows, showing how the finance function fits into the overall scheme of things at the firm.

The chart for the finance function is as follows.

Task 1

From the preceding organisation charts shown in 'How it Works' identify:

(a)   How many people you (Accounts clerk) directly report to

(b)   Who you would ask if you don't know what to do with a memo about a staff member's National Insurance contributions

(c)   Which three members of the financial accounts department have the same amount of authority

(d)   What difficulties might be caused for you by these members having the same amount of authority

(e)   Who you might appeal to if these difficulties were too much for you

(f)   How a member of the R & D function should issue instructions to a member of the Kitchen Appliances production team

(g)   Whether the finance function has 'line' or 'staff' authority to impose a credit control policy in the logistics department

Document and information flows

The organisation structure affects the accounting system, and the role of the accounting and payroll functions, in terms of:

- How information is collected, and by whom

- How information is sent up and down the organisation chain, and across the boundaries between different functions

- How information should be processed and presented, to suit the needs of different users

IDENTIFYING REPORTING LINES

When you work within an organisation you are not working in isolation. As we have just seen, you may have colleagues or peers at the same level, managers of varying levels of seniority, and possibly more junior employees to whom you can delegate tasks.

Your job or role description often sets out the reporting and REPORTING PROCEDURE for that role. For whom are you doing tasks? Who needs particular data or documents next? To whom are you accountable for performing a task correctly? To whom should you refer questions and problems?

Reporting lines and procedures will differ from organisation to organisation, depending on the formal structure of the business. In a very small business, for example, all employees may report directly to the owner of the business. In a large multinational company, there could be complex organisational structures for the business as a whole, and each country, site or department within it.

Identifying reporting lines for a given job and task

You are most likely to report on a day-to-day basis to a designated supervisor or LINE MANAGER such as the head of your department or section. A line manager is someone who has direct authority over people and activities, down the vertical 'line' of command in the organisation chart. In an accounts department, this is likely to be an accountant or financial controller, or it could be the general office or administration manager.

If you are temporarily working on a particular project, you may report to the PROJECT MANAGER on tasks relating to that specific project. An example might be if you were preparing costings for a new product launch, say, or checking supplier invoices for the installation of a new IT system: such activities may well be organised as a distinct project, with a designated project manager overseeing the work.

You may also find that, on occasion, you are required to do a one-off job for someone to whom you do not normally report. For example, the sales manager may have requested a breakdown of sales by geographical area: in this case, you may report directly to the sales manager on this specific task (by agreement with your line manager).

Organisational policies and procedures may suggest other reporting lines. For example, if you identify a health or safety risk in your work place, the 'appropriate person' to report it to may be the Health and Safety officer or Fire officer.

It is important for you to know to whom you should report both on routine and non-routine matters. For routine tasks, this will most often be your immediate superior, project manager or the person who has asked you to perform a task.

In cases where a matter has to be referred 'above the head' of your immediate superior(s) for decision, you should simply follow the vertical line of command up to the next highest person. An example might be where you cannot resolve a conflict with an immediate superior: if he/she has asked you to do something inappropriate or unethical, say, or has treated you unfairly.

HOW IT WORKS

At Southfield Electronics, there are two accounts clerks – yourself and Amy Laval – employed as a 'shared resource' for two assistant financial accountants and a payroll manager.

Your role includes fulfilling work requests given to you by all three of these individuals, and giving clerical support, as required, to the work of the financial accounts section as a whole.

One day:

- You are struggling to complete a piece of work given to you by Ron Howard, which appears to contain incomplete information.

- You have just finished a batch of payslips, which need checking.

- You have just received a delivery of stationery supplies for the section, but before signing the receipt note, you notice that the delivery does not seem to be complete, according to the copy of the purchase order sent to you by the purchasing department.

- Both Kellie McDonald and Ron Howard have given you urgent tasks to perform the following day, and you know you will not have time to do both of them. You have spoken to both Kellie and Ron about this – but neither of them will back down: they each think their work is most important.

What are the appropriate reporting and referral lines in this situation?

- Your queries about the first task should be referred to Ron Howard, because he was the one who gave you the task.

- The payslips should be given to Jane Chu (the Payroll manager) for checking, because this is the work area for which she is responsible.

- The query about the stationery order should be referred to the purchasing department, since they are responsible for the purchase order, and dealing with suppliers.

- If Kellie and Ron cannot come to agreement, you may have to refer the matter to their superior, who has the authority to decide whose work has priority.

ORGANISATIONAL POLICIES AND PROCEDURES

Organisational policies and procedures will influence most aspects of your everyday working practice, both in technical matters (ie how accounting and information-processing tasks should be carried out) and in regard to your behaviour in the workplace (including areas such as health, safety and security, timekeeping, dress, confidentiality of information, recycling and other 'green' practices – and so on).

A POLICY is a statement of how an organisation wants and expects activities to be carried out. They provide strong guidelines for action, decision-making and problem-solving. Equal opportunities policies, for example, are statements of the organisation's attitude to eliminating discrimination in the workplace, and how this should be done in selecting people for jobs, training, rewards and promotions.

A PROCEDURE is a standard sequence of steps or operations necessary to perform an activity. An organisation will have formal or informal procedures relating to a wide range of matters such as: the handling of cash receipts, the recording of payroll details, the processing of expenses claims, the authorisation of payments and the secure storage of data.

Why is it important to adhere to policy and procedure?

Often, policies and procedures are regarded as routine – or even as a nuisance, if there are more convenient 'short cuts' in performing a task. However, it is important to adhere to formal organisation requirements – and to know *why* you are doing so.

Policies and procedures are put in place to:

- **Support efficiency**. They enable people to perform routine, repetitive or foreseeable tasks correctly, without having to waste time and resources analysing and planning them afresh every time: in other words, you don't have to 'reinvent the wheel'.

- **Support compliance**. They generally build in the requirements of law and regulation, ensuring minimum standards of practice (and possibly 'good' practice).

- **Protect people**. Health, safety and security policies and procedures, for example, are put in place to protect you, others working around you and people visiting your workplace.

- **Protect finance, property, information and other assets of the organisation**. Financial control procedures, for example, are established to minimise temptations and opportunities for fraud and mismanagement of resources.

Procedures may also incorporate rules. If a policy is 'the way it should be done', and a procedure is 'the way it is done', a rule is 'the way it must be done (in order to be done correctly)'. Examples of rules include: maintaining the confidentiality of financial information; seeking required authorisations for transactions; and keeping fire doors clear and closed.

Let's look briefly at some of the organisational policies and procedures that are most likely to affect your work in an accounting or payroll environment.

Health and safety

Most policies and procedures for health and safety in the workplace are based on provisions set out in law such as the Health and Safety at Work Act 1974 and related regulations.

Health and safety at work is about the prevention of accidents and ill-health caused by working conditions and work practices.

All organisations with five or more employees must have a written Health and Safety Policy, continually updated and circulated to all employees. As an employee, you have a duty to study this document: you will normally be asked to sign a form stating that you have read it and are willing to take responsibility (in relevant areas) for complying with the policy.

Specific occupational health and safety policies may cover a range of issues such as:

- The duty of all employees and managers to contribute to a healthy and safe work environment

- The use of safety measures and equipment, where required

- Non-smoking

- The participation of staff in regular fire and evacuation drills

- The reporting of risks and accidents to appropriate officials (eg a Health and Safety or Fire officer)

There should be detailed procedures for operations such as:

- The use of fire alarms and equipment
- The evacuation of the premises in the event of fire or other threats
- The labelling, storage and handling of potentially dangerous workplace chemicals
- The safe use and maintenance of electrical equipment and dangerous tools
- The reporting of identified health and safety hazards
- The recording of accidents (eg in an accident book)

HOW IT WORKS

Southfield Electronics has a range of policies and procedures, which are published in Procedures Manuals for each function and work site, and also posted on the corporate intranet for employees to consult on their computer terminals.

Its Evacuation Procedure, for example, appears as follows.

EVACUATION OF THE PREMISES IN THE EVENT OF EMERGENCY

In the event of an emergency such as fire or terrorist threat all employees are required to leave the building by the designated route as quickly as possible. They are advised to remain calm and not to linger to gather personal belongings.

Employees are advised not to use the lifts in the event of a fire emergency, as lifts may cease to operate at any time. Particular attention should be paid to evacuees who have special needs (for example, those in wheelchairs or with impaired sight or hearing), and members of staff should help them out.

Once they have left the building, employees and visitors should go immediately to the designated Assembly Point and ensure that any visitors or others on the premises at the time of evacuation, who do not know where to go, are directed and assisted to the Assembly Point by members of staff.

Employees should wait at the Assembly Point. The Safety Officer will carry a roster of everyone signed in as being in the building, and will 'call a roll' at the Assembly Point. Each person should respond when their name is called.

No-one is permitted to return to the building until instructed to do so by a senior official or the Safety Officer.

Task 2

You are the accounts clerk at Southfield Electronics, and you have noticed that several members of the accounts department have been taking the lifts, or even staying in the offices, during fire evacuation drills. You have a word with your supervisor about this, and she refers you to the Safety Officer.

(a) For each action provided, select whether they are correct or incorrect actions to carry out during a drill (according to the evacuation procedure).

Action	Correct/Incorrect
Leave the building by the designated route as quickly (but calmly) as possible, not lingering to gather personal belongings	▼
Use lifts in the event of a fire emergency	▼
Go immediately to the designated Assembly Point and ensure that any visitors are directed and assisted	▼
Pay particular attention to people with special needs (eg those in wheelchairs or with impaired sight or hearing)	▼
Stay quiet when your name is called by the Safety Officer who will 'call a roll' of everyone signed in as being in the building	▼
Do not return to the building until instructed to do so by a senior official or the Safety Officer	▼

Picklist

Correct
Incorrect

(b) Explain the importance of complying with the procedure during drills.

Security

Security policies and procedures are designed to protect the physical security of assets (such as computers or petty cash); the physical security of employees (eg from attack or intimidation); and the security of information (eg from unauthorised access, theft or tampering).

Security measures in an office environment can range from simple rules about locking doors, windows, filing cabinets and petty cash boxes at the end of the day – to more complex procedures for:

- Controlling access to areas of a building (eg using security doors, sign-in procedures and identity badges or security cards)

- Controlling access to the computer system (eg using passwords and authorisation codes)

- Training staff to handle potentially unsafe situations, and to report unidentified strangers and intruders in the office

Working hours and time-keeping

Policies will generally be laid out in regard to issues such as:

- Working hours
- Office opening hours
- The taking of lunch breaks (and holiday entitlements)
- Time-keeping and punctuality

There may be detailed procedures for clocking on and off, filling out time sheets, operating flexi-time schemes and other forms of flexible working – and so on.

Such issues are important for:

- The efficiency of the organisation, ensuring that it can plan for adequate staffing – and rely on those plans, once made

- Fraud prevention, ensuring that people work the hours they are paid for

- Effective working relations, ensuring people honour their commitments to the team and 'pull their weight'

- Individual wellbeing, ensuring some 'work-life balance' – which also supports long-term productivity

- Individual work planning and scheduling, ensuring that workloads are planned within the hours available in the day! (We look at this in more detail later in the Combined Text and Question Bank)

Maintenance of your work area

Your personal WORK AREA may include your desk, the area around your desk, and other areas of the office in which you regularly move and work.

Your immediate work area will often be your own responsibility, in general terms. It will, to some degree, define you to your colleagues – and external visitors. If your desk is tidy and documents are filed away, this gives an impression of a tidy mind and an efficient employee. Conversely, an untidy work area may create the impression of someone who does not care about their work. A tidy and organised work area also ensures that you – and others around you – can work effectively and efficiently: we look further at this later in the Combined Text and Question Bank.

There may be departmental rules or guidelines as to how your work area should be organised and maintained, mainly aimed at ensuring that offices maintain a professional image, and reflect the corporate image of the organisation, particularly in areas which are visited by outsiders.

Organisations often have rules regarding personal effects displayed in work areas, such as photographs of family and friends, posters or postcards. This will often depend upon the type of environment in which you work. In a large open plan office which rarely receives visits from external parties such as customers, suppliers or the general public, it might be quite acceptable to have family photographs or amusing cartoons displayed (providing that they do not offend those working around you).

However, in an office regularly visited by customers, the desire to convey professionalism may lead to organisational restrictions on the type or number of personal possessions allowed in the workplace.

Even if there are no formal 'rules' regarding such matters, there may be informal 'understandings'. Ask colleagues or your supervisor, or observe the work areas of your colleagues to find out what is appropriate.

Another important aspect of this is that tidiness supports data security. You will generally be expected to tidy away confidential documents once they are finished with, or likely to be left unattended. However, in some organisations, there may be an explicit CLEAR DESK POLICY, which requires that everything must be cleared from your desktop at the end of each day, in order to ensure disciplined work practices and to reduce the vulnerability of data to theft and espionage.

Confidentiality of information

In an accounting role, you will come across a variety of confidential information – and you must be extremely careful how you deal with it. As we saw earlier in this chapter, you have a key role in co-ordinating flows of financial information in the organisation. But what information should 'flow' – and to whom? What is 'confidential' information?

Some information (in files, reports, emails or letters, say) may be clearly marked as being 'confidential' (or 'private', or 'limited access' or 'for authorised individuals only').

Certain types of information may be designated as confidential by law, organisational policy and professional codes of practice.

- Details of customers and suppliers must not be disclosed to anyone outside the organisation.

- Personal data about employees, for example payroll details, must be kept strictly confidential, to protect privacy.

- Financial information is likely to be highly sensitive – but there are other categories of information which, if disclosed, could be used for purposes harmful to the organisation or its personnel: there are likely to be strict rules about the disclosure of security procedures and codes, details of legal proceedings, new product plans and so on.

HOW IT WORKS

At Southfield Electrical, the sales manager has forwarded to the financial accountant a letter from an estate agent, requesting financial information about one of the firm's major customers, which is applying to rent a commercial property. The information is needed as soon as possible, by fax or email, in order to secure approval for the rental. The Sales Manager has asked the accounts department to help.

Is there a confidentiality issue here? Yes, there is. The financial accountant would certainly need the customer's permission to disclose any information. Since the request seems inappropriate, she should also confirm the identity of the person making the request. If everything is above board, there is still a confidentiality issue in how the information is sent: fax can be easily intercepted (and so can e-mail). The information should be sent securely, and clearly marked 'private and confidential'.

Task 3

You have been asked for the following information. Should each item be provided?

(Indicate whether you would provide the information or, if not, indicate the reason why.)

	Yes – Provide Information	No – Personal Information	No – Confidential Information
A customer asks for the address and telephone number of another customer	☐	☐	☐
A colleague asks you for the home address of two other employees	☐	☐	☐
The company's security guard asks for the names of the visitors expected by your department that week	☐	☐	☐

Secure storage of data and information

Information held in files, records and computers needs to be protected from accidental or malicious damage, loss, theft, sabotage, interference – and prying eyes. Interference may just be casual – someone playing around with your terminal when you are not there – but it can still result in damage, disruption or loss of data. Potential threats to data security include computer viruses, hacking or 'phishing', systems failure and corruption/loss of data.

It is especially important to keep accounting data secure, because it is needed to run the business properly; it is often commercially sensitive; and (as in the case of personnel and payroll data) it may be private, confidential and protected by privacy and data protection laws.

There will almost certainly be policies and procedures covering data security aspects such as:

- The non-removal of data and equipment from the premises

- The frequent backing-up of computerised data, and the storage of backups separately from the original data, so that there are safe copies in case of systems failure, data corruption or fire

- The use of anti-virus software, firewalls and other protective tools on all computers, to prevent malicious corruption and theft of data

- The use of passwords to prevent unauthorised users from gaining access to computer systems or files (often with additional policies regarding the complexity and regular change of passwords)

- The use of authorisations to control access to security-coded paper-based files

- The non-divulging of passwords, security codes and other data security measures to other parties

Document retention

There will be additional policies and procedures for document retention: the period that documents need to be kept on file. There are legal obligations to keep certain financial documents for prescribed lengths of time.

- Many accounting and banking records (including ledgers, invoices, cheques, paying-in counterfoils, bank statements and instructions to banks) should be kept for six years.

- Employee records (including staff personnel records, time cards and piecework records, payroll records and expenses claims) should also be kept for six years – and accident report books, permanently!

If in doubt, you should consult organisational policy documents, or your supervisor, to check on what these are – and look out for any specific policy information set out in the assessment.

Departmental deadlines

Some activities of financial functions are bound by strict deadlines, and these should be clearly incorporated in relevant plans and procedures.

Payroll preparation is one example. If an employee is to be paid on the 30th of the month, the pay must be in his/her bank account on that date. Any changes to pay rates must be included on the first available payroll. Tax deductions have to be paid over to HM Revenue & Customs by a due date: if payment is delayed, the employer may have to pay interest. Similarly, other deductions, such as pension contributions, need to be paid over to third parties regularly and on time, otherwise the employee's entitlements could be affected.

In financial accounting, there are strict, externally imposed deadlines for the preparation and lodging of statutory financial statements and reports (eg the year-end lodgement date). These, in turn, impose internal deadlines for the gathering and processing of information, auditing and so on.

However, as we will see in later chapters, it is very important to meet *any* agreed departmental or team deadline for the completion of work, because your work impacts on the work of others.

HOW IT WORKS

One of your tasks at Southfield Electronics is to list any cheques received in the post each morning. This listing is then passed on to the cashier, James Thorne, for entry into the cash receipts book and updating of the receivables ledger (sales ledger). He can only carry out his daily task once you have finished yours.

If you do not finish the cheque listing early in the morning (because you have not planned your work routine) or if you mislay the cheque listing for the day (because your work area is untidy or your files disordered), this will impact on James' work for the day as well as yours.

Authorisation procedures

Many accounting and payroll tasks require authorisations, as part of the organisation's system of financial controls to prevent fraud and mismanagement of resources. An authorisation is a point in a procedure at which confirmation or permission to proceed must be obtained from an individual with appropriate authority.

In payroll, for example:

- All variations to the payroll must be properly authorised, including temporary variations such as overtime. Permanent variations, such as salary increases, will usually be authorised by senior managers and it is likely that you will be familiar with their signatures. However, overtime is likely to be authorised by line managers. The employee's record or contract of employment will let you know if (s)he is entitled to overtime payments – but how do you know if the actual overtime figure has been correctly authorised?

- Most large organisations will have a list of AUTHORISED SIGNATORIES for each department. This is a list of people authorised to approve changes to the payroll, together with a specimen signature. The list should also indicate whether the person can authorise permanent and/or temporary changes, to what value, for what department, and to what grades of employee. If you are a payroll clerk, you will need a copy of this list so that you can check that variations are correctly authorised!

- If variations are not correctly authorised, you will need to bring this to your supervisor's or line manager's attention. (Do not assume that it is an innocent mistake: the employee could be trying to obtain an increased salary or overtime payments fraudulently...)

Similar policies and procedures (involving authorisations and designated signatories) will invariably be in place for operations such as:

- The issuing of purchase orders
- The preparation of cheques and other payments
- The processing of expense claims
- The processing of petty cash

These policies may vary from organisation to organisation, but the principles will be similar.

Task 4

What information will you need to know, and check, to ensure that authorisations comply with procedure?

You should be informed of the specific policies and procedures applicable to your work role, via policy documents and procedure manuals (and their online equivalents) and/or by induction, training and coaching within your department.

The most important point is that individuals working in financial roles need to:

- Find out what the applicable policies and procedures are

- Ensure that they understand the requirements (or seek help to understand them)

- Ensure that they follow or adhere to the requirements, in all relevant situations

HOW IT WORKS

Southfield Electronics has a policy about authorising expenditure.

Ian Hamilton, an employee in the Sales department, has been asked to organise the office Christmas party. He has booked caterers for the event, but they require a deposit of £150.

Ian must fill in a cheque requisition form, giving details of the payment, and attach a VAT invoice or receipt as evidence of the payment. Ian doesn't have such documentation, so just puts 'None' in the space on the cheque requisition form.

The form is sent to the sales supervisor for authorisation. However, she knows that for amounts between £100 and £500, requisitions must be authorised by a department manager. The form is therefore forwarded to the Sales manager – who signs it, and sends it to the Financial Accounts department.

Jenny Faulkner calls the sales manager to point out that the requisition should not have been authorised, and cannot be processed, in the absence of evidence of payment. The requisition form will be returned to Ian. Jenny advises that Ian, or the Sales manager, can pay the deposit himself – and then fill out a cheque requisition for reimbursement, attaching the VAT receipt for the expense. However, they will have to bear in mind that correctly completed and authorised cheque requisition forms must be with the accounts department by 10 am to guarantee that a cheque is prepared on the same day.

Meanwhile, the company also has a written agreement with its bank regarding who is allowed to sign the organisation's cheques. The bank will only accept cheques that have been signed by the authorised signatories. For cheques up to a value of £8,000, the signature of a director is required. Cheques for more than this amount require the signatures of two directors.

CHAPTER OVERVIEW

- Organisation structure reflects the grouping of tasks into units and functions; the flow of authority and responsibility; and lines of communication and co-operation between individuals and units. This can be depicted in organisation charts.

- The organisation structure partly determines reporting lines, in establishing a 'chain of command'. Your designated supervisor or line manager is your direct superior in this chain, to whom you report most directly.

- Reporting lines and relationships are also based on: who asked you to perform a given task; who is the manager of the project to which the task contributes; and who is the most appropriate person to deal with a given matter. Some matters may need to be 'referred upwards' to a superior manager.

- Organisational policies and procedures will influence most aspects of your everyday working practice. It is important to adhere to them, to support efficiency and compliance – and to protect people and assets.

- Some key examples of policies and procedures in an accounting environment include: health and safety; security; working hours and timekeeping; maintenance of your work area; confidentiality of information; secure storage of data and information; document retention; adherence to departmental deadlines; authorisations and designated signatories.

Keywords

Organisation structure – the 'shape' of an organisation, made up of defined units, levels of authority and communication lines

Chain of command – the line down which authority flows in the organisation structure

Organisation charts – diagrams depicting the formal structure of an organisation

Accountable – the duty of a subordinate to report to a superior on the outcome of the tasks (s)he has been given

Line manager – your immediate superior in the line or chain of command

Cross-functional teams – teams which include members from different functions in the organisation, for the purpose of co-ordination (eg in carrying out projects)

Reporting procedure – the channels through which an employee reports to a superior official

Project manager – the manager appointed to run a particular project

Policy – a statement of how an organisation wants and expects activities to be carried out

Procedure – a standard sequence of steps necessary to perform an activity

Work area – your desk, chair, surrounding furniture and space

Clear desk policy – an organisational policy that all desks must be left clear at the end of each working day

Confidentiality – the duty not to disclose restricted, private or otherwise sensitive information to unauthorised parties

Authorised signatories – people who are authorised to sign the organisation's cheques and to authorise other operations

TEST YOUR LEARNING

Test 1

Given below are examples of types of information that flow either down the organisation structure or up the organisation structure. Tick the appropriate boxes to decide whether this is a downward flow or an upward flow.

	Downward	Upward
Instructions	☐	☐
Exception reports	☐	☐
Briefings	☐	☐
Queries and questions	☐	☐
Plans	☐	☐
Routine reports	☐	☐
Decisions	☐	☐

Test 2

You have been asked to prepare a 'To Do List' for the Accounts department, in relation to the relocation of the company's offices. This is being managed as a cross-functional project by the Office manager. Because of the pressure of work from the Accounts supervisor, you are not sure you will be able to complete the 'To Do List' in the time given to you. Who should you report to about this?

Picklist

Office manager
Accounts supervisor

Test 3

Most employees like to personalise their work area with personal objects. In which of the following work areas would this be most acceptable?

Picklist

Sales department where regular meetings are held with customers
Accounts department where there are rarely any visits from non-employees
Reception area which is open to the public

Test 4

Would you supply the following information? Enter Y for yes, N for No.

Your supervisor asks you for details of the latest R & D
expenditure on new products

A telephone caller, saying she is a financial journalist,
asks you for details of your upcoming plans for new products

A customer calls asking for the bank details of one of your
fellow employees, stating that the customer wishes to pay
a cheque into her bank account

One of the senior accounts assistants has asked you
to photocopy the notes for a training course that another
rival company uses. You notice that the course notes
have the copyright © symbol on them

Test 5

Complete the following sentences.

[▼] are points in a procedure at which confirmation or
permission to proceed must be obtained from an individual with appropriate
authority.

[▼] are people who are authorised to sign documents (eg
for authorisation purposes) or company cheques.

Picklist

Managers
Policies
Designated signatories
Accountants
Requests
Authorisations

chapter 4:
COMMUNICATION SKILLS

---

chapter coverage 📖

This chapter, together with Chapter 5, will develop the knowledge and skills required to communicate effectively in a range of formats and contexts. Chapter 5 covers the presentation of information in reports, letters, memoranda and emails.

In this chapter, we focus on communicating clearly, using business language, and demonstrating numeracy skills appropriate to your role.

This chapter explains numeracy skills you may require in the assessment. You should use the tasks within the chapter and the questions at the end to practise and develop your skills.

The topics covered are:

✎ Effective business communication

✎ Message content

✎ Presentation

✎ Business language

✎ Numeracy skills

EFFECTIVE BUSINESS COMMUNICATION

What is business communication?

As we saw in Chapter 2, working effectively in accounting and finance is fundamentally about the effective preparation, giving and receiving of information. As we will see in later chapters, it is also about working effectively with other people to achieve shared objectives. All of this means: communication!

COMMUNICATION is, at its most basic, the transmission or exchange of information: putting across a message. However, there are many different purposes for doing this:

- To inform: to give people data they require

- To persuade: to get others to agree to, or do, something

- To request: to ask for something

- To confirm: to check that data is correct and that different parties have the same understanding of it

- To build effective working relationships

All of these activities underpin efficient working and constructive working relationships.

The communication process

Effective communication is a two-way process, often shown as a 'cycle'. Signals or messages are sent by the communicator and received by the target recipient, who sends back some form of confirmation that the message has been received and understood.

Some means of communication are more appropriate and effective than others in different business contexts. If you get the choice of whether to carry out a communication task using a letter, memo, email, report or informal note – or, in real working life, a telephone call or face-to-face discussion – you will need to consider factors such as: whether speed is important; whether there is the need for written confirmation; which format will best support you in getting your message across to the recipient; and which is the most efficient method in terms of time and cost. This is considered in more detail in Chapter 5.

Task 1

Suggest the most effective medium for communication in the following situations using the dropdown list.

Situation	Medium
New stationery is urgently required from the office goods supplier	▼
The managing director wants to give a message to all staff	▼
A member of staff has been absent five times in the past month, and her manager intends to take action	▼
You need information quickly from another department	▼
You have to explain a complicated procedure to a group of people	▼

Picklist

Face to face conversation
Meeting
Telephone
Notice board/intranet

Communicating effectively, clearly and appropriately

This Unit requires you to demonstrate that you can 'communicate effectively, clearly and appropriately' in a range of work-related tasks. So what makes communication effective, clear and appropriate?

Attribute	Explanation
Using appropriate formats	Selecting the right format (letter, email, memorandum etc) for the job
Observing format conventions and house style	Using formats correctly: observing conventions of structure, format and style, within organisational guidelines and 'house style'
Professionally presented	Ensuring that documents are neat, legible, concise, helpfully structured and smartly presented: showing competence and awareness of business needs

Attribute	Explanation
Technically correct	Ensuring that content is accurate, appropriately detailed (for different levels of requirement) and checked for factual/data and typographical errors
Clearly understandable	Tailored to the writer's purpose in communicating (so that a clear message is sent) and to the information needs, language and capabilities of its audience (so that the message can be received)
Projecting the appropriate corporate image	Reflecting a general image of professionalism and competence – including appropriate formality – and the specific desired image or 'character' of the organisation
Achieving its purpose	Obtain feedback to check that the communication has been *effective*. Has it 'done its job'? Has it got the response it aimed for? If not: adjust and try again!

MESSAGE CONTENT

Technically correct

The information you provide, in an accounting role, is likely to be relied on by others, and factual and numerical errors may have serious consequences for their decision-making and results – and for your performance evaluation, credibility and reputation!

This should go without saying, and it is perhaps unlikely that you would knowingly give out information that is technically incorrect. However, there is always the possibility of unknowingly conveying inaccurate information, or making careless errors – and you should be aware of this at all times.

- You may need to verify information, by checking the accuracy of the source, or cross-checking with other sources.

- If you are not confident in your knowledge or competence in a particular area, you may need to check with a more expert colleague, or with your supervisor.

- Always check the assumptions, logical processes and numerical operations (or 'workings') behind a piece of work, before submitting it.

Clear and understandable

It is always the responsibility of the sender of a message to ensure that the message has been received and understood: don't expect your target audience to do your work for you!

Take care with the language and terminology you use: tailor it to the needs and abilities of the person with whom you are communicating. In some cases you will be giving information to others in the Accounting department who are, like you, familiar with accounting terminology. However, if you are giving information to customers, or to the Marketing department, say, you could not take for granted that your accountancy knowledge will be shared!

Avoid JARGON: technical terms or buzz words that only fellow technicians will know. Think about whether any diagrams you use will be meaningful to another person – and add labels and explanatory notes if you think a reader will need help 'decoding' your meaning.

When planning communications, think about your:

- **Purpose**: what do you need to get across? How do you need the other person to respond?
- **Audience**: what language will they understand? What are their needs?
- **Structure and Style**: what format, order, layout and language will be most helpful in achieving your purpose, given your intended audience?

(You might like to remember this as a checklist for message planning, with the helpful mnemonic: PASS!)

HOW IT WORKS

Clare Francis is one of the assistant management accountants at Southfield Electronics. She has received a request from Kate Saltmarsh (the management accountant) and Taylor Smith (a new sales manager) for a summary of the comparison of the monthly sales per product type to budget for November. Both Kate and Taylor have requested the information to be sent via email.

Although Clare is sending the same information to both people, she decides to word the messages slightly differently. Kate is an accountant with detailed knowledge of accounting terminology, whereas it is unlikely that the new sales manager would have such detailed knowledge of the subject. The two emails might look like this.

EMAIL

To: ksaltmarsh@southfield.co.uk

From: cfrancis@southfield.co.uk

Date: 8 December 20X8

Subject: Sales variances – November

In response to your query, the following sales variances by product type were incurred in November:

Product	Variance
MP3 players	£14,300 adverse
Portable DVD players	£2,700 favourable
DVD/VHS combo players	£21,600 adverse
Digital TVs	£18,600 favourable

If you require further detail, let me know.

Clare

EMAIL

To: tsmith@southfield.co.uk

From: cfrancis@southfield.co.uk

Date: 8 December 20X8

Subject: Comparison of actual sales to budgeted sales – November

---

In response to your query, I have compared the *actual* sales per product type for November to the *budgeted* sales for that product, with the following results:

MP3 players	– sales were £14,300 less than budget
Portable DVD players	– sales were £2,700 more than budget
DVD/VHS combo players	– sales were £21,600 less than budget
Digital TVs	– sales were £18,600 more than budget

Clare

Keep it short and simple!

Here's another helpful mnemonic: KISS! Business people have limited time in which to peruse communications – and that time is worth money to them and their organisations. So business communication, while never abrupt or discourteous, should always be short, to the point, and easy to use. 'Keeping it Short and Simple' may mean:

- Ensuring your message is well structured (eg in clear topic paragraphs)

- Making it easy to read (eg legible and well spaced on the page, and written in reasonably short sentences)

- Being unambiguous (without potential misunderstandings from double-meaning words or vague phrases)

- Avoiding the use of jargon

- Eliminating unnecessary words and phrases

- Separating out detailed data, which would interrupt the flow of your main information or argument. Detail can be placed in appendices or attachments, or summarised in tables or diagrams

Verbal or visual?

Consider what format will make your information clear, easy to use, professional-looking – and, if you are trying to be persuasive, impactful.

Verbal communication (using words or text) is useful for conveying the thread of an argument, and the meaning of information. However, it can overload readers with limited time to read and absorb. You might like to use visual elements – such as headings and bullet points – to organise textual information into more manageable 'chunks', with clear signposts for the reader.

Detailed data may be more clearly organised in a table, or headed columns, to show the reader how it is grouped and classified. Even more visual formats, such as charts, graphs and diagrams, may be used to highlight aspects such as comparisons, correlations and trends. (We look at the use of diagrams in Chapter 5, when we discuss report writing.)

PRESENTATION

Professionalism and corporate image

Written communications may be the first or only contact people have with you in a business situation – and first impressions count! A letter or email is like an 'ambassador' for you, your organisation and your department.

In order to convey professionalism, the presentation of your message should show the following qualities.

- If handwritten, it should be legible (readable), neat and free of excessive visible errors and corrections (such as crossings out or Tippex). Neatness and legibility are the absolute minimum requirement in a professional context. Do not compromise on this!

- It should demonstrate competence in using word-processing or email software, and whatever tools you are using (including the use of diagrams).

- It should demonstrate some regard to the needs of the user, such as clear diagram labelling, cross-referencing of appendices, and citing of information sources.

- It may even display some features of good 'design', such as creative use of space, and the use of devices such as <u>underlining</u>, **bold** or *italic* type, for headings and emphasis.

Communications also create or reflect the image that outsiders have of an organisation: its CORPORATE IMAGE. Your organisation may seek to project itself as creative, youthful and informal – or as reliable, mature and traditional. Your communications should reflect that image, and there may be CORPORATE IDENTITY and house style guidelines to help you in doing this. You may, for example, be instructed to include corporate logos; to use specially designed letter, memo or email stationery; to use particular layouts, colours or typefaces; and/or to include certain standard elements (such as blocks of text accompanying your signature at the bottom of letters and emails).

If such guidelines exist – follow them.

Task 2

Which of the following are advantages are of using a computer word-processing package for producing business documents and communications? Tick the boxes which are advantages.

Documents can be saved and edited easily	☐
They provide the personal touch	☐
The writer can make corrections and changes which are 'invisible' to the reader	☐
Documents can be tailored to individual circumstances but this takes time – often quicker to write from scratch	☐
Standard or 'template' documents can be created	☐

BUSINESS LANGUAGE

Formality

Styles of communication range from extremely informal and friendly through to extremely formal and impersonal. It is important that the right style is used in appropriate contexts!

There is the basic requirement that *any* business communication must be courteous, businesslike and professional. This does not necessarily mean 'formal': if you work in an organisation where all levels of employees and managers are on first name terms, the style of communication will tend to be less formal than in an organisation where all managers are addressed by their title and surname, eg as Mr Jones or Ms Smith.

Even in relatively informal settings, however, the appropriate style for business communication will be significantly more formal than you might use in a note, email or text message to a friend. You *must* bear this in mind – both at work and in your assessment!

Formality expresses respect for the position and professionalism of the person you are dealing with, and signals the seriousness with which you take your own work role. Formality is also important in getting your message across, since many people find text-message-style abbreviations and slang terms not just disrespectful and unprofessional – but difficult to decode!

A businesslike formal style is written in full, grammatical sentences, avoiding 'text-message'-style abbreviations, and even abbreviated forms such as 'there's' or 'we've'. (The full form 'there is' or 'we have' are preferable.) Your language should be direct (not ambiguous), accessible (but not clichéd) and factual (not too emotional or 'colourful'): avoid colloquial or slang expressions. You should keep to the point and avoid unnecessary digressions. Your tone should be appropriate for business relationships: not overly 'familiar' or friendly in tone, or personal in content, and referring to people by their title and surname – unless they have expressly invited you to be more informal.

Task 3

Allocate *(CBT: Drag and drop)* the 'Do's and Don'ts of acceptable business style into the appropriate columns.

Do.....	Don't....

Drag and drop choices:

Write in full sentences

Refer to people by their title and surname, in more formal relationships – or where their expectations about formality are unknown

Use direct, commonly used and factual language

Use colloquial or slang expressions

Use 'text message'-style abbreviations

Remove digressions, rambles and unnecessary words and phrases: keep to the point

Be overly 'familiar' or friendly in tone, or personal in content, unless the other person has expressly invited this

Use abbreviated forms such as 'There's', 'I'm', 'We've': use the full forms (there is, I am, we have) instead

NUMERACY SKILLS

You should already have been developing your numeracy skills in your studies for other Units, such as *Basic Accounting*. So you won't be starting from scratch in preparing to demonstrate your competence in this assessment!

The important thing here is to recognise when your numeracy skills are being called on, select the right techniques and tools to use – and apply them carefully and accurately.

Addition and subtraction

Addition is used in sub-totalling and totalling amounts: columns of debits and credits, for example, or itemised costs, or the total output of team members, or an amount payable after the addition of VAT.

Subtraction is used for operations such as calculating net pay after deductions, or amounts payable after deduction of a discount.

Addition and subtraction should, with practice, be a fairly straightforward operation (with or without a calculator). However, you do need to think carefully that you are selecting the right items or numbers to add or subtract, from a list of data.

Multiplication and division

Multiplication is used in operations such as calculating annual costs from monthly costs (multiplying by 12), or calculating total costs from unit costs (cost per unit multiplied by the number of units). It is also used when dealing with fractions and percentages of an amount.

Division is used in operations such as calculating the cost 'per' unit (total cost divided by number of units).

Multiplication and division should, similarly, become a fairly straightforward operation with practice (although in this case, a calculator certainly helps). Again, however, you need to think carefully about whether multiplication or division are required, and which items of data to select for the operation. We will look at some practical examples in a moment.

Fractions

A FRACTION is a ratio of two numbers. ¼ means 'one part in four': it also means 1 *divided by* 4.

To find 'a fraction of' something, you simply use multiplication. Say the cost of 20 invoiced items is £360, but you only ordered and received eight items. You need to work out the cost of eight out of the 20 items.

$8/20 \times £360 = £144$

When working with fractions (especially if you aren't using a calculator), it helps to use the simplest version of the fraction, with the lowest numbers. You can do this by a process called 'cancelling down': simply divide the top and bottom numbers of the fraction by the same amounts, until they won't go any further.

Because fractions are ratios or relationships, they stay the same as long as you multiply or divide the top and the bottom numbers *by the same amount*.

$$\frac{8}{20} = \frac{4}{10} = \frac{2}{5} \qquad \frac{24}{30} = \frac{12}{15} = \frac{4}{5}$$

In these examples, you might like to stop cancelling down at 4/10 – or use equal top-and-bottom multiplication to convert 4/5 into 8/10, because tenths are very easy to work with, and easy to convert into decimal points (8/10 = 0.8) and percentages (8/10 = 80/100 = 80%).

If you are using a calculator, you will need to familiarise yourself with the 'fraction button' (if any) and how it is used.

HOW IT WORKS

You are investigating inaccuracies in the work of the Accounts section at Southfield Electronics. You have been told that three out of every 12 invoices in the section's work contain an error, and you want to calculate how many errors that makes over a whole day's work of 88 invoices.

You could rephrase the problem as follows.

$$\frac{3}{12} = \frac{?}{88} \qquad \text{Cancelling down:} \qquad \frac{1}{4} = \frac{?}{88}$$

What do you have to multiply 4 by to get to 88? Division is the reverse operation to multiplication, so you work backwards: 88 ÷ 4 = 22. Now you know you have to multiply the bottom of the fraction by 22, and in order to keep the ratio the same, you have to do the same to the top.

$$\frac{1 \times 22}{4 \times 22} = \frac{22}{88}$$

If three out of 12 invoices are faulty, then – at the same rate of errors – 22 out of the daily total of 88 invoices may be faulty!

There is another way of thinking about this. You could say that 3/12 or ¼ (one quarter) of all invoices have an error. 3/12 of 88 invoices is calculated as:

3/12 × 88 = 22

So 22 invoices out of 88 will have an error.

Percentages

A PERCENTAGE is a proportion or rate per hundred parts (per cent). It is used to express any proportion in relation to a whole: fractions can also be expressed as percentages, by multiplying by 100.

$$\frac{1}{4} \times \frac{100}{1} = \frac{100}{4} = 25\% \qquad \text{or} \qquad 0.25 \times 100 = 25\%$$

Percentages are quite easy to calculate, using multiplication.

$$4\% \text{ of } 900 = \frac{4}{100} \times 900 = 36 \qquad \text{or} \qquad 0.04 \times 900 = 36$$

The same method can be used to calculate:

- The amounts of VAT (20% of a total amount) to be added to an invoice, or the amount of a percentage discount (say 10% of a total amount) to be deducted from a total cost.
- The size of segments of pie charts, and other relative proportions (eg the percentage of total training costs incurred by a particular training programme).
- Changes (eg in sales, costs or output) from one period to another. If your accounts department processed 288 invoices in March and 300 invoices in April:

  $$\text{Its output grew by } \frac{300 - 288}{288} = \frac{12}{288} \times 100 = 4.2\%$$

Task 4

A particular training programme costs £2,300. Your department's total training budget is £11,500. Answer the questions below, entering each answer to the nearest whole number.

(a) What percentage of the total budget is represented by this training programme?

[　　　　　　] %

(b) If you were to draw a pie chart showing this percentage, how many degrees (of a 360-degree circle) would it represent?

[　　　　　　] degrees

(c) If your department was eligible for a 15% discount on all training programmes over a value of £2,000, what would be the amount of the discount, and what would be the net amount payable?

Amount of discount　£ [　　　　　　　　]

Net amount payable　£ [　　　　　　　　]

Rounding

Rounding is a way of making numerical data easier to use by reducing the accuracy (or detail) of numbers to an appropriate level. If you are compiling average numbers of trainees on courses, for example, it may not be helpful to talk about 6.8 trainees being away from work at a given time: it would make more sense to round up to 7 (whole) trainees!

Similarly, if you have 7 trainees on courses costing a total of £699, and were asked for the 'cost per trainee', you know that you need to divide the cost by the number of trainees – and your calculator will tell you that you get £99.8571428. This is not particularly digestible or helpful information – particularly since in monetary units, you really only need two decimal places to give you pounds and pence.

To round to two decimal places, just look at the three numbers after the decimal place: in our example, 857. We are looking to round to the nearest 10, and this means rounding up to 860 (since 57 is closer to 60 than to 50). We can then knock off the final zero, to give us £99.86.

To round to three decimal places, look at the four numbers after the decimal place: 8571. We can round down to the nearest 10 (because 71 is closer to 70 than to 80): this gives us 8570 – and we can knock off the zero for the rounded number £99.857.

HOW IT WORKS

Back at Southfield Electronics, you have been asked to do some VAT calculations. You know that these calculations require the use of percentages, fractions, multiplication, division, addition, subtraction and rounding – so you are determined to work through the calculations carefully.

The net amount (sales price) shown on one invoice is £235.46. How much VAT should be charged on this amount? You know that VAT is 20% of the sales price and is rounded down to the nearest whole pence.

$$20\% \times £235.46 = \frac{20}{100} \times £235.46 = £47.092 \text{ (rounded to £47.09)}$$

The total amount (including VAT) will therefore be:

£235.46 + £47.09 = £282.55

On another invoice, you see that the gross amount (the total price of goods plus VAT) is £375.80. How much VAT is included in this price, and what is the net price of the goods? The total price includes the added 20%, so it totals 120% of the net price. The VAT is, of course, 20% of the total price. So:

$$\text{VAT} = \frac{20}{120} \times £375.80 = £62.6333 \text{ (rounded to £62.63)}$$

To get the net price of the goods, you then subtract the VAT from the VAT-inclusive price. £375.80 – £62.63 = £313.17.

Task 5

Goods with a list price of £2,450.00 are to be sent to a customer. The customer is allowed a trade discount of 15% and VAT is to be charged at 20%. What is the invoice total?

£ [   ]

Averages

An AVERAGE is another way of reducing the level of detail in numerical data to a usable level, based on finding a value that is 'typical' or representative of a larger set of data.

There are three different types of averages.

- The **arithmetic mean** is found by adding up all the items in the set, then dividing the total by the number of items in the set.

  Say there were the following customer complaints about invoices over a six-month period.

January	February	March	April	May	June
0	26	0	5	3	2

  The average number of complaints is:

  $$\frac{0 + 26 + 0 + 5 + 3 + 2}{6} = \frac{36}{6} = 6 \text{ per month}$$

  The problem with this is that *extremes* (like 26) distort the average: the actual monthly complaints are not as bad as 6 in five of the months – the average also disguises the fact that there was a real problem in February!

- The **median** is the middle value, when you arrange the data in ascending order. (If there is an even number of items, the median is mid-way between the middle two.) Here are our monthly complaints, re-ordered:

  | 0 | 0 | 2 | 3 | 5 | 26 |

  Median = 2.5

- The **mode** is the most frequently occurring value in a set of data. So the mode for our monthly complaints is 0.

Task 6

You are trying to compare the costs of training courses offered by two different providers, for a Continuing Professional Development plan.

The course costs are as follows.

	Provider 1	Provider 2
	£	£
Legal Compliance	250	340
Payroll Procedures	590	375
Spreadsheets	260	290
VAT Update	300	350
Effective Communication	200 per day*	210 per day**

* 3 day course
** 2 ½ day course

(a) What is the mean value for each provider?

Provider 1 [   ]

Provider 2 [   ]

(b) What is the median value for each provider?

Provider 1 [   ]

Provider 2 [   ]

(c) Based on your answers to (a) and (b) discuss which provider offers best value in terms of cost.

Selecting the right numeracy tool

One of the tricky things about being set numerical tasks is that they are often set in words! You have to work out what numerical operation is required to get the information you are being asked for.

- To calculate work output 'per' month, for example, you need to divide the total output by the number of months under consideration.

- On the other hand, if you are asked to calculate work output in a particular month, you may need to add up the output of different team members in that month.

- If you are told how many tasks a team member can complete in an hour, and the number of hours she worked in a day, you will need to multiply the hours by the hourly output to get her total daily output. You could multiply this by the number of days worked in the month, to get this team member's monthly output.

- If you know the total monthly output and the monthly output of each team member, you could also calculate the percentage of the total monthly output represented by each team member: team member output divided by total output multiplied by 100. For ease of use, you might round this percentage to one or two decimal places. (You could then re-calculate them as percentages of a 360º circle and draw a handy pie chart, to motivate the team with a bit of healthy competition!)

- Now, say that a team member's time costs '£50 per half day' when she is away on a training course, and that she does '1 day' of training per month'. How would you manipulate this information to calculate the total overtime cost over a year? First of all, notice the different units we've been given to work with: half days, days, months, years. Let's get them all into a common unit: days.

  £50 per half day = £100 per day.
  1 day per month × 12 months in a year = 12 days per year.
  Now it's easy: 12 days × £100 per day = £1,200 per year.

- What if you then found you were eligible for a 10% discount from the training provider because your spend exceeded a particular threshold? You would have to calculate the *percentage* (10/100 × total spend) – and then deduct it from the total.

Accuracy in numerical tasks

One of the great problems in accounting and payroll work is the need for a high level of accuracy – particularly avoiding silly mistakes such as adding a number instead of subtracting it, using the wrong tables or making an arithmetical error. This is also a problem in assessments! So what can you do to minimise the risk of errors?

- Always check your work before finishing and submitting it.

- Don't see tasks as mechanical processes: try to understand what the numbers represent, so that you know (a) what needs to be done with them and (b) whether answers are plausible or likely.

- Perform credibility checks, such as using mental arithmetic to see approximately what you expect the answer to be.

Task 7

Calculate the cost of each employee's travel expenses as a percentage of the total cost of travel expenses. Calculate the percentage to 3 decimal places.

Travel expense

	£
Anne	45
Jaitinder	71
Benjamin	86
Chloe	32
Vimal	59
	293

Anne   [＿＿＿＿＿＿] %

Jaitinder   [＿＿＿＿＿＿] %

Benjamin   [＿＿＿＿＿＿] %

Chloe   [＿＿＿＿＿＿] %

Vimal   [＿＿＿＿＿＿] %

CHAPTER OVERVIEW

- Communication is, at its most basic, the transmission or exchange of information. It is at the core of the role of the accounting and payroll functions within an organisation.

- You are required to demonstrate that you can communicate effectively, clearly and appropriately in a range of situations. This broadly means: using appropriate formats; observing format conventions and house style; presenting information neatly and professionally; ensuring that content is technically correct and clearly understandable (bearing in mind the needs and capacities of your audience); projecting an appropriate corporate image; and achieving your purpose in communicating.

- When planning a communication, you want to PASS: know your Purpose and Audience, and use the right Structure and Style.

- Keep It Short and Simple (KISS) is an important guideline for business communication.

- The formality appropriate for business communication is considerably greater than you might use in non-work settings, and you must bear this in mind.

- You are required to demonstrate a range of numeracy skills appropriate to this level, including (but not limited to) addition and subtraction, multiplication and division, fractions, percentages, and rounding to a certain number of decimal places.

- Other important numeracy skills are (a) working out what numerical operation is required to get the information you are being asked for, (b) checking the accuracy of your calculations and (c) formatting your work in a clear way.

Keywords

Communication – a method of putting across a message and ensuring that the message is understood

Jargon – technical terminology which may not be understood by non-specialists

Corporate image – the image of itself which the organisation seeks to project to the outside world

Corporate identity – guidelines for how the organisation presents itself visually in its communications

Fraction – a ratio of two numbers – for example, $\frac{1}{4}$ means 'one part in four'

Percentage – a proportion or rate per hundred parts – for example, 20% = 20 parts per hundred or $\frac{1}{5}$

Average – a value that is typical, representative or 'middling' for a set of data

TEST YOUR LEARNING

Test 1

Complete the following sentence using the picklist below.

[▼] is the response of a person with whom you are communicating, which indicates whether your message has (or has not) been received and understood as you intended.

Picklist

Feedforward
Budget control
Exception reporting
Feedback

Test 2

It is 15 May and you have just received an invoice for 2,000 kg of raw materials. Inclusive of VAT (sales tax) the invoice totals £4,580 and the VAT rate is 20%.

Next month you need another 2,000 kg of the same raw material but you know the VAT exclusive material price is set to rise by 3% by the start of June.

What will the VAT value be on the 2,000 kg to be purchased in June rounded to two decimal places?

£ [   ]

Test 3

Your Accounts department processed £16,600 worth of invoices in January and £20,916 worth of invoices in February. What percentage increase in revenue does this represent?

[   ] %

chapter 5:
PRESENTING INFORMATION

chapter coverage 📖

In this chapter, you will develop the knowledge and skills required to produce professional informal business reports, letters, emails and memos. You will learn to use standard formats correctly and effectively, within organisational guidelines.

The chapter also explains how to structure informal reports, letters and other business documents and the appropriate use of diagrams and charts.

You should use the tasks within the chapter and the questions at the end to practise and develop your skills, and to prepare you for the assessment.

The topics covered are:

✍ Choosing communication formats

✍ House style, guidelines and policies

✍ Informal business reports

✍ Using diagrams and charts

✍ Business letters

✍ Memos and business emails

CHOOSING COMMUNICATION FORMATS

There are a variety of possible methods of communication for presenting business information, and you must select the most appropriate method for the circumstances, for the target audience, and for the type of message that is to be relayed.

Face-to-face communication (in meetings, interviews, discussions or presentations) allows you to express yourself fully, to be sensitive to the other person, to take advantage of on-the-spot question-and-answer, and to gain immediate feedback to make sure your message is getting across. However, a face-to-face meeting is often not possible due to time constraints or physical location. It is also often the case that, particularly with a complex subject, it is better to communicate the details in writing so that the recipient has time to consider the details and complexities and has a copy for reference/confirmation.

If immediate feedback or personal sensitivity is required but face-to-face communication is not feasible, the next best option is a telephone call.

Short notes are good methods of passing on information and providing a reminder (eg asking someone to carry out a task) in informal settings (eg among colleagues).

Letters are often used in formal, person-to-person business communication where urgency (given the lead time for postal delivery) is not a factor. Letters can be made confidential by stating 'private and confidential' on the envelope and at the top of the letter, so that only the target recipient should open the message.

Informal reports are often used in business communication to convey larger amounts of information in a clear, structured, easy-to-use way.

Memos are a standardised, efficient way of sending messages within an organisation. They may be the approved internal format for notes and short informal reports.

EMAIL is extremely versatile: it can be used to send notes, memos, letters, reports, forms and all sorts of other messages. Email has the huge advantages of speed (provided the recipient picks up the message when it is sent) and electronic format (so it can be easily filed, edited, copied and sent to multiple recipients all at once). It can also have other documents (reports, diagrams, schedules and so on) 'attached', if this would be helpful in backing up the main message.

HOUSE STYLE, GUIDELINES AND POLICIES

As we saw in Chapter 4, business communication needs to be more planned, more formal and more efficient than everyday communication, in order to:

- Make best use of the time of all parties involved

- Avoid misunderstandings or communication failures, which could be detrimental to the achievement of deadlines and objectives

- Establish and maintain positive relationships with colleagues, customers, suppliers and other stakeholders in the business

For this reason, organisations often issue guidelines for their staff on how to use various communication methods efficiently and effectively, and how external messages should be presented.

Communication policies

Organisations often publish policies and guidelines on how to use – and how not to abuse – communication tools such as the telephone and emails.

There may be restrictions on making personal calls or using email and internet for personal purposes at work. There will often be strict warnings about the unacceptability of offensive or illegal content in messages – although we hope this would be common sense! In an accounting and finance setting, there will almost certainly be policies about confidentiality: what information can and cannot be given, to whom, and by what means, to protect the integrity and security of information.

There may also be helpful guidelines for staff about issues such as: data security when using email (eg the use of anti-virus software); the rules of email 'etiquette'; when to use (and not to use) email; what 'signature' information should be added to the end of emails; and so on.

House style

Organisations seek to communicate a consistent, coherent image to the outside world – and, ideally, also one that reflects the corporate identity, self-image and style. If every member of the organisation presents letters and emails differently, according to their own preferences, a consistent image will be difficult to maintain!

'HOUSE STYLE' is an expression of how the organisation wants to present itself in its communications. It may include aspects such as the use of standardised letterheads and memo pads; how letters and memos are laid out; what headings and formats are used for reports; and the logos, typefaces and colours used as part of the corporate identity. It may also include more subtle aspects such as a tendency towards informality or formality in the tone of writing, or creativity or traditionalism in the style of presentation.

House style may be developed informally, as 'the way we do things around here', which people pick up through modelling their messages on existing examples. House style may also be formally expressed in guidelines and rules for communication – and if this is the case, in your work organisation you should seek to adhere to the guidelines set for you.

HOW IT WORKS

At Southfield Electronics, there is a House Style manual for all communications sent to external parties.

Standardised stationery is available for handwritten and word-processed documents – and also for email messages. The corporate letterhead appears as follows.

SOUTHFIELD ELECTRONICS LTD
Tomorrow's technology for today's homes

Micro House
Newtown Technology Park
Innovation Way
Middx NT3 OPN

Every email must be 'signed off' with a standard block of text called a 'signature block', which is inserted automatically by the email software:

[Sender's Name]
[Sender's Position]

Southfield Electronics Ltd
Micro House, Newtown Technology park
Innovation Way, Middx NT3 OPN, UK

Tel: +44 (0)20x xxx xxxx * Fax: +44 (0)20x xxx xxxx * Web: www.southfield.com

This message and any attachments are confidential and may contain information that is subject to copyright. If you are not the intended recipient, please notify us immediately by replying to this message and then delete it from your system. While we take reasonable precautions to prevent computer viruses, we cannot accept responsibility for viruses transmitted to your computer and it is your responsibility to make all necessary checks. We may monitor email traffic data and the content of emails to ensure efficient operation of our business, for security, for staff training and for other administrative purposes.

General guidelines for effective written communication

We have already looked at these in Chapter 4: be ready to apply them to specific formats such as reports, letters, memos and emails. In order to create clearer communications and foster more effective working relationships:

- Take into account your purpose in writing: what are your aims and objectives? What response or action do you want as a result of your message?

- Take into account the requirements of your target recipient or audience: their information needs and capacities (including their limited time, and familiarity/unfamiliarity with technical jargon).

- Structure your communication in such a way as to make it easy to read and understand.

- Keep it short and simple (KISS) and aim for clarity and ease of understanding.

- Present your material in a way that demonstrates professionalism and reflects the desired image of the organisation.

We will now look at some of the main tools for presenting information in the accounting and finance environment.

INFORMAL BUSINESS REPORTS

'Report' is a general term, which covers a wide range of formats. If you inform someone verbally or in writing of facts, events, actions you have taken, or suggestions you wish to make – you are reporting. In this sense, you can make a report in a meeting or phone call, letter, memo or email.

If you are asked for an INFORMAL REPORT, however, this will usually mean a relatively short written document, in which information is presented in a direct and structured way.

Informal report structure and style

A formal report can be a massive, complex and highly-structured affair, presenting and analysing high-level concepts and information. An informal report is generally used for less complex reporting tasks, so it does not require elaborate referencing, structuring and layout. However, it still needs to have a clear structure and layout, to help the user to 'navigate' through the information.

There are some important points to note about the written style of an informal business report.

BPP
LEARNING MEDIA

The language is still more formal than that used in everyday speech, or in informal messages to colleagues. Avoid slang and colloquialisms. Write grammatically in full sentences. Do not take short cuts: use 'there is' rather than 'there's', and 'I have' rather than 'I've'.

The key objective is ease of understanding, and ease of navigation through the information, for the user. A good report will:

- Avoid technical language for non-technical users.

- Organise material logically – especially if it is designed to be persuasive, leading up to a conclusion or recommendation!

- Signal relevant topics by using appropriate headings.

- Use tables or diagrams, where this would be helpful in highlighting important points (such as comparisons or trends), or in organising raw data (eg into a table).

- Include background or supporting detail into an APPENDIX or appendices: attaching relevant documents at the end of the report, in order to keep its main body concise and flowing.

There are seven key sections of an informal report you need to know about for the assessment. These are as follows.

- Title (or title page)

- Executive summary (sometimes just referred to as the summary)

- Introduction

- Main body/detailed findings (divided into a series of meaningful subsections)

- Conclusions

- Recommendations

- Appendices (as mentioned above)

Now we will look at what each section includes and how a report might look.

REPORT TITLE ('Report on [topic]')

To: Requester/recipient of the report

From: Compiler/writer of the report

Date: Date of submission

Executive summary

The executive summary (or summary) should be a short overview setting out the main findings of the report along with a summary of the key conclusions and recommendations. Although presented at the start, it is often written last as this is the best time to assess what the most important 'headline' points are.

Introduction

The introduction should explain the contents, purpose and scope of the report, along with any relevant background information.

Findings (main body)

Then comes the main body of the report which contains the detailed results, findings or observations. This will be structured in sections, with clear headings. There are different ways of dividing the body of the report into sections, such as:

Section headings: as dictated by the report brief

Report sections may reflect a list of topics you were asked to cover in the report 'brief', or request for information. If you are given a number of issues to report on, it makes sense to use these as your report sections.

Section headings: as dictated by the subject matter

A subject will often have topic areas to provide report headings. You might report on a process, for example, under the headings of its various stages or steps. You might report on data security under the headings of particular security risks (viruses, phishing, systems failure, loss of data).

Section headings: as dictated by the task

If you are asked to investigate an issue, give your findings and make recommendations, it would make sense to have sections headed: Background; Investigation; Findings; Recommendations.

Conclusions

This section will collate the key points arising from each of the preceding sections in the main body of the report, discuss them and explain the conclusions reached as a result. The report brief may not have specifically asked for conclusions, but it will still be helpful to the report user to have at least one overall conclusion including what facts, decisions or options the report has led to. An overview of the key conclusions will be included in the Executive Summary at the start of the report.

> ### Recommendations
>
> There is sometimes a separate section containing any recommendations if not already covered in earlier sections, or to collate all the recommendations in one place. The most important recommendations may also be summarised in the Executive Summary.
>
> ### Appendices
>
> Supporting data and documents can be attached to the report, where useful. Such documents should be numbered and referred to in the body of the report, so the user can locate the data: eg '… based on September sales forecasts (See Appendix 1)' or '… as set out in the attached Schedule (Appendix 2)'.

HOW IT WORKS

You have been at Southfield Electronics for a while now, and you are becoming frustrated by the tendency for staff members to 'cut corners' on organisational policies and procedures, such as correct authorisation of cheque requisitions; respect for the confidentiality of other staff members' personal details; and attendance at fire evacuation drills.

You mention this in conversation with Jenny Faulkner, the financial accountant, and she asks you to observe and record any further instances over the next month and to write an informal report covering: incidences of non-compliance, reasons for concern, and how Southfield can improve compliance. Having observed further non-compliances throughout August 20X0, you draft the following.

 SOUTHFIELD ELECTRONICS LTD

REPORT: COMPLIANCE WITH POLICY & PROCEDURE

Executive summary

During August 20X0 there have been a number of cases where staff members have not complied with company policy, including staff submitting incorrect cheque requisitions, breaches of confidentiality and lack of participation in fire drills. This culture of non-compliance jeopardises efficiency, employee safety and data security. The situation can be remedied by reminding staff of company policy, better staff training and increased monitoring and enforcement of employee compliance by managers.

1 Introduction

This report sets out observations of non compliance with organisational policies and procedures in August 20X0. It was compiled by Your Name, Accounts Clerk, at the request of Jenny Faulkner, Financial Accountant, and submitted on 23 September 20X0.

2 Non-compliance with policies and procedures

In August 20X0, I witnessed several cases where staff members failed to comply with formal policies and procedures.

- Cheque requisition forms have had to be returned to the originators because they were incorrectly completed or authorised. (See copies attached: Appendix 1.)

- There is an apparent lack of respect for the confidentiality of other staff members' personal details, in verbal and written communication with third parties. In some cases staff members' details have been provided to third parties by colleagues without obtaining the relevant employee's permission.

- A number of staff members failed to take part in fire evacuation drills. Those that did take part, failed to comply with proper procedures (for example, by taking lifts and leaving fire doors open). (See the Safety Officer's report on the most recent drill: Appendix 2.)

3 Reasons for concern

The 'lapses' in compliance are of concern, for several reasons.

Policies and procedures, such as the ones mentioned, have been put in place to ensure the efficiency of operations such as cheque requisition; the confidentiality of information which may be used to the detriment of the organisation and/or its staff; and the safety of staff and visitors in the event of an emergency.

4 Conclusions

Non-compliance in such areas jeopardises efficiency (by necessitating re-work), data security and personal safety.

By themselves these may be small things, but I have come to the conclusion they reflect a culture of 'corner cutting' which may eventually result in more serious consequences and immediate action is needed.

5 Recommendations - How Southfield can improve compliance

I would like to make the following recommendations for management's consideration.

- All staff should be reminded of their responsibility to comply with organisational policies and procedures.

- Where necessary, training should be given to reinforce awareness and competence in relevant procedures.

- Managers at all levels should seek to monitor and enforce compliance more strictly, and to model compliance in their own conduct.

I hope this information is helpful, and I would be willing to discuss it further – and to present more detailed evidence of my observations – at your convenience.

Appendix 1: Incorrectly completed cheque requisition forms (attached)
Appendix 2: Safety Officer's Report for August 20X0 (attached)

USING DIAGRAMS AND CHARTS

If you are preparing a report (or perhaps preparing slides for a presentation), you may need to use visual aids of some kind. Diagrams are useful in conveying large amounts of data more accessibly and in adding interest and appeal to a document.

In addition to the numerical competences required to organise your data, there are some key principles of effective 'graphic' communication.

- Give each diagram or chart a concise and meaningful title.

- Cite the source of the data, where relevant.

- Clearly label all elements of the diagram, either on the diagram itself, or in a separate 'key' to the colours or symbols used.

- Keep textual elements (labels, explanatory notes) brief.

- Keep the presentation as simple as possible: cut down on unnecessary lines and elements, to avoid overcrowding, clutter and confusion.

- Make the diagram large enough so that it is easy to read.

Let's look briefly at some examples of visual elements you might use in an informal report.

Tables

Tables are a good way of organising information. The use of columns and rows allows the data to be classified under appropriate headings, clearly organised and labelled, totalled up in various ways (across rows or down columns) and so on.

You might use a table format to organise data about a list of trainees, say, as follows.

Staff member	Training undertaken	Training provider	Duration of training (days)	Cost of training
John				
Amy				
Fred				
Total:				

Bar charts

Bar charts are useful for showing or comparing magnitudes or sizes of items: for example, sales revenue or expenditure on a month-by-month basis, or training costs per department.

- The diagram needs to be labelled to indicate what it shows.

- The positions of the bars are labelled to show what they represent (eg months or departments).

- The height of the bars, drawn against a specified scale, indicate the magnitudes of the different items (monetary value or number).

- The bars can be subdivided to show components of the total magnitudes (eg breakdown of monthly expenditure by department or category).

Sales Revenue 20X0

Pie charts

Pie charts are useful for showing the relative sizes of component elements of a total value or amount, represented by the 360° of the circle or 'pie'. An example might be showing the breakdown of the time you spend on different tasks during a day, or the breakdown of monthly sales revenue by product or customer. Below are the steps involved in providing a pie chart in relation to this.

Step 1   Calculate each item as a fraction and/or percentage of the whole. (If handling emails takes you five hours out of your 40-hour week, say, that's 5/40 or 1/8 or 12.5%.)

Step 2   Translate each fraction/percentage into fractions of a circle. (The 'slice' occupied by handling emails would be 1/8 of the pie.) If you want to draw very accurately, using geometric instruments, you would calculate the exact number of degrees of the circle occupied by each slice, as a fraction or percentage of 360° (1/8 × 360° = 45°).

Step 3   Draw a circle, and divide it up using the fractions (or, to be more accurate, degrees) calculated for each slice.

Step 4   Label each slice with what it represents, and its percentage of the total. Check that it adds up to 100%!

HOW IT WORKS

Jenny Faulkner has asked you to report on the breakdown of your 40-hour working week, to check whether your being a 'shared resource' for the assistant financial accountants and payroll manager is working.

You work out that in an average week, emails take 5 hours (12.5%); your work on payroll takes 20 hours (50%); and your work on ledgers takes 15 hours (37.5%). In presenting this data in your report to Jenny, you decide it will be most helpful in graphic form. You calculate as follows:

$5/40 \times 360$ = $45°$ (1/8 of the pie)
$20/40 \times 360$ = $180°$ (1/2 of the pie)
$15/40 \times 360$ = $135°$ (3/8 of the pie)

And you draw the following simple pie chart, for inclusion in your report.

Line graphs

Line graphs are useful for showing the relationship between two variables (represented by the horizontal and vertical axes of the graph), by plotting points and joining them up with straight or curved lines. These are particularly useful for demonstrating trends, such as the increase in departmental output as more time/money is invested in training and development – or fluctuations in revenue or expenditure (or other values) over time.

Here's a very simple example.

Such a graph could be used to highlight variations in work throughput.

Task 1

The table below shows a company's sales figures for the first six months of 20X0.

Product	Jan £'000	Feb £'000	Mar £'000	Apr £'000	May £'000	Jun £'000	Total £'000
A	800	725	725	400	415	405	
B	210	210	180	150	175	160	
C	25	50	60	95	125	140	
Total							

(a) Add up the rows and columns to insert the totals.

(b) What kind of graph or chart would you use to show the fluctuations of monthly sales figures across the six months?

Picklist

Pie chart
Bar chart
Line graph

Have a go at drawing the graph.*

(c) What kind of graph or chart would you use to show the proportion of total sales represented by each product?

Picklist

Pie chart
Bar chart
Line graph

Have a go at drawing the graph.*

*Note that you will not be asked to produce a graph/chart in the CBT. However drawing these graphs for this task will aid your overall understanding of when and how to use each particular graph/chart type.

BUSINESS LETTERS

A letter is a very flexible and versatile medium of written, person-to-person communication. It can be used for many business purposes: requesting, supplying and confirming information and instructions; offering and accepting goods and services; conveying and acknowledging satisfaction and dissatisfaction (eg complaint and adjustment letters); and explaining what else is in an information package via a covering letter.

The modern business letter contains various standard elements and you will need to know what these are and where they are located on the page. Below, you will see a skeleton format and a full example.

Letterheads (the logo, name and contact details of the organisation sending the letter) are often pre-printed on office stationery, or built into word processor templates. If not you should reproduce the name and address details given at the top of the letter page.

A letter should include:

- The name and address of the target recipient

- The address of the sender

- Date

- Greeting (or 'salutation')

- Subject heading (a brief, helpful 'cue' to what the letter is about)

- An opening paragraph

- The main body of the letter

- A closing paragraph

- Sign-off (or 'complimentary close')

- Signature: If an assistant is signing a letter on behalf of the writer, the writer's name must be preceded by 'For' (or its equivalent from legal terminology: 'pp' which stands for per procurationem)

- Enclosure reference: 'enc' (or 'encs' for more than one item), if something other than the letter is included in the same envelope – such as a cheque, price list or leaflet

- Copy reference: 'copies to' or 'cc' plus the names of any third parties to whom copies of the letter have been sent

ORGANISATION LETTERHEAD
(may be pre-printed on stationery)
(includes sender's address)

Confidentiality warning *(if applicable)*

Recipient's name
Designation
Address   Date

Greeting (salutation),

Subject heading

Introductory paragraph: explaining the context and reason for writing.

The main body of the letter, set out with clear separate paragraphs for each sub-topic or new phase of your message.

The content may be tackled in chronological order (if you are narrating or explaining a sequence of events, say) or in any other appropriate order for the subject matter.

Closing paragraph: summarising the content and purpose of the message, and making clear what course of action (if any) you want the reader to take. Putting this last makes it most impactful and memorable.

Complimentary close *(matched to the salutation)*,

Author's signature (handwritten)

Author's name
Author's position

Enclosure reference *(if something is in the envelope with the letter)*
Copy reference *(if a copy of the letter has been sent to another person)*

SOUTHFIELD ELECTRONICS LTD

Tomorrow's technology for today's homes

Micro House
Newtown Technology Park
Innovation Way
Middx NT3 OPN

Confidential

J M Bloggs
Administrator
Wallend Retail Ltd
Wood Lane Industrial Estate
Sussex BN1 4PW

3 September 20X0

Dear Mr Bloggs,

Account No 0139742

Thank you for your letter of 28 August 20X0 regarding credit payments owing to your account as a result of product returns.

I have looked into the matter that you raised and I am afraid that your earlier letter of 26 July was indeed overlooked, due to the temporary absence of the member of staff to whom you addressed it.

I apologise for the delay in processing your credit payment. I have arranged for your account to be credited with the sum of £346.99, and I enclose a print-out of your account status confirming the balance.

If you have any further queries, please do not hesitate to contact me.

Yours sincerely,

Your Name

pp Kellie McDonald
Assistant Financial Accountant

enc.
cc: Kellie McDonald

Appropriate salutations

You need to demonstrate that you can use an appropriate greeting or salutation for the type of relationship you have with the person you are writing to: this may be formal or informal, in recognition of the other person's status, the familiarity of the relationship, and the customs of the organisation (such as calling managers by their first names – or not!).

By convention, the following greetings (or 'salutations') and sign-offs (or 'complimentary closes') should be used together, and you need to demonstrate that you can match them correctly.

Salutation	Close	Context
Dear Sir/Madam/Sirs (name not used)	Yours faithfully	Formal situations Recipients not known
Dear Dr/Mr/Mrs/Ms Bloggs (formal name used)	Yours sincerely	Established relationships Friendly but respectful (eg with superiors, customers, suppliers)
Dear Joe/Josephine	Yours sincerely Kind regards	More personal, informal relationships (eg with colleagues)

Task 2

You have been asked to write a letter to the following people. What salutations and closes will you use?

(a) The accounts department of a firm you are dealing with for the first time.

Salutation [   ]

Close [   ]

(b) A female customer whose name you know to be Georgia Brown, but whose marital status you do not know.

Salutation [   ]

Close [   ]

(c) A sales representative called Mark Stein, whom you know well and with whom you are on first name terms.

Salutation [   ]

Close [   ]

(d) The managing director of your firm, whose name is Sir Joshua Holmes.

Salutation [   ]

Close [   ]

Professional image

A letter may be the first contact a person has with your organisation, so it needs to make a positive impression. As discussed in Chapter 3, this generally means: legibility, neatness, conciseness and businesslike tone. If a letter is handwritten, you will need to minimise crossings out (or Tippex). If it is word processed, it will still require attention to spelling errors, 'typos' and other problems (such as faint or blotchy printing) which may spoil the image of professionalism you are trying to create.

House style

An organisation may have its own stationery and letterhead. House style or custom may also dictate where the standard letter elements are arranged on the page.

- Our example shows what is called a 'semi-blocked' layout, with the date at the top right-hand side of the page, and the subject header centred.

- You will often see the simpler 'fully blocked' style, with everything against the left-hand margin.

At work, you should follow the layout used in your own organisation.

Well structured

A letter (and indeed, any written message) should have a beginning, a middle and an end.

- The opening paragraph is important, because the reader will not be as familiar with the context or reason for the letter as you are! Offer a brief explanation of why you are writing, an acknowledgement of relevant correspondence received, or other introductory background details.

- The middle paragraph(s) should contain the substance of your message. If you are making several points, start a new paragraph with each, so that the reader can digest each part of your message in turn.

- The closing paragraph is important, because it is the best opportunity to make clear to the reader what you hope to have achieved. Summarise your point briefly, or make clear exactly what response is required.

Task 3

Suggest some opening lines for the following letter situations.

(a) You are replying to an agreement you made by phone to send someone a brochure detailing your services.

(b) You have had a phone message from one of your sales reps, George Brown, saying that a person wants to enquire about job openings in the accounts department, and would like to be contacted by mail.

Suggest some closing lines for the following letter situations.

(c) You already have a meeting scheduled to discuss the matter further.

(d) You have just provided the person with answers to questions.

Clearly written

Again, remember the KISS principles we discussed in Chapter 4. Your written style needs to be helpfully structured (in well-spaced paragraphs), easy to read, unambiguous, free of jargon, free of cliché (without meaningless 'stock' phrases), and concise (without unnecessary words).

We can't really teach you to do this. You will have to develop your skills at letter writing by modelling your style on the examples given in this Combined Text and Question Bank – and by evaluating what does and does not work in the letters you encounter.

MEMOS AND BUSINESS EMAILS

Memos

A MEMO or 'memorandum' performs the same function internally as a letter does in external communication by an organisation. It can be used for reports, brief messages or 'notes' and any kind of internal communication that is most easily or clearly conveyed in writing.

Memos are generally written on stationery pre-printed with appropriate headings – or typed into a word-processor template. The standardised headings are designed to make writing more efficient, given that the message is for internal use.

The following shows the standard elements of memo format.

MEMO	
To: [Recipient's name, designation]	**Reference:** [File reference]
From: [Sender's name, designation]	**Date:** [In full]
Subject: [Concise statement of main theme or topic of message]	

The main text of the memo is set out in correct, concise, readily understandable English, in spaced paragraphs following a clear, logical structure. Note that no inside address, salutation or complimentary close are required.

Signature or initials [optional]

cc: [To indicate recipient(s) of copies of the memo, if any]
enc: [To indicate accompanying material, if any]

Nowadays, memos have generally been replaced by internal email messages, which have much the same features – except that you are typing into an electronic form created by email software.

HOW IT WORKS

Following your informal report on non-compliance with Southfield Electronics' policies and procedures, Jenny Faulkner has been investigating, and one morning you receive the following memo.

 SOUTHFIELD ELECTRONICS LTD

MEMO

To:	Your Name, Accounts Clerk
From:	Jenny Faulkner, Financial Accountant
Date:	11 September 20X0
Subject	Abuse of telephone procedures

I have been looking into instances of non-compliance with procedures, and I believe I have identified an additional matter that would be worth investigating further. As you know, our telephone costs have risen significantly over the last quarter, and I have identified three main causes.

1.   There are more telephones in the office than are necessary for efficient communication.

2. Staff have become accustomed to making personal calls on office apparatus.

3. Many calls are made at expensive charge rates and at unnecessary length.

I would like the accounts team to come up with some ideas for action to prevent further cost increases. Is this something that you might be interested in taking on as a project?

Meanwhile, let me know if you have any initial thoughts on the matter.

Thanks.

JF

Task 4

(a) Write Jenny a brief memo replying to the memo sent to you in the 'How It Works' section above.

(b) Write a brief letter to an office equipment company (TeleComs Ltd, 6 Park Way, Brighton, Sussex BN3 4PW) asking for information about models and costs of electronic switchboards and devices for the logging of telephone calls from handsets.

Email

EMAIL is a method for sending electronic messages from one computer to another, either internally within the workplace or to an external party. Email is easy to use, extremely fast and relatively cheap. It is also particularly flexible, because photos, diagrams, computer files or spreadsheets can be sent (with the email as a kind of 'covering letter') as attachments.

To use email, you simply log onto the email software (one of the most common being Microsoft Outlook), and press 'Create email' or 'New mail'. This presents you with a standard email 'page', which looks a bit like a memo form with extra option buttons!

If you have access to email facilities, you simply type data into the fields on the on-screen email page. When the recipient receives your message (and/or when you print it out), the various headers will be included in the print-out, and the sender address and date will be inserted automatically.

You may be asked to complete an email in a CBT task during the assessment by entering the recipient's email address and selecting appropriate words based on accompanying information.

The standard elements for an email are much like a memo.

EMAIL

To: *[Recipient's email address: name@company.co.uk or similar]*

Cc: *[Email addresses of parties to whom the message is copied]*

From: *[Sender's email address]*

Date: *[Today's date]*

Subject: *Concise statement of main theme or topic of message.*

Attach: *[Name of file attached to the message]*

The main text of the email should be written in correct, concise, readily understandable English, in spaced paragraphs following a clear, logical structure and a simple format – avoid the use of **bold**, <u>underlined</u>, *italic* or CAPITALISED text (capitals in an email give an impression of you shouting, which is not professional).

Name/initials (optional)

Signature block (inserted automatically, if used)

Using email effectively

Email is so widespread, it is easy to forget that it has some limitations as a medium of communication!

It is not as secure as you might think (particularly if you accidentally send it to the wrong address or multiple addresses): think carefully before using it for private and confidential messages.

Email is fast and easy to use: think carefully before 'dashing off' messages which may damage relationships (eg by being offensive or inappropriately informal) or have practical implications (eg making commitments to a customer or supplier which you can't later fulfil).

As some email programmes remove formatting, it is best to avoid anything fancy in an email that you send, such as **bold**, <u>underlined</u>, *italic* or CAPITALISED text, since these may not actually be seen by the recipient. Also to be avoided because of the unprofessional impression they give are 'emoticons' such as smileys ☹.

When you have finished the message, always check it through thoroughly: once it has been sent there is no retrieving it!

You should familiarise yourself with the email format (and any guidelines for use) of your organisation.

Making best use of the subject line

The subject line is more or less compulsory in emails (sometimes the software won't let you send a message without one), because if you don't signal what the message is about, the recipient may think it is SPAM (an unsolicited mass marketing message) or some kind of fake message carrying a computer virus: any message without a relevant subject line should be deleted unread!

The subject line is helpful in letting the recipient know whether the message is worth reading; whether it is high or low priority; and whether it has been directed to the right person (or needs to be forwarded). It also directs the recipient to the subject of the message, like a very brief 'executive summary', so that (s)he can be mentally prepared, and read the message more efficiently.

So use the subject line wisely. Use a short phrase that will most effectively convey the seriousness, relevance and topic of the message to a user who may not be expecting it. ('Hi there' or 'read this' probably won't do the job...)

If you are replying directly to an email sent to you (by pressing the 'reply' button), the email software will insert the subject line: 'RE: [the subject of the original message]'. So if you reply to a message 'Monthly totals', the subject line will automatically read: 'RE: Monthly totals'.

HOW IT WORKS

Back at Southfield Electronics, you are working on your analysis of the customers that have been allocated to you. Just to check that you are doing it correctly, you would like a copy of an analysis which your colleague Amy Laval has already completed. You send her a quick email.

EMAIL	
Date:	[inserted automatically]
To:	alaval@southfield.co.uk
From:	yname@southfield.co.uk
Subject:	Customer analysis

Amy,

I'd be grateful if you could send me a copy of a customer analysis that you have already completed, so that I can check that I am doing it correctly.

Thanks.

Your Name

Task 5

Compose an email from Amy to you, in reply to your email to her in the 'How It Works' example above.

CHAPTER OVERVIEW

- Workplace communication methods include face-to-face discussion, telephone calls, informal notes, memos, emails, letters and informal reports.

- Organisations often issue guidelines for staff on how to use various communication methods efficiently and effectively, and how external messages should be presented. 'House style' is an expression of how the organisation wants to present itself in its communications, and house style conventions and guidelines should be adhered to, to ensure consistency and coherence.

- Informal reports are relatively short written documents, in which information is presented in a direct and structured way. They should follow a clear logical structure, and be written in an easy-to-understand and appropriately businesslike (relatively formal) style.

- Diagrams and charts (including bar charts, line graphs, pie charts and flow charts) may be used in reports to illustrate key points of data. They should be carefully drawn and labelled for ease of use.

- Business letters are highly versatile for person-to-person written communication. They contain various standard elements. You will need to know what these are and where they are located on the page in different 'house style' layouts. It is particularly important to use appropriate salutations (greetings) and closes.

- Memos cover a wide range of internal written messages. They are generally written on stationery with pre-prepared standard headings.

- Email is a method for sending a written message from one computer to another. Email software, like memo stationery, has pre-prepared headings into which you can input sender/recipient and subject information. You need to make good use of the subject line.

- Regardless of format, all reports, letters, memos and emails must conform to house style guidelines and the attributes of effective communication.

Keywords

Email – an electronic method of sending a note, letter, memo or other information via computer

House style – the distinctive way an organisation seeks to present itself in its communications

Informal report – a relatively short written document, in which information is presented in a direct and structured way

Appendix – a separate section attached to a report, with supporting data or documents referred to in the report

Memo – a structured message sent within an organisation via internal mail

TEST YOUR LEARNING

Test 1

For each of the following situations, which would be the most appropriate method of communication? Choose from the picklist below.

Situation	Method	
Detailing a telephone message left by a supplier for a colleague		▼
Informing an employee that his work has not been up to standard recently		▼
Requesting a customer's sales ledger account balance from the credit controller		▼
Requesting production details for the last month from the factory manager where the factory is situated five miles away		▼
Sending monthly variances to the sales manager		▼

Picklist

Email
Informal note
Face to face discussion

Test 2

What information is usually contained in the three sections of a report shown below (on the left hand side)? Indicate your selections by drawing lines between the relevant information (on the right) and the section in which it would appear (on the left).

Report section

Executive summary

Main body

Introduction

Content

Detailed results and findings

Summary of key conclusions

Purpose and scope of the report

Overview of key findings

Test 3

A fellow member of your AAT local branch recently asked you for advice on report writing, and specifically on the use of appendices. Draft a short letter (making up appropriate details of your and the other person's address) explaining the purpose of an appendix, and what (s)he needs to do to ensure that (s)he uses appendices effectively. Use a fully blocked letter layout.

chapter 6:
WORKING INDEPENDENTLY

chapter coverage 📖

In this chapter, you will develop the knowledge and skills required to plan and manage your own workload effectively. We discuss important issues in personal effectiveness such as prioritising, flexibility, confidentiality and meeting deadlines. We also examine the use of a range of planning aids and organisational tools.

This chapter explains how to prioritise and schedule tasks and to plan the use of your time: these are all tasks you could be expected to perform in the assessment. It also includes a section on the importance of meeting deadlines.

The topics covered are:

- ✍ What is involved in a 'job'?
- ✍ Time management
- ✍ Setting and managing priorities
- ✍ Planning aids
- ✍ Monitoring plans
- ✍ Meeting deadlines
- ✍ Adhering to working practices and policies

WHAT IS INVOLVED IN A JOB?

A 'job' is a collection of tasks and responsibilities allocated to an individual. Some organisations allocate a defined set of tasks to individuals in particular positions, while others allow teams to allocate tasks among themselves more flexibly (within the constraints set by the team's goals and targets for performance).

Job description

A key element in being able to work effectively is knowing exactly what is required of you (and what you are not necessarily expected to do). In most cases, an employee will be given a JOB DESCRIPTION when (s)he enters a position. This should include a job title and an outline of the main tasks and responsibilities involved in the job.

HOW IT WORKS

When you started work at Southfield Electronics, you were given the job description shown below.

JOB DESCRIPTION	
Job title:	Accounts clerk, financial accounting
Location:	London office
Job summary:	General financial accounting duties
Key responsibilities	Providing administrative and clerical support to the Assistant Financial Accountants and Payroll Manager, including filing, answering the telephone and dealing with post
	Undertaking work as requested, including: obtaining quotes from suppliers; preparing daily cheque listings, sales invoices, credit notes and monthly sales summaries; and checking purchase invoices to goods received notes
	Using own initiative to deal with enquiries in the absence of the Assistant Financial Accountants
	Being aware of the importance of maintaining strict confidentiality in all aspects of work

Reporting structure:	Financial accountant
	Assistant financial accountants (2) and Payroll manager
	Accounts clerk
Hours:	9:00am to 5:30pm Monday to Friday 1 hour for lunch
Training:	Induction training will be provided Continuing Professional Development encouraged
Prepared by:	Head of HR
Date:	March 20X0

TIME MANAGEMENT

Time is a resource – the same as money, information, materials and equipment. You have a fixed and limited amount of it, and various demands in your work (and non-work) life compete for a share of it. If you work in an organisation, your 'time is money': you will be paid for it, or for what you accomplish with it.

Time, like any other resource, needs to be managed if it is to be used efficiently (without waste) and effectively (productively).

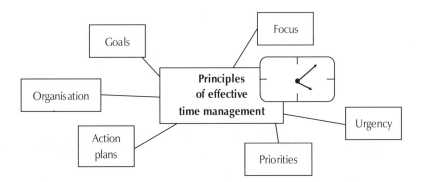

The key principles of TIME MANAGEMENT (according to John Adair) can be summarised as follows:

- **Set goals** for all aspects of your work, so that you know what you want to achieve – and can tell when you have done so.

- **Formulate action plans** that set out how you intend to achieve your goals: the timescale, deadlines, the tasks involved, resources required and so on. (We will look at various planning aids later on.)

- **Set priorities**: decide which tasks are the most important – what is the most valuable use of your time at this moment? – and list them in the order in which you would tackle them. (We discuss how to do this below.)

- **Focus**: give your attention to one thing at a time, if possible. Make sure that everything you need for the task is available, avoid interruptions if you can – and then concentrate.

- **Urgency**: do not put off tasks because they are difficult or large. (They will only get worse as the deadline approaches!) Work on any task you are doing as if it were urgent.

- **Organisation**: develop positive work habits which minimise the time and effort spent (and wasted) on tasks. Do similar tasks (eg photocopying) in batches to avoid multiple trips to the photocopier. Keep your filing up-to-date, so you know where to find things. Manage your in-tray: don't let things 'pile up' without dealing with them or making a plan to do so.

Routine tasks

Much of your day at work will revolve around the carrying out of the ROUTINE TASKS that will have been summarised in your job description. Some of these will be daily tasks, such as opening the post, doing the filing and dealing with incoming emails. Other tasks may be weekly tasks, such as paying suppliers' invoices or monthly items, such as preparing the bank reconciliation statement.

HOW IT WORKS

Every day at Southfield Electronics, you are (as stated in your job description) required to open the post in the morning. You have to list any cheques received from customers and give the cheque listing to Kellie McDonald. If any purchase **invoices** are received from suppliers, you retain them for checking against 'goods received' documentation during the week. Once checked, you hand them over to Kellie McDonald each Friday morning for payment.

You distribute any other post received to the in-trays of the relevant people each morning.

During each day, you will receive despatch notes from the Stores department, for goods which have been sent out to customers. Each day, you are required to prepare sales invoices corresponding to these despatch notes, which are then sent to the financial accountant, Jenny Faulkner, for checking by the end of each day: they are then sent out to the customers the next day.

You will also receive goods returned notes from the Stores department. By the end of each week, you must have produced, and sent to Jenny Faulkner, a credit note for each goods returned note.

At the end of each month, Jenny Faulkner requires a listing of all invoices and credit notes sent out during the month.

A number of times per week, you will receive purchase requisitions which have been authorised by Jenny Faulkner. Your task is to email the appropriate suppliers, requesting quotations, and to prepare purchase orders from approved suppliers.

All copy invoices, credit notes, purchase invoices and purchase requisitions should be filed each day.

As office junior, you are also (informally) expected to ensure that there is tea, coffee, milk and biscuits in the office kitchen.

In order to keep track of all these routine tasks, you summarise them in a helpful format, as follows.

Daily	■ Open post
	■ Prepare cheque listing
	■ Distribute other post
	■ Check emails and respond
	■ Prepare sales invoices
	■ Filing
	■ Check kitchen supplies
Weekly	■ Check purchase orders – ready for Friday morning
	■ Send quotation requests and purchase orders
	■ Prepare credit notes
Monthly	■ Prepare sales invoice/credit note listing

Unexpected tasks

As well as the general, routine tasks that are part of your role, you may also be asked to perform non-routine or unexpected tasks. These may be one-off special jobs, cover for an employee who is off sick, or assisting a colleague to complete his or her task. They may also include the handling of enquiries or queries from customers, suppliers or other staff members.

Such tasks are part of general working life, and you will need to fit them into your work schedule. This is why the guidance notes for this Unit refer to 'changing priorities as appropriate': in other words, adjusting your plans and priorities to take account of changing demands.

Task 1

Place each of the tasks below in the relevant box using the drag and drop list below.

Routine tasks	Unexpected tasks

Drag and drop choices:

Preparing a special report for your manager
Performing the weekly bank reconciliation
Preparing sales invoices daily
Dealing with petty cash as the petty cashier is off sick
Listing cheques received in the post each morning
Showing a visitor around

Urgent tasks and important tasks

Some tasks will be URGENT TASKS: they need to be completed for a deadline in the near future. For example, the marketing director may request a breakdown of sales by product for a meeting first thing tomorrow morning.

Other tasks might be classified as IMPORTANT TASKS. These are jobs that have major value or potential consequences for the organisation: for example, preparing cost estimates for a major purchase, or a report for a high-level meeting. A task will be classed as important if:

- Other people or tasks rely on its timely completion (a task which is relatively unimportant to you may be an important part of someone else's work); and/or

- The consequences of non-completion are high (in terms of costs, damage, delay); and/or

- It has been requested by an individual or body which has high power (eg a senior manager or government agency)

It is natural to think that an urgent task is important – or that an important task is urgent – but this is not necessarily the case. You may have time to devote to the important task – or you may have to 'drop' an urgent task because it is not as important as another requirement. This is a question of priority.

Task 2

It is the first day of the current month. Indicate whether each of the following tasks is urgent or 'important'. (Select urgent if you think the task is both urgent and important. If the task is important but not urgent, select 'important'.)

Task	Important/Urgent
Preparing a credit note listing for your manager due by the end of the month	▼
Producing a staff analysis for the Personnel Director for a meeting this afternoon	▼
Producing product costings for the production manager for a meeting first thing tomorrow morning	▼
Checking purchase invoices to goods received notes	▼

Picklist

Important

Urgent

SETTING AND MANAGING PRIORITIES

Even with routine tasks, it may be necessary to plan the order in which you will carry them out on a given day or week. When unexpected tasks are introduced as well, this form of planning becomes even more important. The process of determining the order in which tasks should be carried out is known as PRIORITISING. So how do you go about it?

Prioritising by urgency and importance

Clearly, urgent tasks are higher-priority than non-urgent tasks, and important tasks are higher-priority than unimportant tasks. You might therefore use a simple framework of four categories.

Urgent and important	Tasks that must be done in the very near future and which are important to you and to other people in the organisation. (For example, you are asked to produce a report for a manager for a high-level strategy meeting tomorrow morning.)
Not urgent but important	Tasks which are important but not immediately due. (For example, today is Monday and the project manager has asked for some product costings for Friday.) Beware, however, if you leave non-urgent tasks too long, they become urgent!
Urgent but not important	Tasks which are urgent – but will not be a major problem if not completed in time. (For example, there is no milk in the kitchen, and the shops are about to close. The worst that can happen is some grumbling, until you can find time to shop the following morning.)
Not urgent and not important	Tasks that can be slotted into the gaps between higher-priority tasks. (For example, periodically you may pack up out-of-date files to be stored in the archives.)

HOW IT WORKS

As well as your routine duties at Southfield Electronics (detailed earlier), you discover that a number of other tasks are required of you today, Thursday, when you come into work.

- There is no milk in the fridge, and it is your responsibility to replace it.

- Jenny Faulkner has left a note on your desk saying that she needs the November sales figures by lunchtime, for a meeting with the Managing Director.

- Kellie McDonald requires photocopies of the cheque listings for the last two weeks by Friday lunchtime.

Remember that you also have your routine duties to carry out. How should you plan your day? To start with, you could categorise your tasks according to their urgency and importance.

Category	Tasks	Comments
Urgent and important	Open and distribute post Produce daily cheque listing Check emails Plus November sales figures (today)	Although the routine tasks are not as important as the job for Jenny, they are still important: your colleagues rely on you completing them.
Not urgent but important	Prepare sales invoices Check purchase invoices ready (Fri) Check credit notes prepared Plus copy cheque listings (Fri)	There should be time to fit these in around the urgent/important tasks – but keep an eye on them, because they will become urgent if left too long.
Urgent but not important	Buy milk	May be important to colleagues, so perhaps persuade one of them to do you a favour (in their own interests) and go to the shop!

Your day can now be organised with the tasks undertaken in the order suggested by the above analysis.

Other prioritising techniques

If tasks are of equal urgency and importance, or there are no particular issues of priority, the following are some other possible criteria for determining the order in which tasks should be completed.

- Arrival time: performing tasks in the order in which they are requested.

- Most nearly finished: starting with the task nearest completion. (It is satisfying ticking off finished tasks – and frustrating to interrupt a nearly-complete task to start something else.)

- Shortest task first: enabling you to get lots of tasks out of the way quickly.

- Longest/most difficult task first: enabling you to get some momentum on tasks you might otherwise procrastinate over!

- Difficulty of handover: if you are about to go on holiday, say, you should tackle the things that it will be most difficult for someone else to take over while you are away.

Task 3

It is 4:00pm on Friday afternoon and the office will shut at 5:30pm. You are in the process of printing off the sales invoices for the day, to be checked by the accountant and sent out this evening. Your supervisor approaches you and asks you to print out and bind a confidential report that she requires for a meeting on Monday at 12:00 noon. There is only one printer in the Accounts department. You estimate that there are still another 30 minutes of sales invoice printing, and that the high resolution report will take about two-and-a-half hours to print and bind.

Which of the following actions should you take now?

Continue printing the sales invoices ☐

Interrupt the sales invoice printing in order to print the confidential report instead ☐

In the assessment you could be provided with a number of work requests and deadlines, which you would then have to prioritise and organise in order to ensure that they will all be completed on time.

Dealing with changes in priority

Just because you have planned your tasks for a day or a week does not mean that they are fixed in stone! As other unexpected tasks come along, you may well need to change your priorities – and therefore the order in which you carry out your jobs.

HOW IT WORKS

You have been working hard in the Financial Accounts department at Southfield Electronics this Thursday morning and by 11:30am, you have produced the November sales figures for Jenny, opened the post, prepared the cheque listing and distributed the post. You also managed to persuade Amy Laval to go out and buy the milk. However, you are just about to check your emails when Jenny Faulkner comes over to your desk.

She tells you that Sam Piper, the new accounts assistant, has gone home ill. One of Sam's most urgent tasks today was to prepare statements for two large customers who are querying the amount that they owe. As you have done this before, Jenny asks you if you will perform this task for Sam and get the statements to her by 4:00pm for checking and sending out in the post tonight.

You now have to change your priorities, as this task is both urgent and important. Your day will now look as follows:

- Prepare customer statements by 4:00pm at the latest
- Check emails – deal with any that are urgent
- Photocopy the cheque listings for Kelly McDonald
- Prepare sales invoices for the day
- Check that purchase invoices will be ready for Friday morning
- Check that all credit notes have been prepared

A pretty full day!

Scheduling tasks

Once you have a list of priorities, you will need to SCHEDULE tasks, by determining when you will tackle them.

Determining the time that it will take to do a task is easy if it is a routine procedure that you have done many times before: simply note how long it takes you, on average. With non-routine tasks, particularly substantial ones, it can be far more difficult to determine how long to allow. You can ask someone with more experience than you, or you might be able to break the task down into smaller stages whose duration you can more easily estimate. The important thing is to be realistic!

Time schedules can be determined by different methods.

- Forward scheduling: adding the estimated duration of each task from its scheduled starting time/date, to give you the target completion time/date. This is useful for scheduling routine tasks.

- Backward scheduling: subtracting the estimated duration of each task from its deadline or completion time/date. This gives you the latest start from which you'll get the job done in time – so schedule an earlier start where possible! This method is useful for meeting deadlines and for complex tasks, where each stage depends on the timely completion of the previous stage.

- Slotting your tasks into appropriate start dates/times, in order of priority – and fitting lower-priority tasks around higher-priority ones. Remember to check that your daily schedule only adds up to the number of working hours in your day (allowing for lunch breaks, routine daily jobs and scheduled meetings). Tasks which don't 'fit' can then be moved to a bigger 'slot' (if they have to be done all in one go) or carried over for completion on another day.

Task 4

An accounts assistant works from 9:00am to 5:00pm (with a lunch break between 1:00pm and 2:00pm). The assistant has the following routine daily duties which are listed in order of priority below (most important shown first) with the maximum expected duration of the task shown in brackets.

- Respond to customer queries from the day before (1 hour).
- Enter sales invoices/credit notes (45 mins).
- Enter purchase invoices/credit notes (45 mins).
- Enter cash receipts and payments (1 hour).
- Print daily cheque run (30 mins).
- File all sales and purchases invoices and credit notes (1 hour).

On arriving at work on Thursday, the assistant notices two messages on her desk.

- The first is from the accountant asking for a statement to generated and sent via email to a major customer as soon as possible. It will take a maximum of 30 minutes to complete this task.

- The second is from the HR manager asking the accounts assistant to attend a compulsory meeting for all employees to take place in the HR office at 3.30 pm, expected to last an hour.

At 2:00pm the assistant picks up an email from the managing director asking for the balances and recent activity on the accounts of eight customers which he urgently requires for a meeting at 9:00am tomorrow.

The director says extracting this information will probably take about 1 hour, but the assistant is more familiar with the computer system and is almost certain the task will take an hour and a half.

Using the picklist below indicate the order in which the accounts assistant should have carried out the tasks for the day.

THURSDAY tasks		Order of task completion
	▼	First task
	▼	Second task
	▼	Third task
	▼	Fourth task
	▼	Fifth task
	▼	Sixth task
	▼	Seventh task
	▼	Eighth task

Picklist

Print daily cheque run

Generate eight customer balances for MD meeting

HR Meeting

Enter purchase invoices/credit notes

Enter cash receipts and payments

Enter sales invoices/credit notes

Respond to customer queries from the day before

File all sales and purchases invoices and credit notes

Generate statement and send to major customer

Protecting your time

In addition to planning your time, time management requires you to control – and sometimes protect – your time, in the face of changing and competing demands.

- You may need to delegate less important tasks which can be done by other people, in order to free up your time for more important tasks which only you can do.

- You may need to develop skills in assertiveness (stating clearly, firmly but calmly what you feel, need or want), in order to ask for help when you need it – or to say 'no' when others inappropriately make demands on your time.

We look at this, in the context of working as part of a team, in Chapter 7, but it is important to remember that if a colleague or manager tries to add something to your planned and agreed schedule, this may cause a conflict of priorities, and you will have to negotiate solutions to such conflicts. As we have seen, the solution may be to re-prioritise your schedule, if it is flexible enough, or to ask for assistance or extra time where necessary.

However, it may be that the only solution is to say 'no' to requests, if they are unreasonable. In a professional setting – and particularly if the requester is in a position of authority – this will have to be done courteously and positively (proposing alternative ways of getting their demands met if possible), but also firmly.

PLANNING AIDS

There are a wide variety of PLANNING AIDS that can help you to ensure that all of your tasks are remembered, scheduled, monitored and completed on time.

To Do List

The simplest planning aid is a 'To Do List', tick list or checklist. Here you simply write down each task that is required of you for the day, preferably in prioritised order. Then as each task is completed, you tick it off from the list – the satisfying part!

At the end of the day, anything left un-ticked on the To Do list can be carried over to tomorrow's To Do list and fitted into tomorrow's tasks and priorities.

Another advantage of this technique is that, if you have to hand your tasks over to someone else, it is easy for them to see where you are 'up to'.

Diary or timetable

The purpose of the diary or timetable is to slot events, tasks or meetings into clearly labelled time 'slots' (hours or days), where they become an easily used reminder (and signal that that time is 'taken' and cannot be used for other scheduled items).

Diaries also offer a useful follow-up system, because you can schedule questions, checks and follow-up actions: for example, to check that you have received the data you requested on the day it was due.

Diaries and timetables can be paper-based or electronic (eg using a PDA, electronic personal organiser, mobile phone or computer). Software such as Microsoft Outlook and Palm Desktop is often used to combine a diary, alarm clock (notifying you of the time for diarised events), To Do list (with reminders as you approach deadlines) and address book (in case you need to contact other people involved).

You might like to experiment with such tools if you have access to them. The limitations of such systems are: they do not guarantee efficient or organised working; it is easy to grow dependent on them (to the point where loss or damage creates chaos); and they can take quite a lot of time to use effectively!

Planning schedules and charts

Schedules and charts are often used for more complex tasks or projects. They tend to be used when a project involves a number of separate tasks, some of which must be completed before others can be started. Longer-term planning schedules may be conveniently set out using charts or monthly/yearly 'planners'.

Bar charts are often used to 'block out' periods of time on a calendar, to show when tasks are scheduled, or when staff members are on holiday. This has the advantage of clearly showing where tasks fall in the month/year, what order they fall in, where they overlap and so on.

A PLANNING SCHEDULE is a form of bar chart, but each division of space represents both an amount of time and an amount of work to be done in that time. Lines or bars drawn across the space indicate how much work is scheduled to be done and/or how much work has actually been done.

This makes it easy to measure your progress, and whether you are ahead of schedule or behind schedule. Here's an example of a planning schedule for a small furniture maker, showing work in progress against schedule at the morning break time on Thursday 8 March 20X0.

Task 5

What can you tell from this planning chart about the furniture maker's progress on the scheduled tasks for the week?

Choose from the picklist below.

Table ▽

Shelves ▽

Kitchen units ▽

Bed ▽

Picklist

Completed on schedule
Ahead of schedule
Behind schedule
Not due to start

HOW IT WORKS

Management accountant, Kate Saltmarsh, has to produce the quarterly cost accounts for the quarter ending 30 November for the finance director by Monday 13 December. From experience she knows the following:

- Once she has all of the information to hand, it will take her two full days (around her other tasks) to produce the accounts.

- She will need a variety of information from the assistant management accountants and this will take them two days to prepare.

- The typing of the accounts can be done in half a day and then there will be another half day of proofing and checking.

- The accounts must be sent to the general office for binding which will take a further day.

If Kate is to have the accounts on the Finance Director's desk by the morning of Monday 13, she will have to start work some time in advance. So she draws up a To do list, backward scheduling based on having the accounts fully bound at close of business on Friday 10 December.

To Do List

- Friday 10 December – binding
- Thursday 9 December – typing and proofing
- Tuesday 7 and Wednesday 8 December – preparation time
- Friday 3 December – request information from assistants

Kate then realises that she will be out of the office all day on Tuesday 7 December, and will need to allow for this as well. The final planning schedule for the preparation of the cost accounts will therefore be as follows.

	December						
	Thur 2	Fri 3	Mon 6	Tues 7	Wed 8	Thurs 9	Fri 10
Request information	■■						
Preparation of accounts			■■		■■		
Typing and proofing						■■	
Binding							■■

From this Kate will also be able to warn the typist to be ready for the work on Thursday 9 December, and warn the general office to be ready for the binding task on Friday 10 December.

Task 6

At the end of Friday 5 October, your in-tray includes a number of work requests for the following week. You collate them to draw up a To Do List. (The 'job codes' are the initials of the person who requested each task, plus a number, so that you can slot them into a timetable more easily.)

Job code	Task	Approx time	Deadline (end of:)
AB1	Project cost analysis	7 hours	Wed 10
AB2	Depreciation figures	5 hours	Wed 10
AB3	Presentation slides	8 hours	Thur 11
AB4	Check inventory (stock) figures	12 hours	Mon 15
Train	Training course	6 hours	Fri 12: 8am – 3pm
AB5	Collect staff CPD plans	2 hours	Fri 26
CD1	Check statements	6 hours	Tues 9
EF1	Aged receivables (debtors)	6 hours	Tues 9
EF2	Bank reconciliations	4 hours	Mon 8

(a) Complete the timetable that follows, indicating what task you will work on for each hour of each working day. (Note that overtime has been authorised for a maximum of two hours each day.)

(b) Identify any task(s) where you may have difficulty meeting the deadline.

TIMETABLE					
	Mon 8	Tues 9	Wed 10	Thurs 11	Fri 12
[8.00 – 9.00]					
9.00 – 10.00					
10.00 – 11.00					
11.00 – 12.00					
12.00 – 13.00					
13.00 – 14.00					
14.00 – 15.00					
15.00 – 16.00					
16.00 – 17.00					
[17.00 – 18.00]					

Task(s) carried over to week beginning 15 October:

-
-

Action plans

An ACTION PLAN is an even more detailed planning tool which can be used for complex and usually longer term projects. It contains a considerable amount of detail and is monitored on a regular basis to ensure that things are going to plan and, if they are not, to devise how the situation can be rectified. An action plan normally contains:

- Details of each task which is part of the project
- Start date of each task
- Completion date for each task
- Person responsible for each task
- (In some cases) expected and actual costs

MONITORING PLANS

Plans are all well and good – but things do not always 'go to plan'! It is important that schedules are monitored to ensure that everything is happening as and when expected. If not, adjustments may have to be made either to how the task is being done (if extra effort or resources are required) – or to the plan or deadline (if it was unrealistic, say).

All individuals must maintain checks and controls over their work, to ensure that stages of work are 'on track', that jobs have in fact been completed at the deadline (or payments made when they fall due), and that agreed follow-up actions are not forgotten.

Checklists are useful for monitoring what has been done and what hasn't. Diary systems may also be used. Some computer-based organiser systems issue alert messages when the scheduled event or completion time approaches.

You should keep copies of work plans and schedules, and any work request forms (or other communications in which you are asked to perform tasks). This will enable you to:

- Check that your work is on track with your current schedule

- Review and keep track of original work requests, plans and priorities, as the situation changes

- Monitor the need for follow-up action

- Review your scheduling and workload management, perhaps with your supervisor or learning coach, to see how effectively you have translated work requests into plans and schedules

MEETING DEADLINES

A DEADLINE is a set or agreed time when a task must be completed. It is important to realise that deadlines are set for a reason. Some are obvious reasons: the sales director has a meeting with a large customer this afternoon, say, and needs a printout of the sales to this customer for the last six months. The time of the meeting is the (obvious) deadline.

Other reasons for deadlines may not be so obvious. Your line manager has asked for some figures for Wednesday, because she has to write a report for Monday morning: you don't necessarily know that it will take her two days to complete the report – but she does.

Missing deadlines

If you fail to complete the task by the deadline, this will affect the person who has asked you to undertake the work – and has then relied on you to do so.

There may be occasions when it will become apparent that you are going to struggle to meet a deadline. This could be for a number of reasons.

- Your workload may be too great for you to finish on time.

- Colleagues who are providing you with required information may have failed to meet their deadlines for doing so.

- You may not have planned effectively or worked efficiently enough.

- Unexpected, higher-priority demands may have been placed on your time, pushing lower-priority tasks back.

Reporting problems in meeting deadlines

Whatever the reason, if you become aware that you may not meet a deadline you must report the fact immediately to the appropriate person. This may be the individual who has requested the work, your supervisor or line manager, or a colleague who is relying on the work.

It is never easy to admit to someone that you are not able to complete a task on time, but it is important that you do so as soon as you anticipate difficulties.

- The person expecting the work may find that if you miss your deadline, they will miss theirs – and they will need time to adjust their plans or warn others.

- A manager may be able to take action to enable you to meet your deadline.

This second point is particularly important. Provided that you report any anticipated difficulties in meeting a deadline early enough, there are actions that can be taken to help! The manager can:

- Put pressure on any other employees who are holding you up by not producing the information you require.

- Lighten your existing workload in order to free up time to meet the deadline.

- Provide you with additional resources, such as extra computer time or another colleague's time.

- Adjust plans, so that you will have more time.

Seeking assistance with problems

The first stage is to recognise that you are not going to be able to complete the assignment without some additional help. Be prepared to admit this to yourself, if necessary!

When you ask for assistance, try to identify what resources you require: extra time to get the task done yourself, say – or additional computer time or help from a colleague.

If you are in a position to delegate work to more junior team members, they may provide the extra resources required. However, in many cases you will have to approach a more senior manager or colleagues and request assistance. You will need to explain why you need the assistance and what you think is required.

You may need to negotiate: persuading the other person to help you, by showing how it will benefit them, or by offering something they want in return.

Once you have been granted assistance, it is important that it is in fact a help – not a hindrance! Helpers need to be properly briefed on what is required. At the same time, assisting you should not become a burden or disruption to the other person's work.

ADHERING TO WORKING PRACTICES AND POLICIES

We discussed some of the legal, policy and procedural requirements for accounting and payroll – and why it is important to adhere to them – in Chapters 2 and 3.

It is important to adhere to any agreed working practice, even if it is just 'customary', because other people will be basing their plans and conduct on their expectation that you will do so. If you depart from accepted procedures and practices, you are creating a risk of disruption to plans and damage to working relationships – as well as, perhaps, risks to health and safety, confidentiality, the integrity of data and so on: all the things the procedures and practices are designed to protect.

Communicating with your line manager or supervisor

In general, you will need to adhere to instructions and departmental practices for maintaining communication with your supervisor or line manager, in a range of situations including:

- Providing information, and reporting on work progress and results, where this is routine or requested

- Reporting by exception: that is, reporting when there has been some deviation or variance from the plan or budget

- Seeking advice and assistance for decisions or actions beyond your competence to perform effectively

- Seeking authorisation for decisions or actions beyond the scope of your authority to deal with

- Receiving information and instructions, perhaps as part of regular or occasional team briefings

- Seeking and receiving feedback on your work performance

- Seeking learning and development opportunities in your work, eg if your supervisor is willing to act as an on-the-job coach, or has responsibility for authorising your development objectives and plans

You will need to observe established customs and protocols for how this communication takes place. Your manager may exercise informal 'management by walking around'; you may have defined opportunities for communication (eg in regular meetings, briefings or 'open door' hours); or you may need to put information and queries in writing, using email or memoranda.

Organising and maintaining your own work area

As we mentioned in Chapter 3, the maintenance of your work area is often the subject of organisational policies, mainly aimed at ensuring that offices maintain a professional image, and reflect the corporate image of the organisation, particularly in areas which are visited by outsiders.

However, it is also your responsibility to organise your work area so that it helps with – and does not interfere with – efficient and effective work habits. This might mean:

- Positioning your desk (where possible) to ensure that you have sufficient space for your activities

- Ensuring that you and others can move efficiently and safely around the work area, without obstructions or hazards

- Positioning chairs for visitors, printer tables and filing cabinets for efficient use

- Organising your desk top and shelving to ensure that items you use regularly are within reach – and that your space is generally tidy, so that you and others can easily find items when required. Aids to organisation include: document trays, desktop organisers, devices to keep electrical wiring out of the way, pin boards (where you can stick reminders etc) and filing systems

- Ensuring that you tidy away all sensitive and confidential documents (and their computer equivalents) when you leave your desk unattended, and especially when you leave work at the end of the day, in order to protect the security of the data

Respecting confidentiality

We covered the need for confidentiality (and data security) in Chapter 3, but it is always worth repeating! In order to work effectively in accounting and finance, you must be aware of – and adhere to – all work practices and procedures involving rules of disclosure and non-disclosure, the protection of confidentiality, and the secure handling and storage of sensitive data.

CHAPTER OVERVIEW

- An employee's job will usually consist of a variety of tasks which may be set out in a job, role or competence description.

- A typical job will be made up of a number of daily/weekly/monthly routine tasks plus other unexpected tasks to which schedules must be adapted as required.

- Tasks can be categorised as urgent or non-urgent and important or unimportant when setting priorities.

- You must be able to deal with changes in priorities and therefore changes to your planned work schedule.

- A variety of planning aids can be used to ensure that all tasks are completed on time: eg to do lists, diaries or timetables, planning schedules and action plans.

- If it appears that a deadline may not be met, it is important to report the difficulty to the appropriate person as soon as possible, and to negotiate assistance where possible.

- Time management is a combination of effective work planning and control of time (eg through delegation and assertiveness).

- Legal and policy constraints apply to your working practices in areas such as maintaining your own work area and respecting confidentiality. (Recap your learning from Chapter 2 if you need to.)

Keywords

Job description – a written summary of the main duties and tasks required as part of a particular job

Time management – ensuring that work is carried out efficiently and effectively, so that all tasks are completed on time and within the time available

Routine tasks – the general daily, weekly, monthly tasks which make up a job

Urgent tasks – tasks for which there is a deadline in the near future

Important tasks – tasks which affect other people or outcomes; on which others depend; or which have significant (positive or negative) impact

Prioritising – ordering tasks according to their degree of urgency and importance

Schedule – the allocation of tasks to appropriate times/dates when they will be tackled or completed

Planning aids – tools, formats and techniques for organising tasks and projects

Planning schedule – a form of a bar chart, but each division of space represents both an amount of time and an amount of work to be done in that time

Action plan – detailed record of all of the tasks involved in a complex project – normally including start and finish dates and responsibility for each task

Deadline – a set time when a task must be completed

TEST YOUR LEARNING

Test 1

For each of the following tasks, select their priority category from the picklist.

Task	Category
Preparing a petty cash summary by the end of next week	▼
Packing up out of date files to be archived	▼
Preparing a report for a meeting tomorrow	▼
Replenishing the milk in the kitchen this morning	▼

Picklist

Urgent and important
Urgent but not important
Not urgent or important
Not urgent but important

Test 2

Complete the missing terms using the picklist below.

A(n) [▼] is a simple short-term planning tool and consists of a checklist listing the tasks that need completing for a particular day.

A(n) [▼] is a detailed planning tool which can be used for complex longer term projects.

Picklist

action plan
to do list

Test 3

You have been asked to prepare a report for your manager which must be with her on Wednesday 22 August. You will need to requisition some files for this, which will take a day to arrive. You estimate that the research will take you three days and the analysis required another two days. The report will be with the typist for a further day and then you will need one final day for checking and proofing.

The latest date on which you could start work on this report is [   ].

chapter 7:
WORKING AS PART OF A TEAM

— chapter coverage 📖 —

In this chapter we consider the benefits and problems of working as part of a team, and how you can best contribute to efficient and effective team working.

We also consider the problem of conflicts and dissatisfactions within your work role and environment, and how they can be resolved.

The topics covered are:

✐ Teams and team working

✐ Working as part of a team

✐ The impact of your work on colleagues

✐ Conflict and dissatisfaction at work

✐ Resolving conflicts and dissatisfactions

TEAMS AND TEAM WORKING

In most work situations, you will find that you are not working in isolation, but as part of a work group. This work group might be a department such as the Accounts department, or a section of a department such as the Payroll section. If this group works closely together, and has a strong sense of shared goals and identity, it may be thought of as a TEAM.

A team is a small number of people with complementary skills who are committed to a common purpose, performance goals and approach, for which they hold themselves jointly accountable.

People working together in organisations need to recognise their mutual obligations to each other, and their shared tasks and objectives. They need to recognise their roles and relationships with respect to each other, as determined by their position and function in the team and in the organisation. They need to treat each other with mutual respect, within guidelines of acceptable and professional behaviour. They need to resolve any differences and conflicts that may reduce personal and team effectiveness. That's what team working is all about.

Advantages of team working

There are a number of advantages to working as part of a team rather than on an individual basis.

- **Additional resources**: a team provides extra skills, information, ideas and work hours, compared with working on your own.

- **Inspiration**: teams are particularly useful for generating ideas and solving problems, because different people's ideas and viewpoints can influence the work and thinking of others.

- **Motivation**: the shared efforts of a team and the help and support of its members can often provide additional motivation and satisfaction to team members in their work.

- **Communication**: team working is a great way to get people talking about how their tasks depend on each other, and how they can work together to solve problems. Teams are a key tool for CO-ORDINATION in organisations, especially where team members (for a project, say) are drawn from different functions or units, so that there is plenty of lateral or cross-functional communication.

- **SYNERGY**: for all the above reasons, teams can often accomplish more than the same individuals working alone. The concept of synergy describes how sometimes, two heads are not just better than one: they are better than two! When people work together effectively, $2 + 2 = 5$.

The downside of team working

Team working is often not easy! Individuals have different skills, personalities and working styles, and although this can contribute to team ideas and decisions, it can also cause frictions and conflicts within the team. Conflicts and disagreements (as we see later) can get in the way of effective team performance.

Some other disadvantages of team working are that decision-making takes longer (because of the need to take different views into account) and the process of working together and maintaining good relationships can actually distract team members from the task at hand.

WORKING AS PART OF A TEAM

Effective team working requires a number of elements:

- A mix and balance of people in the team
- Clear shared objectives and performance feedback
- Co-ordination, collaboration and communication

Team members

In order for a team to function well together, and to fulfil its task objectives, it needs to have a mix and balance of:

- Required skills, experience and knowledge, which people can contribute to the task. Different people will have varying strengths and weaknesses: team working helps to even this out – and fill any gaps!

- The way people contribute to the functioning of the team. These are sometimes called 'team roles'. Some members will be leaders; some 'ideas' people; others will be better at implementing or following through the ideas; still others will be the ones who help team discussion along and act as peacemakers if there is conflict. All these roles are needed in a well functioning team.

It is important for you to identify your own role in the team's performance and maintenance. What does the team need you to do, competently and reliably, in order to achieve its objectives? What does the team need you to contribute, in order to maintain effective team working?

Do not underestimate the importance of small contributions to good working relationships, like replenishing the biscuit tin, or offering support to a colleague. Conversely, do not underestimate the negative affect on team working of letting conflicts fester, failing to 'pull your weight' in the team, or failing to honour your commitments to other team members.

Objectives and feedback

In order for a team to work well, it must have a well-defined and well-understood purpose and objectives, which apply to all its members. This ensures that all members are working towards the same goals. Each member should have clearly set out (or jointly agreed) responsibilities – but essentially, the focus is less on individual achievement than on contributing to group achievement.

In some cases, the objectives of a team will be set for it by the nature of its work, and the team leader's goals for how the work should be carried out.

However, where a new team has been set up for a task or project, it may be necessary to negotiate and jointly agree objectives, targets and standards for the team.

The team will require regular feedback: information on its progress and results, so that it can learn, correct or adjust its performance – or celebrate its successes.

Let's consider the accounts department as an example of a team with objectives. The accounts department will have the standing objective of preparing monthly cost accounts and annual financial accounts, invoicing and receiving money from customers, paying suppliers and other expenses – and so on. There are also likely to be specific targets and standards for how quickly, efficiently and accurately these tasks are carried out – which can be used for performance measurement and management.

Collaboration, co-ordination and communication

Team working is about collaboration (working together) and co-ordination (making sure that each member's work 'fits' with the work of others and contributes to the team's objectives). The key point is that the work that you do impacts upon the work of other people: positively or negatively!

Information that you provide will be used by other members of the team. They may not be able to complete their tasks until you have completed yours. Therefore, schedules and working methods must be set by the team leader – or by negotiation among the group – to ensure that the work of all members is co-ordinated and integrated.

As we saw in Chapter 6, it is always important to meet deadlines and commitments: within a team, it is even more important that each individual fulfils his or her responsibilities, according to agreed schedules and working practices, in order for the team to achieve its objectives.

If any team member anticipates trouble meeting his or her commitments, (s)he must inform the team leader and affected colleagues, and work with them to devise options to resolve the situation.

In general, the more communication between team members – and between the team and its leader – the more effective its performance will be. Among other things, this means that conflicts between team members must be resolved, so that they don't interfere with communication.

HOW IT WORKS

A few months into your time at Southfield Electronics, you are asked by Jenny Faulkner, the financial accountant, to form a small project team with Amy Laval (accounts clerk), Sam Piper (the new accounts clerk), Kellie McDonald (assistant financial accountant) and John Yeo (sales manager).

This morning, Friday 3 March, you, Amy, Sam, Kellie and John had a meeting with Jenny to discuss the purpose of the project team and the work that is to be done.

Jenny explained that the company is looking into changing its credit terms to credit customers and, in particular, is reviewing its policy of offering prompt payment discounts to some customers. This will require a wide-ranging analysis of credit sales, and the payment patterns of all credit customers, in order to forecast the effect of the change of policy on sales. Jenny handed out the following briefing notes.

CREDIT SALES PROJECT: BRIEFING NOTES

OBJECTIVE

Analysis of credit limits and payment patterns of all credit customers – to be produced by Kellie McDonald by Friday 31 March.

TASKS

Accounts clerks to analyse each credit customer's account for the last year. Analysis to be prepared as follows:

- Credit limit
- Number of times credit limit exceeded
- Average amount by which credit limit exceeded
- Total credit sales for the year
- If prompt payment discount offered, percentage of total credit sales on which discount is taken
- Monthly average of outstanding amount which has been due for more than 60 days and more than 90 days

[Your Name] – credit customers from A to G
Amy Laval – credit customers from H to N
Sam Piper – credit customers from O to Z

[Your Name] is also to set up a computer spreadsheet for the analysed data. Amy Laval and Sam Piper are to input the data to the spreadsheet. Kellie McDonald is to write the final report summarising the findings regarding credit limits and payment patterns, with comments on key findings by John Yeo, where relevant.

RESOURCES

Computerised receivables ledger
Monthly aged receivables listing
Manual customer data file

TIMETABLE

Computer spreadsheet to be completed by Friday 10 March
Accounts assistants' analysis to be completed by Monday 20 March
Completed spreadsheet to Kellie McDonald by Friday 24 March

You realise that, given your existing workload, you cannot possibly set up the spreadsheet and analyse all of your assigned credit customers by the due dates. You voice this concern to Jenny, and explain that you will also need test data to be input into the spreadsheet.

Jenny agrees that perhaps this is asking too much and assigns customers beginning with E and F to Amy and customers beginning with G to Sam, leaving you with a more manageable workload. Jenny also decides that Sam should have the analysis for 30 credit customers ready for you to input as test data on 13 March.

Kellie agrees to supervise the analysis and sets up a weekly meeting every Friday morning at 10:00am in order to assess the team's progress.

THE IMPACT OF YOUR WORK ON COLLEAGUES

Members of an accounting section are generally interdependent: their work objectives and outputs are often linked to each other. This is even more evident in fully team-based activities and projects, where tasks, or components or stages of tasks, are shared among team members. The outputs of one person's activity will become the inputs to another's.

The most important aspect of this is that if one team member fails to complete his/her allotted/agreed tasks, or fails to complete them on time, there will be an impact on other team members and their work.

Task 1

From the learning you have already completed in Chapter 6, explain three impacts on a team of one member failing to meet an agreed deadline for project work.

Deadlines

We covered the importance of meeting departmental deadlines, and what to do if you encounter problems in meeting deadlines, in Chapter 6. There, we were looking at deadlines faced when working independently – but we emphasised that your work is almost always intended for use by someone else, who may rely on its timely completion. The same thing applies in team working – only more so, because of the need to co-ordinate the work of more than one person.

Refresh your memory about the importance of meeting deadlines, and what to do if you encounter problems, if you need to, by re-reading the relevant section of Chapter 6.

Mutual assistance and support

There will undoubtedly be occasions when a team member realises that (s)he cannot fulfil a work commitment, because the schedule turns out to be unrealistic, or because unforeseen factors have created a lack of time or resources.

On such occasions, other members of the team should be prepared to provide assistance or support, as required. For example, if one team member is running out of time to carry out a task, another could offer to help (if he/she has extra time available) or could allow the person struggling to have first option on equipment time, say. Provided that it does not impact negatively on your own work, or become a recurring pattern, 'doing a colleague a favour' can contribute to good working relationships and team performance.

In some cases, support will be personal as well as practical. Team members may support each other when they are struggling, through empathetic listening, collaborative problem-solving, encouragement, constructive feedback and so on.

HOW IT WORKS

Let's return to the Southfield Electronics credit sales project. On 10 March at 10:00am, the first project progress meeting is held. You report that you have the spreadsheet set up and are ready for the test data to be input on Monday. Kellie checks with Sam to ensure that the test data will be ready by Monday morning. Unfortunately, Sam has to admit that he is struggling with the analysis so far and has only analysed data for 18 customers: he asks for assistance. Kellie asks you and Amy about your workloads.

You feel that you have to get on with your analysis of credit customers, as your time has been taken up by the spreadsheet. Amy also feels that in order to meet the deadline of 20 March for her analysis, she has no spare time. However, as Amy has already completed analysis of 29 customers, she suggests that the remaining 12 analyses required for the test data are simply taken from her customers. Kellie agrees and it is further agreed that you will input the test data on Monday as originally planned.

Task 2

On Monday 22 March 20X0, you are asked to take part in a team project that will take about one month – as well as your normal tasks for the financial accounts section. The team is to provide detailed costings for a new line of children's toys. It is made up of three accounts assistants (including you), a senior accounts assistant and the team leader (the cost accountant). The costings must be ready for the monthly Board meeting on Wednesday 21 April.

On Tuesday 6 April, at the weekly project team meeting, one of the other accounts assistants timidly admits that she had forgotten that the following weekend was the Easter holiday: she will not be able to meet her stage deadline. She believes that she can analyse the figures by the next day, but will not have time to input them to the computer on Thursday, the last working day of the week.

You know that you are likely to have some spare time on Thursday, as you are ahead with your routine tasks and have already completed your project tasks. However, you do not expect to have any spare time before Thursday.

What should you do in this situation? (tick the correct box)

Offer to help input the figures on Thursday ☐

Ask the other accounts assistant to complete the work in her own time outside of work ☐

Offer to help analyse the figures on Wednesday ☐

Do nothing as it is not really your problem ☐

Being appropriately assertive

As we mentioned in Chapter 6, it is important to protect your time and scheduled priorities – in order to avoid having them disrupted by the demands of other team members.

Your ability to do this, and what course of action is appropriate in a given situation, depends on a number of factors. You will need to consider:

- The authority of the person making an unexpected demand on your time. Does this person have the 'right' to ask you?

- The nature of the request: is it appropriate and reasonable, and in the best interests of the effectiveness and efficiency of the department – or can you propose a better course of action?

- The impact on other people and tasks, if you go ahead with the demand: for example, will it prevent you from meeting other deadlines?

- Which of the people making conflicting demands on you has the most authority? If they have equal authority, you might be able to ask them to negotiate a compromise between them – or you may have to refer the matter upwards to a higher authority for a decision.

- What is the most courteous, respectful, professional and assertive way to resolve the problem – without inappropriately sacrificing your own needs and interests?

ASSERTIVE COMMUNICATION means standing up for your own rights, needs and opinions (ie not being passive or a 'doormat') – without dismissing the rights, needs or opinions of others (ie not being 'aggressive').

You have a right to say 'no' to inappropriate or unreasonable demands – but you can choose to do this in a way that is calm, courteous, professional, positive and co-operative. The key is to state clearly and directly what the problem is, and what you want or do not want to happen. If possible, explain why you cannot comply with a demand because of its impact on your work or the interests of the team: this should defuse any suspicion that you are just being 'selfish'! You might then be able to propose alternative solutions to meet the other person's needs (can you perform their task later, or get the assistance you need to fit it in, or propose someone better placed to do it than you?) – or invite them to make alternative suggestions, which you will consider positively.

HOW IT WORKS

Back at the Southfield Electronics credit sales project, it is now the end of the day on Wednesday 22 March. You are finalising the spreadsheets for Kellie McDonald, ready to submit them to her, as requested, on Friday.

Just as you are packing up for the day, Ron Howard, another of the assistant financial accounts to whom you report, comes and asks you to do a task for him first thing tomorrow. He estimates it will take you about half a day – and it will enable him to take the morning off to take his wife to the doctor.

You are aware that you do not have half a day to spare, if you are to complete your spreadsheet work for the project. So you say, calmly and courteously to Ron:

'I'm sorry, Ron, but I have an important deadline coming up on the credit sales project. I simply don't have any time to spare tomorrow. I would love to be able to help you out – but if I don't get the spreadsheet done, Kellie and John Yeo will not have time to work on their final report.'

Ron says loudly that his work should take equal priority to Kellie's – particularly since it is genuine Accounts department work, 'not some project thing'. Obviously, you cannot take this view, since you have agreed your schedule with Kellie, who has equal authority to Ron – and also the backing of Jenny Faulkner.

Without backing down, you continue to calmly offer constructive options, suggesting that if Ron were to speak to Kellie and explain the situation, she might be able to stretch your project deadline a little – or one of the other accounts clerks might be able to help him.

Task 3

Discuss how effectively have you handled the situation in the 'How It Works' scenario above. What are the key points of the argument you make for protecting your time in this scenario?

Task 4

Which of the following is the best description of assertive behaviour?

Dismissing the rights, needs or opinions of others ☐

Standing up for your own rights, needs and opinions ☐

CONFLICT AND DISSATISFACTION AT WORK

CONFLICT is the clash of opposing 'forces' – including the personalities, interests and attitudes of individuals and groups. In any working relationship or team, there are bound to be disagreements and conflicts of various kinds. There are also likely to be times when you are dissatisfied with something at work: for example, unresolved problems, frustrations, poor working conditions or unfair treatment.

Your aim in the workplace is to be able to handle disagreements, conflicts and dissatisfactions constructively, so that you can maintain good working relations and efficient individual and team working.

Causes and types of conflict

In any working relationship or team, there are bound to be conflicts on occasion. Such conflicts may be due to:

- Differences in personality (eg an outgoing person irritating a quiet, reflective person)

- Differences in working style (eg if one person likes to plan ahead and the other doesn't)

- Differences in status (eg if team members feel powerless or micro-managed by a powerful boss, or unable to raise problems because a manager is seen as 'unapproachable')

- The interdependency of work (eg if one person or team is frustrated by delays caused by another's missed deadline, or someone within the team isn't 'pulling their weight' and leaves others with more work to do)

- Competition between groups or departments for limited resources (including office space, finance, information, status and power). This is a major cause of conflict, whether we're talking about individuals or nations!

- Unfair treatment (eg a manager gives an unfairly harsh evaluation, or refuses legitimate requests for help)

- Hurtful treatment (eg a team member is bullying, offensive, sexist or racist)

Differences, frustrations and competition by themselves don't necessarily lead to conflict: they can even be positive forces, helping people to solve problems or to lift their performance. However, they can escalate or deteriorate into harmful conflict if there is a lack of communication and problem-solving – or if work demands put pressure on people and situations.

Disagreement

It is important that you are able to disagree with someone – and still maintain good working relations! For example, suppose that your supervisor believes that one method of dealing with purchase invoices is the most efficient, but you have a different view. If you have tried to persuade your supervisor that your method is more efficient, but have failed to do so, you need to accept the superior authority, forget the argument and continue with your tasks. It is more important to be effective than to be right!

More serious conflicts

Other disagreements or conflicts may be more serious: someone may be disobeying agreed rules or procedures, say, or behaving in unacceptable or even illegal ways (eg in the case of sexual harassment, bullying or breaking safety rules).

You need to be aware of the limits of your authority to deal with such problems. You may be able to sort some out yourself (eg by having an honest talk with a colleague about how his or her behaviour affects you or the team). In some instances, however, you may need to take it to a higher authority: a process called 'ESCALATION'. We will consider a range of conflict resolution options below.

Effects of unresolved conflict and dissatisfaction

If conflict and dissatisfaction are allowed to go unresolved, or to get worse, they can have a negative impact on the functioning and effectiveness of the team.

- Individuals with unresolved dissatisfactions may become resentful, de-motivated and unco-operative. They may withdraw their contribution to the group – or actively seek to sabotage it.

- The cause of the dissatisfaction may itself be a barrier to effective performance (eg lack of resources).

- Unresolved conflict between individuals can result in reduced communication, co-ordination and co-operation between them.

- Conflict between individuals may split the team into 'factions', escalating rivalry and hostility within the team.

- Conflict can polarise differing viewpoints, causing people to hold extreme views, and to dig their heals in, in disagreements. This may make it impossible to 'agree to disagree' – and create unbalanced and risky decisions.

In other words, unresolved conflict can significantly interfere with team working! On the other hand, the effective management of conflict and dissatisfaction can contribute to better team work – and to more productive working relationships.

Law and policy frameworks for positive working relations

Major legislation in the UK and EU is directed at preventing harassment and discrimination against people at work due to their sex or sexual orientation, race or ethnicity, religion, age or disability. This is broadly called 'equal opportunity' law.

Employers must not discriminate in giving people access to jobs, promotion, training or benefits, and you may have rights as a job applicant or employee in these areas. However, employees are also required not to 'harass' others in the workplace by using language or behaviour which intimidates, denigrates or offends.

It is said that 'the law is a floor': it only sets minimum standards of acceptable behaviour. Organisational policies and practices (together with professional codes of conduct) may go beyond basic non-discrimination, to try and foster positive values for working relationships, such as: courtesy, respect, professionalism and team work.

RESOLVING CONFLICTS AND DISSATISFACTIONS

Dealing with dissatisfactions

Some dissatisfactions at work may be within your competence and authority to resolve yourself, or by informal negotiation with your supervisor or colleagues. If your workload is too heavy, for example, you may be able to adjust your schedule or work plans, or ask a colleague to help you. If you get headaches from inadequate light at your desk, you may be able to re-position your desk, or requisition a desk lamp, or ask colleagues' permission to keep window blinds open.

Some dissatisfactions, however, may be beyond your competence or authority to resolve yourself. In such cases, you may need to take the problem first to your immediate supervisor or line manager, who may be able to propose or mobilise solutions to the problem.

You may be advised to refer the problem to another appropriate person. If your dissatisfaction is with poor training, for example, you may be advised to approach the Training or HR manager. If you are frustrated by the performance of the office cleaners, you might be advised to communicate with the office manager.

Conflicts you can resolve yourself

Conflicts can be managed informally in several ways.

- If you have a problem working with someone, you might initially attempt direct, informal discussion with the person concerned. Where there is a personality or style clash, this gets the problem out in the open and gives an opportunity to clear up any misunderstandings.

- Problems of incompatible working styles or excessive work demands are matters which can be taken to your supervisor, who will be able to help you develop solutions to the problem.

- If your conflict is with someone in authority over you, you may have to discuss the matter with someone higher up in the organisation. This is probably best handled using more formal channels, called 'grievance procedures' – discussed later.

Where the interests or styles of different parties are genuinely incompatible, you may need to work together to explore a range of options that will at least partially satisfy both parties. This is a process called NEGOTIATION. You may have to give or concede something the other party wants in return for getting something that you want: a process of bargaining, which often results in a mutually acceptable compromise.

However, the best approach – most satisfying for both parties *and* most likely to preserve positive relationships – is to attempt to find a mutually satisfying or 'win win' solution. The 'win win' model states that there are three basic ways in which a conflict or problem can be worked out:

- One party gets what (s)he wants at the expense of the other: 'win lose'. For example, if two parties are fighting over an orange, one gets the orange, and the other gets nothing. However well-justified the solution, there is often lingering resentment on the part of the 'losing' party.

- A compromise solution is found, so that neither party gets what (s)he really wanted: 'lose lose'. For example: both parties get half an orange each. However 'logical' such a solution is, there is often lingering dissatisfaction on both sides.

- Both parties work together to understand each other's needs and concerns, and generate options to try and get as close as possible to what each party really wants: 'win win'. A 'win win' result may not be possible, but in the process of working together and trying to get the best outcome for both sides, new options may be created – and co-operation will be enhanced. So for example, it may come out in discussion that one party likes orange juice, while another wants the zest of the orange to make a cake: there is now a way of dividing up the orange that leaves both parties satisfied!

Task 5

Two of your team members are arguing over who gets to use the desk by the window.

Of the following options, which is the only one which may result in a 'win win' situation?

The team members get the window desk on alternate days or weeks ☐

Find out why each wants the window desk and look for solutions to meet their needs ☐

One team member gets the window desk and the other doesn't ☐

If personality clash is the main source of conflict, you may have to arrange (or request) a way of working with the other person as little as possible. If the problems persist, you may need to refer them upwards: to have your supervisor (or another appropriate third party) mediate – or arrange for you to work in different areas or teams.

Referring conflicts upwards

In many cases, conflicts and dissatisfactions can be dealt with by the individuals involved. In other cases, however, they may be beyond your authority or ability to resolve, and may require escalation.

It may be necessary to report the incident or conflict to a more senior person for help in handling it. Your supervisor or manager may be able to make decisions to resolve the matter (eg by reallocating resources or changing schedules), or may be in a position to enforce rules and procedures – or may simply be more persuasive getting a point across than you are!

In the first instance, you should go to your supervisor – or whoever has authority over both parties in the conflict. For a conflict within a project team, for example, you might talk to the team leader.

If your conflict is with your own supervisor or line manager, the problem may have to be escalated 'up the line' to his or her immediate manager. Obviously, you will have to think carefully about whether and how you do this. Is the issue serious enough to risk damaging your working relationship with your boss? Do you have a strong, reasonable 'case', supported by evidence, for any allegations you feel you need to make? Can the issue be put in a positive light, with the aim of co-operative problem-solving, in the interests of improving working relationships and work performance?

HOW IT WORKS

Back at Southfield Electronics, Ron did not take well your courteous refusal to take on extra work at short notice. He shouted at you and stormed out of the office. The following day, when he came in late, he was rude to you, and blamed you loudly for his being behind on his work. He says that your 'unco-operative behaviour' will be reflected on your performance appraisal.

What should you do?

You calmly but assertively explain to Ron that you did in fact attempt to be as helpful as possible, but that you had prior work commitments that could not be broken. You refer him, once again, to Kellie McDonald, so that they can resolve the 'time-sharing' issue between them.

If Ron continues to be aggressive and hostile in his manner towards you, you will seek a confidential meeting with Jenny Faulkner (the financial accountant) to explain the situation to her.

Jenny may be able to meet with Kellie and Ron (to resolve the issue of how your time is allocated) and perhaps with you and Ron (to resolve the conflict between you). She will be able to discipline Ron, if necessary, for his inappropriate behaviour.

Formal grievance procedures

In some cases, the matter may be so serious that a more formal approach needs to be adopted.

A GRIEVANCE is a formal complaint by an individual who feels that (s)he is being wrongly or unfairly treated by a colleague or manager at work. Such complaints may include:

- Harassment or bullying
- Unfair or discriminatory treatment by managers due to race, gender or disability
- An employee being given an unfair workload
- An employee being unfairly blocked for promotion

All organisations should have a written GRIEVANCE PROCEDURE which is communicated to all employees. This should state to whom an employee should go with a particular type of grievance. It will often be his or her line manager. If the grievance is against the line manager, or if it cannot be sorted out at that level, a more senior manager will be consulted, and the HR department may become involved.

If the grievance cannot be sorted out internally, the employee may have to take the problem before an Employment Tribunal, which works as an independent informal court.

CHAPTER OVERVIEW

- Team working, as opposed to working individually, can provide additional resources, inspiration, motivation and communication (for co-ordination).

- When a team is set up, it is important to establish a mix and balance of members; shared, appropriate resources; and agreed working methods, time scales and schedules.

- It may be necessary to provide assistance or support to other team members from time to time, in order to achieve the objectives of the team.

- There will often be conflicts in working relationships, which may be caused by differences in personality, working style or status, or work demands.

- In general, disagreements or conflicts should be dealt with in such a way as to maintain relations and relationships. This requires positive, assertive communication.

- In some cases, conflicts can be satisfactorily dealt with between individuals, but in more serious cases an employee may have to report a matter to a line manager with the authority to resolve matters or enforce rules.

- Employers should have a written grievance procedure policy which employees can follow if the grievance needs to be properly investigated and arbitrated by senior management.

Keywords

Team – a group of employees working together to meet shared objectives

Co-ordination – the process by which the work of different individuals and teams is linked together to achieve shared objectives

Synergy – a process in team working by which 'the whole is greater than the sum of its parts' – or 2 + 2 = 5

Assertive communication – a style of communication based on respecting your own rights – without trampling on the rights of others

Conflict – opposing forces or interests, causing disagreement, competition or hostility

Escalation – taking a problem to a higher level of management for resolution

Negotiation – a process of bargaining to reach a solution in a situation where there is a conflict of interests

Grievance – a complaint brought by an employee who feels wrongly treated by colleagues or managers

Grievance procedure – an employer's formalised procedure for investigating and resolving a grievance

TEST YOUR LEARNING

Test 1

Which two of the following might be teams operating within an accounting function? Tick the correct boxes.

Receivables ledger team ☐

Inventory control section ☐

Human resources team ☐

Payroll section ☐

Test 2

Give examples of roles that people might occupy in a well-balanced team.

Test 3

If a team is working to complete a particular project, why is it important that all schedules and timetables are (a) agreed and (b) met?

Test 4

Explain how mutual assistance within a team can provide synergies.

Test 5

You have recently joined the accounting department of a company and have found one of your fellow accounts assistants to be extremely rude to you and constantly demanding that you fetch the coffee, clean up the kitchen etc.

Which of the following would be the best course of action in the first instance?

Do nothing ☐

Discuss your concerns with your colleague ☐

Complain to your line manager ☐

Resign from your position ☐

Test 6

You and a colleague both need access to the same file at the same time. You both need it to compile reports for your managers, for the following morning. It is now 3.00pm and each of you will need it for two hours to do this work. Suggest (a) a win-lose, (b) compromise and (c) a win-win solution in the scenario. What result can you foresee from each solution?

Test 7

Which of the following would be examples of possible 'grievances' in the workplace? Tick the correct boxes

Sexual or racial harassment ☐

Unfair treatment or discrimination due to race,
gender or disability ☐

Having to share a printer with another department ☐

An argument with a fellow employee over the tidiness
of their work space ☐

An employee being given an unfair workload ☐

An employee being blocked for promotion ☐

chapter 8:
DEVELOPING SKILLS AND KNOWLEDGE

chapter coverage 📖

This chapter considers how each individual can develop the skills and knowledge required to meet both their own and the organisation's needs.

It explains how to identify your own development needs and to formulate your own personal development plan. It also contains information regarding the importance of continuing professional development and on monitoring your own development progress, which you may need to refer to when carrying out the tasks in your assessment.

The topics covered are:

- ✍ Continuing professional development
- ✍ Identifying your development needs
- ✍ Defining your development objectives
- ✍ Learning and development approaches
- ✍ Monitoring and reviewing your progress
- ✍ Your personal development plan

CONTINUING PROFESSIONAL DEVELOPMENT

Let's start with some useful definitions.

- TRAINING is a process of using learning experiences to achieve more effective performance in particular work activities or roles.

- DEVELOPMENT is a broader process of growth in knowledge and capabilities. In addition to education and training, individuals may be encouraged to gain experience of different roles in an organisation, and increasing challenges (perhaps through promotion within the organisation, or 'career development').

- CONTINUING PROFESSIONAL DEVELOPMENT (CPD) is a systematic process of planning for the future and of gaining experience and training relevant to the directions in which they want to develop – both within the current job role, and in future career progression.

Members of professional bodies (such as the AAT, CIMA or ICAEW) are required to complete a certain amount of CPD as a condition of continuing membership. This ensures that their knowledge and skills are always up-to-date and of a good standard. This, in turn, protects the interests of their clients and employers, as well as the standing and credibility of the professional bodies and the accounting profession.

As we will see, Continuing Professional Development (CPD) can be pursued in a number of different ways. Individuals may undertake vocational training through the NVQ framework, or further education through universities and colleges. They may study for progression to membership of a professional body (like the AAT). They may receive instruction, training or coaching in the workplace. Or they may plan for self-development by a continual process of identifying their weaknesses, seeking opportunities to practice, gathering feedback, and learning from their mistakes.

A key feature of the CPD approach is that the responsibility for development lies mainly with the individual, in collaboration with his or her employers, and other parties such as the professional bodies.

You are responsible for maintaining CPD appropriate to:

- Your current job role: helping you to meet the requirements of the role better – and ensuring that you stay up-to-date with the changing requirements of the role, and/or changing developments in your field

- Your career aspirations: equipping yourself with the knowledge and skills you will require for higher-level roles, and enabling you to seek more challenging job opportunities.

Why is training and development important?

Training can represent a significant cost to a business – in terms of training costs (training providers and resources), staff time spent in training, and resulting lost production – or the costs of covering training absences with replacement staff or overtime working.

It is, therefore, important to be able to justify training effort and expenditure on the basis of sound business benefits!

The on-going development of skills and knowledge has significant benefits for the learners/trainees themselves, and for the organisation in which they work.

Benefits for the individual	Benefits for the employing organisation
Greater confidence and flexibility	More competent job performance
Improved job performance (perhaps leading to increased rewards and recognition)	Competent performance achieved more quickly by new recruits
Greater job security	Less supervision required
Ability to take on more challenge and responsibility in the job	Increased efficiency and productivity, through faster, more skilled work
Increased prospects of promotion	Reduced cost of errors, reduced non-compliance with regulations/laws
Enhanced skills, which can be used outside the job (eg communication skills)	Supports employee initiative, ideas, flexibility and innovation
Satisfaction from greater contribution	Improved staff motivation and morale
Greater 'employability' and value in the job market	Enhanced ability to recruit and retain high-quality employees

Task 1

You have recently prepared, and agreed with your supervisor (Mrs Hoff), a Personal Development Plan, showing targets and activities for your learning over the next six months. Having submitted this plan to the HR Manager (Mr Bolt), you receive the following email.

EMAIL	
From:	a.bolt@reeves.co.uk
To:	y.name@reeves.co.uk; g.hoff@reeves.co.uk
Date:	*[Today's date]*
Re:	Personal Development Plan

Thank you for submitting Your Name's PDP for the next six months.

I am somewhat concerned at the cost of such plans for the Accounts department as a whole. Every member of the department has submitted requests for training – and also for 'professional development' activity which does not seem to be directly related to their current job roles.

I am not sure that this can be justified, and will have to review the PDPs and training requests in this light.

Mrs Hoff asks you to email Mr Bolt in reply, explaining the importance and benefits of Continuing Professional Development.

IDENTIFYING YOUR DEVELOPMENT NEEDS

Learning needs and career goals are highly specific to each individual – and to particular work contexts and roles. Obviously, we can't tell you what your career aspirations are (or should be), what your strengths and weaknesses are, or what areas of knowledge or skill you may need to develop further. What we can do is to give you the tools to work these things out for yourself – whether in your workplace, or in your assessment.

Identifying learning needs in your current job

The most obvious starting point for identifying learning needs may be: how well do I fulfil the requirements of my current work role?

To answer this question, you can simply think through what it is that you do on a day-to-day basis, or consider feedback you have received from your supervisor or line manager about your performance. You may receive more formal feedback reports, setting out recommendations for learning and development, from performance reviews or appraisals.

For a systematic 'start-from-scratch' analysis, you might start with two key documents used by organisations to define the requirements of a job and of a job-holder.

- Your JOB DESCRIPTION or role description, which sets out what a person in your job should be able to do. It describes the requirements of the job.

- The PERSON SPECIFICATION for your role, which sets out what sort of personal qualities the organisation is looking for in your role. It describes the requirements of the job-holder.

Having got to grips with what is required of you in your job, you can ask yourself some questions. Do I have the knowledge and skills necessary to perform my tasks competently? What tasks in my job description am I not yet able to perform well? What desirable attributes in the person specification for my role do I currently lack? Putting this all together: what are my strengths and weaknesses in this role?

HOW IT WORKS

When you joined Southfield Electronics, you were shown the following documents relating to your job role.

JOB DESCRIPTION	
Job title:	Accounts clerk, financial accounting
Location:	London office
Job summary:	General financial accounting duties
Key responsibilities	Administrative support for the financial accounts section, including opening post and handling telephone and email enquiries
	Obtaining quotes from suppliers
	Preparing daily cheque listings, sales invoices, credit notes and monthly sales summaries (using computer spreadsheets)
	Monthly receivables ledger control account reconciliation
	Responsibility for petty cash in the cashier's absence

Reporting structure:	Financial accountant
	|
	Assistant financial accountants (2) and Payroll manager
	|
	Accounts clerk
Hours:	9:00am to 5:30pm Monday to Friday 1 hour for lunch
Training:	Induction training will be provided Continuing Professional Development encouraged
Prepared by:	Head of HR
Date:	March 20X0

PERSON SPECIFICATION		
CRITERIA	**ESSENTIAL**	**DESIRABLE**
Qualifications	GCSE English Language (Grade A* – C) GCSE Mathematics (Grade A* – C)	Undertaking AAT qualification Word processing qualification Level 3 Spreadsheets
Experience	Basic computer use General office procedures	Previous accounts or clerical/administrative experience
Communication	Ability to communicate effectively in a range of situations Understanding of the importance of confidentiality	Familiarity with different communication formats
Team working	Ability to work flexibly in a team Understanding of deadlines	Previous experience of working in a team
Personal skills/ attributes	Personal integrity Attention to detail Ability to handle pressure	Ability to work without supervision when required

You now want to put together some ideas about your training needs, for your up-coming review. You decide to start with your current job performance. Is there room for improvement in the way you fulfil the requirements set out in the job description and person specification?

You make the following notes in your Personal Development Journal.

- *Do I have the knowledge and skills necessary to perform my tasks competently?*

  I still struggle with the monthly receivables ledger control account reconciliation, which I know takes me longer than it should. This is not helped by the fact that I am not confident about double entry bookkeeping. Whenever I have to prepare a computer spreadsheet, I have to ask one of the other accounts assistants for help, as I don't know how to do it on my own.

- *What tasks in my job description am I not yet able to perform well?*

  I should be responsible for petty cash when the cashier is absent, but I have never been asked to do this nor do I know how to.

- *What desirable attributes in the person specification for my role do I currently lack?*

  The holder of my role should ideally have a Level 3 qualification in Spreadsheets, and I have not yet attained this.

From these answers, you are able to draw up a list of your most immediate learning needs.

Learning needs to improve in my current job

- I would benefit from help from a senior colleague to show me how to perform the receivables ledger reconciliation more efficiently.

- I would benefit from studying a textbook on double entry bookkeeping – or perhaps a short bookkeeping course.

- I should plan to attend a computer spreadsheet course or get instruction from a colleague, with a view to working towards a Level 3 qualification.

- I should ask to spend some time with the cashier being shown how she deals with petty cash claims, and, perhaps, perform the task a few times under her supervision.

Strengths and weaknesses analysis

A more general approach to identifying your learning needs would be to review the requirements of your role and your performance in the role, and then to ask, simply: what are my strengths and weaknesses in this role?

- Identified strengths are areas that you can build on. They may represent a foundation for further learning – or areas in which you are ready to ask for more challenge or responsibility.

- Identified weaknesses are areas that need attention in order to bring your competence or confidence up to the required level. They may represent your most immediate learning needs.

HOW IT WORKS

Continuing your learning needs planning at Southfield Electronics, you review your job description and person specification, and note the various requirements of your current role. How well are you fulfilling those requirements?

You reflect on your own performance, remembering particular incidents that have highlighted good and bad points: finishing your workload early so that you could help other members of the project team; mistakes you made in your double entry bookkeeping; having to ask for help with the computer spreadsheets, because you didn't feel confident about doing them on your own...

You note down the feedback you have received from others on your performance: your supervisor's praise for well-written reports and emails; a colleague's comment that the receivables ledger reconciliation is taking you longer than it should...

You look at the tasks in the job description that you are (and are not yet) performing well, and the attributes in the person specification that you do (and do not yet) possess.

You now have a list of good points and bad points, and you decide to pick the three most important of each to build or work on.

STRENGTHS	WEAKNESSES
1. Efficient workload management, prioritisation and flexibility to help others	1. Lack of full competence in double entry bookkeeping and receivables ledger reconciliation
2. Effective communication using emails and reports	2. Lack of confidence in preparing computer spreadsheets: not yet attained Level 3 qualification
3. Good ability to work without supervision and under pressure when required	3. Lack of knowledge/experience of petty cash procedures

Now you can draw up a list of learning objectives which will:

(a) Build on your strengths: you will volunteer to act as secretary to your next project team, in order to develop your communication and workload management skills further.

(b) Address your identified weaknesses: you will plan learning activities to improve your double entry bookkeeping, receivables ledger reconciliation, use of computer spreadsheets, and knowledge of petty cash procedures.

Task 2

Complete the following sentences using the picklist below.

The [▼] for your role sets out what sort of personal qualities the organisation is looking for in your role.

The [▼] sets out what a person in your job should be able to do.

Picklist

job description
person specification

Other tools for learning needs analysis

Some organisations carry out formal learning needs analysis, by testing employees' performance on areas listed in a job description or competence definition, say, or by discussing learning needs as part of their annual performance appraisals.

Other approaches include:

- Keeping a Personal Development Journal, in which you note down any incidents at work which indicate a learning need (eg having to ask for assistance, making a mistake or getting a complaint or negative feedback from a colleague). These are sometimes called 'critical incidents', as they highlight an underlying issue or need.

- Scanning the office notice board, intranet pages or staff magazines for advertised training courses and opportunities which strike you as relevant to your job.

- Gathering feedback or assessments from each training course you undertake, pointing you to 'areas for further improvement' or follow-up learning.

- Asking your supervisor or colleagues for feedback on areas of your performance: 'What do you think I need to learn about or do better?' (An excellent source of information, particularly about your interpersonal skills, or how you work with others!)

Identifying learning needs to fit your future career aspirations

Although you may be happy with your current job role, most people do have ambitions to develop their career, for personal satisfaction and growth – and for higher status and rewards. In order to identify future learning needs, you will need to consider where you are aiming for – whether within your current organisation or elsewhere. What are your CAREER GOALS?

Ambition is a helpful motivator for personal development – but take care to be realistic in your goals. As a first year accounts assistant, it may be realistic to aspire to become an accounts supervisor, but perhaps not to aspire to be Finance Director within two years! Factor in any learning, experience, maturing and trust-earning that may be required to get from where you are to where you want to get to...

It may help to talk informally to colleagues and those in more senior roles about how they got to their positions. It may also be useful to have a more formal conversation with your line manager or the Human Resources manager, to determine the realistic career goals for you as an individual – and what support and opportunities may be available within the organisation.

Once you have identified some goals, you need to plan how to get from your current position to the job that you aspire to.

First, you need to ensure that you are carrying out your current role efficiently and effectively! Then you must consider the requirements of the job that you wish to have.

You may need to talk to your line manager or Human Resources manager in order to find out the details of the knowledge, skills and any qualifications that are required for this job. Once you are armed with this information, you can begin to set yourself realistic and specific development objectives – just as you would for your current job role.

DEFINING YOUR DEVELOPMENT OBJECTIVES

Even if your organisation supports you in training and development planning, it is important that you define your own development objectives, within the context of your own strengths, weaknesses and career goals.

Effective objectives (whether for knowledge and skills development or for career development) are SMART:

S	Specific
M	Measurable
A	Agreed
R	Realistic
T	Time-bounded

Specific

Specificity is necessary in order for a plan of action to be drawn up. 'To improve my use of spreadsheets soon' is far too vague to suggest an action plan – or to get you motivated! 'To pass the AAT Level 3 Spreadsheet assessment by October' is a much better guide to what (exactly) you want to do!

Try to be exact about what you hope to achieve or be able to do.

Measurable

You need to be able to review how you are progressing towards your goals – and whether you've reached them – so you need to state your objectives in a way that will enable you to measure or assess your performance.

How will you (or others) know how much progress you've made? How will you (or others) define completion or success? What test will you be able to pass? What will you be able to do that you couldn't do before? (Note that your Learning Outcomes for this Unit are designed to be measurable in this way.)

Plan up front for when, how often and how your progress towards meeting the objective will be monitored and reviewed.

Agreed

In many cases the achievement of development objectives will require the commitment of resources from your employer: the loss of your time while you study or train, the costs of training, your manager's time coaching you and so on. Therefore, it is important that any personal development objectives are agreed with your supervisor or line manager. (Some matters may be referred to the Training manager or Human Resources manager for further planning and negotiation of goals and resources.)

Realistic

You need to ensure that your objectives are achievable, taking into account the various constraints under which you operate – time, resources, ability and current commitments. Break the objectives down into smaller, manageable chunks, if necessary.

Time-bounded

Include a time scale within which the objective is to be achieved. 'To complete Level 3 Spreadsheets' is the start of an objective but is this within a two-year time scale or a ten-year time scale? 'To complete Level 2 Spreadsheets within six months (or by a particular date)' is a much better development objective. Make sure your time scale is realistic, too!

LEARNING AND DEVELOPMENT APPROACHES

Your learning objectives will in most cases involve acquiring new skills and knowledge for current and future job challenges. So how will you go about this? It will require research into specific opportunities relevant to your SMART objectives, but some of the sources of CPD you may consider are as follows.

Technical briefings and updates

If you want to enhance your knowledge on a topic relevant to your work, or to keep your knowledge up-to-date, you might seek out technical briefings and updates. These may be provided by technical experts within your organisation, or by external bodies. HM Revenue & Customs, for example, may offer update seminars on topics such as VAT, payroll, income/corporate tax, and online reporting. Professional bodies (such as AAT, CIMA and ICAEW) similarly offer technical seminars and local branch events on topics relevant to their field.

You should also look out for technical briefings and updates provided by such bodies in printed form (mailed or emailed to subscribers), or posted on their web sites. Your organisation may keep a library of such resources.

Training courses and seminars

One of the most obvious ways of enhancing your skills and knowledge is by attending training courses and seminars. These may be run internally by your organisation or by external training providers. (External courses can be researched by contacting a local college of further education or by using the internet.) They may be short, stand-alone knowledge or skills-based courses (eg a course in effective communication, team lead or using spreadsheets), or they may be part of a longer scheme of study towards an academic, vocational or professional qualification.

The key advantage of training courses is that they generally give you access to experts, in a structured environment which is designed to maximise learning. There is a disadvantage to 'off-the-job' learning, however, in that it may not be easy to transfer or apply what you have learned in the workplace and of course it tends to be expensive for your organisation.

The internet

The internet can be used to find details of local course providers and CPD events. It may also be a source of information relevant to your learning needs. For example, you could use a search engine such as Google to find articles on assertiveness or managing conflict in the workplace; websites offering technical and legal updates; or tips and tools for various accounting tasks. There may also be web-based courses (or e-learning) in your areas of interest.

Publications

Most industries and professions have specialist journals or trade publications, which may include articles relevant to your learning needs. It may be worth subscribing to a publication of this kind, in order to keep up-to-date with developments in your profession and business sector. Your organisation or department may have a library of relevant journals that you could use, or you may be able to browse the online versions.

Books are another useful learning tool. If you have doubts about your double entry bookkeeping skills, for example, one option is to invest in a textbook and work through it in your own time.

Other research tools

In addition to information searches in publications and the internet, you might consider research tools such as: arranging to talk to (or get instruction from) experts in a topic or skill; or visiting work sites and other places where relevant procedures and practices are demonstrated.

You might also seek out opportunities to try out skills or procedures yourself (where it is not too great a risk to yourself or others to do so!), and then gather feedback on your performance and what you need to do better or differently next time: this is called 'experiential learning' or learning by doing. It is an important tool for on-the-job learning.

Colleagues and coaches

One of the most neglected sources of information and learning is work colleagues. They may be able to give you advice on training courses to attend or books or journals to read. You may also be able to learn new skills from colleagues, through instruction or coaching. Don't forget the 'phone a friend' option!

You may find that you can also simply watch more experienced colleagues at work, to learn from their methods, procedures, techniques and behaviour. This observation may take place informally as you work with colleagues, or on a more formal 'shadowing' or coaching basis.

Task 3

Select the most appropriate learning or training approach for each of the following learning needs.

Learning needs	Suitable approach	
An accounts clerk wishes to work toward becoming AAT qualified		▼
A worker is transferred onto a new piece of equipment and needs to learn how to operate it		▼
A new member of staff is about to join the organisation		▼
An organisation decides that its supervisors would benefit from leadership training		▼

Picklist

Induction training
Internal training course
On-the-job training
External training course

MONITORING AND REVIEWING YOUR PROGRESS

There is no point in setting an objective if you are not prepared to review your progress and achievements on a regular basis. Regular monitoring and review is important in:

- Allowing you to measure your progress towards your goal, so that you are motivated to 'keep on track'

- Allowing you to identify any mistakes or weaknesses in your current performance, so that you can use them in your learning

- Identifying where you are 'off track' or 'behind schedule' on your development plan, so that you can adjust your effort and activity as required

- Identifying where your goals or plans were unrealistic and need adjustment

- Keeping you accountable to your supervisor, coach or line manager for agreed learning goals and progress

- Enabling your supervisor or line manager to justify the costs of your training and development, in terms of proven results and benefits

- Ensuring that the costs of training and development are not being wasted or used inefficiently

- Ensuring that measurable business benefits are accruing to the organisation from your development

- Enabling you to celebrate improvements and attainments (an important part of staying motivated – and reaping the benefits of development)

Informally monitoring progress

You can monitor your own progress against your goals on a regular basis. For example, have you kept up-to-date in your reading on technical changes that affect your job? Have you booked yourself on to the training course that you decided would be a necessary part of your personal development? Are you having to ask for help less frequently? Have you attained the targets you set?

Another review method is to get informal feedback from your supervisor or colleagues. Have they noticed a change in your performance or behaviour? Do they think you have met the targets you set for yourself? How do they think you have improved – and could improve still further?

Formal evaluation and review

In many cases, there will be more formal methods of evaluation and review. Most organisations plan periodic progress reviews (especially in project work and for new recruits). There will also probably be annual PERFORMANCE APPRAISAL for all employees.

You can also use a Personal Development Plan (discussed in a moment) to:

- Set specific criteria for measurement of your progress and attainment

- Gain the co-operation of your supervisor or coach in reviewing your progress at defined intervals or times, and giving you helpful feedback on your progress and performance

- Gain the co-operation of your supervisor in arranging formal testing of your progress or attainment (eg competence assessment, or on-the-job observation)

Such mechanisms allow you systematically to measure your progress against agreed goals, get feedback from your supervisor (and other relevant parties), review your learning objectives, and identify and agree further learning needs.

YOUR PERSONAL DEVELOPMENT PLAN

Having come this far, you have all the tools necessary to formulate a more formal and systematic PERSONAL DEVELOPMENT PLAN or PDP.

A PDP is a clear developmental action plan, which once agreed with the individual's supervisor or line manager, acts as a 'learning contract' between them.

You may have your own preferences for formatting and recording action plans: timetables, diaries, checklists and other methods covered in Chapter 6, for example. Be sure to use any format recommended by your work organisation.

In the absence of such guidelines, feel free to use whatever works for you – but we recommend a simple, systematic format such as the following.

Objective	Methods	Timescale	Monitoring/review
Concise statement of your SMART learning objective	Specific learning methods and activities selected	Target completion date for each listed learning method or activity	How, with whom and how often you will check your progress

HOW IT WORKS

Back at Southfield Electronics, having identified some immediate learning needs to improve your job performance, you prepare the following Personal Development Plan for the next six months, which you agree with Kellie McDonald (your designated Learning Supervisor).

Objective	Method	Timescale	Monitoring/review
To be able to perform petty cash operations	Coaching: instruction and supervised practice with the cashier	By last week of September	Practice tasks under the cashier's supervision and seek feedback
To be able to perform double entry book-keeping tasks with 100% accuracy, without assistance	Reading: review Basic Accounting Textbook Training: short external bookkeeping course	By last week of October Completed by last week of October	Practice tasks, checked by Kellie McDonald End of course competency test
To be able to perform receivables ledger reconciliations efficiently, without assistance	Reading: review Basic Accounting Textbook Coaching: ask Kellie McDonald to instruct and coach me on the process	First week of November By third week of November	Review progress with Kellie during coaching Practice at end October, and seek feedback from Kellie
To achieve the Level 3 Spreadsheets qualification	Training: short computer spreadsheet course	Completed by end of February	End of course competency test Feedback from Ron Howard on application at work

Including your supervisor or line manager in the planning process

Personal Development Planning puts the onus on the individual to define development goals which are relevant to them, and to seek out learning opportunities which suit their needs, preferences and opportunities.

However, it is vitally important to include your supervisor, line manager or designated coach in the process, so that (s)he can:

- Check that your goals are SMART, and of potential benefit to the department and organisation

- Check that the learning activities selected are suitable and cost-effective for the organisation

- Suggest learning methods and opportunities that you might not be aware of

- Mobilise learning opportunities and resources (eg by recommending you for a training course, providing access to publications, or appointing a coach or mentor)

- Authorise and arrange the time off and expenditure that will be required for your training (including cover for your absences, where relevant)

- Plan to participate, as required, in your learning (eg by acting as a coach or providing feedback) and in monitoring and review of your progress

Recording your CPD activity

As we noted at the beginning of this chapter, members of professional bodies are required to complete a certain number of hours of CPD, in order to ensure that they maintain their technical competence and up-to-date knowledge. You must therefore record any CPD activity you undertake, so that you can prove that you have fulfilled the requirements and updated your knowledge and skills appropriately.

Online tools for recording CPD activity are available to AAT members via the AAT web site.

HOW IT WORKS

Southfield Electronics encourages all accounts staff to maintain a CPD log, which is reviewed alongside each individual's Personal Development Plan. The company uses a simple pro forma log sheet for CPD activity.

CONTINUING PROFESSIONAL DEVELOPMENT RECORD

Name:..   Membership no: ....

Covering the period from: ....   to ....

Date(s)	CPD hours	Links to PDP goal	Learning activity	Training provider	Outcomes/ benefits	Follow-up required

Continuing professional development: a continuous process!

Just to finish this chapter it should be noted that the setting of personal development objectives, their review, appraisal and updating will be a continuous process throughout your working career – not simply a one-off exercise!

CHAPTER OVERVIEW

- You need to maintain and update your knowledge and skills to keep pace with technical, legal, technological and other developments affecting your profession and job role. This is called Continuing Professional Development, and it is compulsory for members of professional bodies, as a condition of membership.

- It is important to be able to justify the costs and time devoted to training and development activity. Learning benefits the individual and their employing organisation in a wide variety of ways.

- When considering your own development needs, the best starting point is the current job that you perform. What additional skills or knowledge do you require to carry out your role more effectively and efficiently? What strengths and weaknesses can you identify in the way you fulfil the requirements of your job, as defined by your job description and/or person specification?

- Most employees will have ambitions for career development. Consider your own career goals and what additional skills and knowledge will be required in order for you to achieve them. Remember to be realistic.

- Begin to set your own personal development objectives. Check that they are SMART – specific, measurable, agreed, realistic and time-bounded.

- Sources of CPD activity include: technical updates, training courses and seminars, the internet, journals and trade publications, books, colleagues and observation of others.

- Once personal development objectives have been set, progress must be monitored, reviewed and evaluated. This may be a process of self-review, feedback from others or formal appraisal.

- Be prepared to formulate a Personal Development Plan for your own role, based on your own identified career goals, competences, strengths and weaknesses.

Keywords

Training – a planned process of using learning experiences to achieve more effective performance, in particular, work activities or roles

Development – growth in your knowledge and capabilities, and increasing fulfilment of your potential

Continuing Professional Development – a process of gaining experience and training relevant to the directions in which you want to develop

Job description – a concise statement of the tasks and responsibilities of a particular job

Person specification – a concise statement of the qualities an organisation wants in the holder of a particular job

Career goals – your aims in terms of the job(s) you aspire to in future

SMART – a framework for setting objectives – they should be specific, measurable, agreed, realistic, time-bounded

Personal Development Plan – a learning plan that can be agreed and monitored by your supervisor or learning coach

Performance appraisal – the formal process of regular review of each individual employee's performance, progress and development objectives

TEST YOUR LEARNING

Test 1

Why is CPD important for members of professional bodies?

Test 2

Which of the following are potential benefits of learning and development for an individual employee?

Enables improved job performance	☐
Time consuming	☐
Potential for increased rewards and recognition	☐
Greater job security	☐
Less job satisfaction	☐
Valuable in the external job market	☐

Test 3

Excluding the internet, briefly explain any four methods for acquiring new skills and knowledge for your work.

Test 4

The internet is a good source of technical information, including information on new laws and regulations. However, if the user is not vigilant he or she could end up obtaining misleading or incorrect technical knowledge.

Describe why this problem arises when using the internet as a source for this information and outline the precautions you could take to prevent this from happening.

Test 5

Explain four different ways of monitoring and reviewing your progress against your development goals.

chapter 9:
UNDERSTANDING ETHICAL AND SUSTAINABLE VALUES

chapter coverage 📖

In this chapter, we consider the fundamental principles of ethical behaviour as they apply in the general context of the UK accountancy profession, and the framework set out by the AAT's *Code of Professional Ethics* and the regulatory environment. We also consider the role of sustainability.

The topics we cover are:

✍ What are ethics?

✍ Why behave ethically?

✍ Fundamental ethical principles

✍ Conflicts of interest

✍ Compliance with the law

✍ Business ethics and professional values

✍ Sustainability

✍ Duties and responsibilities of finance professionals in relation to sustainability

✍ Impact and benefits of sustainability

WHAT ARE ETHICS?

Ethics are a set of moral principles that guide behaviour.

Ethical values are assumptions and beliefs about what constitutes 'right' and 'wrong' behaviour.

Individuals have ethical values, often reflecting the beliefs of the families, cultures and educational environments in which they developed their ideas.

Organisations also have ethical values, based on the norms and standards of behaviour that their leaders believe will best help them express their identity and achieve their objectives.

The concept of **business ethics** suggests that businesses are morally responsible for their actions, and should be held accountable for the effects of their actions on people and society. This is true for individual businesses (which should behave ethically towards the employees, customers, suppliers and communities who are affected by them). It is also true for 'business' in general, which has a duty to behave responsibly in the interests of the society of which it is a part.

Some of these ethical values may be explicit: included in the organisation's mission statement, set out in ethical codes and guidelines, or taught in employee training programmes. Other values may be part of the **organisation culture**: 'the way we do things around here', the unwritten rules and customs of behaviour that develop over time as people find ways of working together.

A **code of ethics** often focuses on social issues. It may set out general principles about an organisation's beliefs on matters such as mission, quality, privacy or the environment. The effectiveness of such codes of ethics depends on the extent to which management supports them 'from the top'. The code of ethics often gives rise to a **code of conduct** for employees.

Task 1

Think of some examples of the kinds of behaviour that you consider 'right' or 'wrong' in your personal and professional life.

WHY BEHAVE ETHICALLY?

The AAT has a **Code of Professional Ethics** (the AAT Code) in place, which came into effect on 1 September 2011. This replaced the previous AAT Guidelines on Professional Ethics. The AAT Code is based on the **Code of Ethics for Professional Accountants** produced by the International Ethics Standards Board for Accountants (IESBA) of the International Federation of Accountants (IFAC). AAT is an associate member (not a full member or affiliate) of IFAC.

The AAT Code notes that: 'the decisions you make in the everyday course of your professional lives can have real ethical implications.'

There are several key reasons why an accounting technician should strive to behave ethically:

- Ethical issues may be a matter of **law and regulation**. You are expected to know and apply the **civil and criminal law** of the country in which you live and work – as a basic minimum requirement for good practice. The AAT Code is based on the laws effective in the UK, with which members are expected to comply as a minimum requirement. (It is sometimes said that 'the law is a floor': the lowest acceptable level of behaviour required to preserve the public interest and individual rights.)

- The **AAT** (like other professional bodies) requires its members to conduct themselves, and provide services to clients, according to certain professional and ethical standards. It does this, in part, to maintain its own **reputation and standing** – but this is also of benefit to its members and to the accounting profession as a whole.

- Professional and ethical behaviour protects the **public interest**. The accountancy profession sees itself as having duties to society as a whole – in addition to its specific obligations to employers and clients.

The advice for AAT members, in a nutshell, is as follows:

- Completely avoid even the appearance of **conflict of interest**.

- Be **objective** and act in the **public interest,** because your responsibility is not exclusively to satisfy the needs of an individual client or employer.

- Keep sensitive information **confidential**. Accountants often deal with their employer's or client's most private material.

- Be **straightforward and honest** in professional and business relationships.

- Maintain **professional knowledge, behaviour and skills** at the level required by a client or employer.

- Act within the **spirit and the letter of the law** so as not to bring the profession into disrepute.

FUNDAMENTAL ETHICAL PRINCIPLES

You might have your own ideas about what is 'ethical behaviour'. These ideas will be shaped by your personal assumptions and values, and the values of the culture in which you operate (at work and in the country in which you live). However, there are five **fundamental principles** set out in the AAT Code that underpin ethical behaviour in an accounting context:

Fundamental principle	Explanation
Integrity	A member shall be straightforward and honest in all professional and business relationships.
Objectivity	A member shall not allow bias, conflict of interest or undue influence of others to override professional or business relationships.
Professional competence and due care	A member has a continuing duty to maintain professional knowledge and skill at the level required to ensure that a client or employer receives competent professional service based on current developments in practice, legislation and techniques. A member shall act diligently and in accordance with applicable and professional standards when providing professional services.
Confidentiality	A member shall, in accordance with the law, respect the confidentiality of information acquired as a result of professional and business relationships. A member shall not disclose any such information to third parties without proper and specific authority, unless there is a legal or professional right or duty to disclose. Confidential information acquired as a result of professional and business relationships shall not be used for the personal advantage of the member or third parties.
Professional behaviour	A member shall comply with relevant laws and regulations and avoid any action that brings the profession into disrepute.

Let's look at each of these in turn.

Integrity

On an everyday level, integrity involves matters such as being **open** about the limitations of your knowledge or competence, being **honest** in your relationships and carrying out your work **accurately, conscientiously and efficiently**.

Objectivity

This is a very important principle for the accounting profession because it protects the interests both of the parties directly affected by an accountant's services and of the general public (who rely on the accuracy of information and the integrity of financial systems).

Objectivity is the principle that all professional and business judgements should be made fairly:

- On the basis of an **independent** and intellectually honest appraisal of information

- **Free from** all forms of **prejudice** and **bias**

- Free from factors which might affect **impartiality**, such as pressure from a superior, financial interest in the outcome, a personal or professional relationship with one of the parties involved, or a conflict of interest (where one client stands to lose and another to gain by a particular disclosure)

Task 2

A member who is straightforward and honest in all business and professional relationships can be said to be following the fundamental principle of objectivity.

	✓
True	
False	

Professional competence and due care

Accountants have an obligation to their employers and clients to know what they are doing – and to do it right!

You should understand that you must not agree to carry out a task or assignment if you do not have the competence to carry it out to a **satisfactory standard** –

unless you are sure that you will be able to get the help and advice you need to do so. And if you discover in the course of performing a task or assignment that you lack the knowledge or competence to complete it satisfactorily, you should not continue without taking steps to get the help you need.

In addition, once you have become a member of the profession, you need to maintain and develop your **professional and technical competence**, to keep pace with the demands which may be made on you in your work and developments which may affect your work over time. This may mean:

- Regularly reviewing your working practices against national and international standards, codes, regulations and legislation. Are you complying with the latest requirements?

- Continually upgrading your knowledge and skills in line with developments in accounting practices, requirements and techniques – and making sure that you do not get 'rusty' in the skills you have!

Task 3

Identify the appropriate word to use in the following sentence:

'Continuing professional development (CPD) is important to accountancy professionals as it helps them [▼] competence in their role.'

Picklist:

attain
maintain

Due care is a legal concept that means that, having agreed to do a task or assignment, you have an obligation to carry it out to the best of your ability, in the client's or employer's best interests, within a reasonable timescale and with proper regard for the technical and professional standards expected of you as a professional.

As someone who is knowledgeable about accountancy, you may often deal with others who have little knowledge of accounting matters. This puts you in a position of power, which must never be abused by carrying out your task or assignment in a negligent or 'careless' way.

Confidentiality

Confidentiality is a very important fundamental principle but there are circumstances where the law **allows or requires** that confidentiality to be breached. These circumstances are described in the AAT Code in section 140.7 and are summarised in the table below.

Circumstance	Examples
Disclosure is permitted by law and is authorised by the client or employer.	Providing working papers to a new firm who is taking on the client
Disclosure is required by law.	Providing documents or other evidence for legal proceedings
	Disclosure to HMRC
	Disclosure of actual/suspected money laundering or terrorist financing to the firm's Money Laundering Reporting Officer (MLRO) or to the Serious Organised Crime Agency (SOCA) (in the UK)
There is a professional right or duty to disclose which is in the public interest and is not prohibited by law.	Complying with the quality review of an IFAC member body or other professional body
	Responding to an inquiry or investigation by the AAT or other regulatory or professional body
	Disclosure to protect the member's professional interests in legal proceedings
	Disclosure made to comply with technical standards and ethics requirements

It is vital to appreciate the importance of the fundamental principle of **confidentiality**. You need to respect the confidentiality of information acquired as a result of professional and business relationships. This means that you will not use or disclose confidential information to others, unless:

- You have **specific** and **'proper' authorisation** to do so by the client or employer

- You are legally or professionally **entitled** or **obliged** to do so

It is also worth being aware that personal information shared with you by clients and colleagues at work should be regarded as confidential – unless you are told otherwise: this is an important basis for trust in any working relationship.

Task 4

In which of the following circumstances do you have a legal duty to disclose confidential information concerning a customer of your organisation?

	✓
If they are asked for during legal proceedings	
When your manager tells you to disclose the information	
When writing a report for general circulation within your organisation	

Professional behaviour

The final fundamental principle is professional behaviour.

An example is when advertising their services, members must ensure that they are honest and truthful. They can bring the profession into disrepute by making **exaggerated claims** about services, their qualifications and experience, or if they make **disparaging references or unsubstantiated comparisons** to the work of others.

Applying this principle means **'being professional'**. You'll have your own ideas about what 'being professional' means. Certainly it involves complying with the law and behaving in a way that maintains or enhances the reputation of your profession: bringing it credit – not discredit.

One key aspect of this is **courtesy**. As a professional, you should behave with courtesy and consideration towards anyone you come into contact with in the course of your work and indeed in your personal life.

It is impossible for us to overstate the importance of each of these fundamental principles – you MUST be able to recognise each of them.

HOW IT WORKS

Now that we've considered the fundamental principles in general, let's consider some typical scenarios in which they might be helpful. In each case, we will identify the ethical issues they present, in line with the basic principles discussed so far. For the purposes of these questions you should assume you are an AAT student.

Incident one

You are asked to produce an aged receivables' listing for your manager as soon as possible. However you do not have up to date figures because of a problem with the computer system. A colleague suggests that to get the report done in time you use averages for the missing figures.

There is an **integrity** issue here. Using averages instead of actual figures will almost certainly result in an inaccurate listing. You should report the problem to your manager and ask for an extension to your deadline in order to provide an accurate listing.

Incident two

You have received a letter from an estate agent, requesting financial information about one of your company's customers that is applying to rent a property. The information is needed as soon as possible, by fax or email, in order to secure approval for the rent agreement.

There is a **confidentiality** issue here. You need the customer's authority to disclose the information; you may also need to confirm the identity of the person making the request. You should also take steps to protect the confidentiality of the information when you send it: for example, not using fax or email (which can be intercepted), and stating clearly that the information is confidential.

Incident three

While out to lunch, you run into a friend at the sandwich bar. In conversation, she tells you that she expects to inherit from a recently deceased uncle, and asks you how she will be affected by inheritance tax, capital gains tax and other matters.

There are issues of **professional competence and due care** here. You are not qualified to give advice on matters of taxation. Even if you were qualified, any answer you give on the spot would risk being incomplete or inaccurate with potentially serious consequences.

Incident four

A client of the accountancy practice you work in is so pleased with the service you gave him this year that he offers you a free weekend break in a luxury hotel, just as a 'thank you'.

There is an **objectivity** issue here as the gift is of significant value. Think about how it looks: a third party observer is entitled to wonder what 'special favours' deserve this extra reward – and/or how such a gift may bias you in the client's favour in future.

CONFLICTS OF INTEREST

It is impossible to give guidelines on every possible situation that may arise in the course of your work which conflicts with the fundamental ethical principles. The AAT Code therefore sets out a basic **problem solving procedure,** which you can use in any situation, to give yourself the best chance of complying with the principles. This procedure forms the '**conceptual framework**' which requires the following:

- Identify where there may be a **threat** to a fundamental principle.

- **Evaluate the threat**: how significant is it?

- For any significant threat **apply safeguards** that will eliminate the threat or reduce it to an acceptable level (so that compliance with the fundamental principle is not compromised).

- If safeguards cannot be applied, **decline or discontinue** the specific action or professional service involved or, where necessary, **resign** from the client (if you are a member in practice) or the employing organisation (if you are a member in business).

Identifying and evaluating threats and the application of safeguards all require the application of an accountant's **professional judgement.** Although professional judgement is a **personal view**, based on an accountant's training and experience, it is expected that all members of the profession would act in a broadly similar way given the same circumstances.

We shall now look at threats and safeguards in more detail.

Threats

Many of the threats that may create a risk of compromising the fundamental principles will fall into one of the following five categories.

Threat	Explanation	Examples
Self-interest	Financial or other interests may inappropriately influence the member's judgement or behaviour	Undue fee dependence on one particular client
Self-review	A previous judgement needs to be re-evaluated by the member responsible for that judgement	Tax and accountancy work carried out by the same engagement team

Threat	Explanation	Examples
Advocacy	A member promotes a position or opinion to the point that subsequent objectivity may be compromised	Acting on behalf of an assurance client which is in litigation or dispute with a third party
Familiarity	Due to close or personal relationships, a member becomes too sympathetic to the interests of others	A senior member undertaking an assurance engagement for a number of years for the same client
Intimidation	A member may be deterred from acting objectively by threats (actual or perceived)	Threatened withdrawal of services by a dominant client

Safeguards

The AAT Code defines safeguards as '**actions or other measures that may eliminate threats or reduce them to an acceptable level.**' The Code identifies two broad categories of safeguards that you might use to reduce or eliminate the threats we have described above.

- **Safeguards created by the profession and/or legislation and regulation**. These include:

    – Education, training and experience, as requirements for entry into the profession

    – CPD

    – Corporate governance regulations

    – Professional standards

    – Professional or regulatory monitoring and disciplinary procedures

    – External review of financial reports, returns, communications or information produced by members

- **Safeguards in the work environment**, which increase the likelihood of identifying or deterring unethical behaviour, include:

    – Quality controls, and internal audits of quality controls

    – Mechanisms to empower and protect staff who raise ethical concerns ('whistleblowers')

    – Involvement of, or consultation with, independent third parties (eg non executive directors or regulatory bodies)

- Rotation of personnel to avoid excessive familiarity and opportunities for collusion in fraud
- Opportunities to discuss ethical dilemmas (eg with an ethics officer, committee or forum)

Task 5

Jake has been put under significant pressure by his manager to change the conclusion of a report he has written which reflects badly on the manager's performance.

Which threat is Jake facing?

	✓
Self-interest	
Advocacy	
Intimidation	

COMPLIANCE WITH THE LAW

In the UK, law falls into two categories:

- **Criminal law** – offences relating to persons or property that affect the whole community. Criminal punishment for breach of criminal law (for theft, money laundering, terrorist financing, bribery or fraud, for example) is most likely to result in fines or imprisonment imposed by the state. Criminal cases are **prosecuted** in a criminal court.

- **Civil law** – wrongs relating to conflicts between individuals within the community. There is no involvement of the state. Lawsuits, for breach of contract, negligence and trust, for example, are civil actions and the remedies awarded are designed to place the injured party in the position they would be in were it not for the breach. The concept of punishment does not apply. Civil cases are **heard** in a civil court.

Accountants are affected by a range of laws which they should be aware of. Some of them are not necessarily obvious such as **health and safety legislation,** and **employment protection and equality laws**.

- Members who are employees have duties under health and safety legislation to take precautions against risk of injury and to report potential risks to management. Members who are self employed have duties to protect the health and safety of their employees.

- All employees have a general duty to behave in ways that contribute to, and maintain, a healthy and safe workplace. Reckless behaviour endangers both yourself and others: creating the risk of accidents, fire, security breach and so on.

- Employment protection and equality laws concern rules on whether an employer can dismiss employees without being liable for claims for wrongful and unfair dismissal. It also includes legislation on treating employees fairly, for example without discriminating against them due to their age, sex, religion or sexual orientation.

Remember when deciding whether or not behaviour is ethical, compliance with the law is assumed as a starting point: 'the law is a floor'.

BUSINESS ETHICS AND PROFESSIONAL VALUES

In 'Setting the tone: ethical business leadership' by Philippa Foster Back (2005, published by the Institute of Business Ethics) the author lists some key business values such as truth, transparency, fairness, responsibility and trust.

The importance of business values in a company's culture is that they underpin both policy and behaviour throughout the company, from top to bottom.

Managers usually have a duty to aim for profit. At the same time, modern ethical standards require them to protect the rights of a range of groups inside and outside the organisation who have a legitimate interest or 'stake' in the organisation's activities. These groups are often known as **stakeholders**.

Business ethics are also relevant to **competitive behaviour**: there is a distinction between competing aggressively and competing unethically (for example, by stealing competitors' designs; using buyer power to prevent suppliers from dealing with competitors; or spreading false negative information about competitors).

A consequence of the need for a business to act ethically may be for it to **change its culture** so all employees, managers and directors know that ethical behaviour is expected of them and that the management will take action against unethical behaviour. For example, management might 'turn a blind eye' to employees submitting inflated expense claims, but this is not something an ethical organisation would allow. Therefore the attitude of employees and mangers must be changed so that only accurate expense claims are made

To achieve this a **code of conduct** must be developed and 'sold' to the organisation. The **Institute of Business Ethics** (IBE) was set up in 1986 to encourage high standards of business behaviour based on ethical values.

The IBE's website contains a lot of information on the purpose of ethics policies and programmes and also how to develop a code of ethics and make it work within an organisation.

The IBE also sets out the simple ethical tests for a business decision. Some companies provide their employees with ethical tests to help them make decisions, ie a series of questions to ask themselves. The IBE's simple ethical tests for a business decision are:

- **Transparency** ('Do I mind others knowing what I have decided?')
- **Effect** ('Who does my decision affect or hurt?')
- **Fairness** ('Would my decision be considered fair by those affected?')

SUSTAINABILITY

We saw earlier that accountants are expected to act in the public interest, and in the modern business world, the concept of **sustainability** is increasingly important in this regard.

There are three aspects to sustainability.

Economic sustainability ensures fair distribution and efficient allocation of global resources. Developed countries consume more per capita than developing countries. Economic growth must be balanced with the needs of the developing world.

Social sustainability involves the responsibility to work towards eradication of human inequality, poverty and social injustice. This responsibility falls particularly heavily on Western firms that employ people in developing countries.

Environmental sustainability describes the need for organisations to consider how their activities impact the environment and to take steps to minimise that impact and to conserve energy.

Sustainable development is a core part of an organisation's corporate social responsibility. It can be seen in policies aimed at reducing waste, using less energy and recycling. Companies are increasingly engaging in practices such as encouraging flexible working, cycle-to-work schemes, reducing business travel through the use of technology and sourcing materials from green suppliers. Sustainability is also fostered through research and development, supply chain improvements and innovation.

Another definition of sustainability can be found in the **UN's Brundtland Report**. According to this, organisations must aim to 'meet the needs of the present without compromising the ability of future generations to meet their own needs.'

We shall consider this definition further in the next section.

DUTIES AND RESPONSIBILITIES OF FINANCE PROFESSIONALS IN RELATION TO SUSTAINABILITY

The definition of sustainability from the **UN's Brundtland Report** makes it clear that business organisations have a duty to **protect society** and **future generations**. As part of the business world, finance professionals have a duty to consider the economic, social and environmental aspects of their work in order to support sustainability.

Duties of finance professionals

The diagram below shows how economic, social and environmental issues are linked.

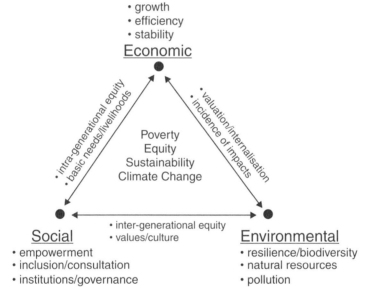

Economic aspects that finance professionals may consider include, supporting their organisation or clients to be profitable, supporting local businesses when deciding on suppliers and paying them on time and looking for ways to improve the efficiency of the organisation's finance operations.

Social aspects may include supporting policies on corporate governance and consulting the local community when making decisions on investing in or relocating operations.

Environment aspects are usually focused on using less energy and creating less pollution. A finance professional should therefore support company policies on the long-term management of resources and facilitating the running of their organisation in a sustainable manner. These may include, for example, not printing emails unless necessary, turning lights off at the end of the day and recycling materials used in their office.

Responsibilities of finance professionals

There are six main responsibilities of finance professionals in regards to upholding the principles of sustainability.

Creating and promoting a sustainable culture

Finance professionals should help senior management create and promote a sustainable culture within their organisation. Primarily it means supporting sustainable policies as they are introduced, but it also means discouraging wasteful or environmentally unfriendly behaviour if they are aware of it.

Championing the aims of sustainability

The aims of sustainability, as identified by the UN's Brundtland Report, should be promoted and followed. However, the finance professional should remain objective at all times. This means that the aims should not be followed blindly, but instead be followed within the context of the organisation's culture and its own policies on sustainability.

Evaluating and quantifying reputational and other ethical risks

Finance professionals have well-developed analysis and evaluational skills. This means they are among the best placed within an organisation to deal with reputational and other ethical risks, including risks to the environment.

Taking social, environmental and ethical factors into account when making decisions

Social, environmental and ethical factors are together known as the 'triple bottom line'. Many organisations demonstrate their commitment to corporate social responsibility (CSR) by including, in their financial reports, organisational performance information based on these factors. Financial professionals have a responsibility to take these factors into account when making decisions so that when organisational position and performance is measured, the business can clearly demonstrate its commitment to CSR.

Promoting sustainable practices

As well as promoting policies in relation to ethical and illegal practices, finance professionals should also support sustainability practices developed by the organisation. Such practices may be in relation to, for example, products and services, customers, employees, the workplace, supply chain and business functions and processes.

Raising awareness of social responsibility

As mentioned earlier, finance professionals should consider the sustainability impacts of their decisions and actions. By doing so, they will help raise awareness of sustainability within the organisation as colleagues, who may be in different departments, see them taking a lead in this area.

Task 6

Think of some examples of sustainability issues in the place that you work.

IMPACT AND BENEFITS OF SUSTAINABILITY

A business may adopt policies and procedures which support sustainability from an environmental and from an organisational perspective.

Environmental perspectives

Environmental areas of focus include the actions an organisation or those within the accounting function can take in respect of:

- Environmental care
- Recycling
- Energy and resource consumption
- Travel efficiencies

Organisational perspectives

Organisational areas of focus include the actions an organisation takes in respect of:

- Its shareholders
- The acquisition and retention of customers
- The acquisition and retention of suppliers
- Delivery of high quality goods and services
- Development of employees

Impacts and benefits

In each case, it should be remembered that there may be costs as well as benefits in pursuing a sustainable solution. A business will need to weigh up any additional costs and compare them with the benefits received.

HOW IT WORKS

Scenario 1

In seeking to care for the environment, a business may decide to abandon the harsh chemicals used in cleaning the business premises and to use environmentally friendly products instead. However, these new products prove to cost more than the original chemicals. This needs to be compared with the positive publicity generated by caring for the environment and the sales generated by new customers attracted by an environmentally friendly business.

Scenario 2

A business may decide to start using recyclable packaging. Its current supplier cannot supply this and so the business has to find a new supplier. This process will take time and may mean that the business does not receive such good discounts as its current supplier gives it. These costs must be taken into account when considering the benefits of the project.

Scenario 3

A business decides that it will save paper by using electronic methods of communicating with its shareholders. It needs to remember that some shareholders may not have access to computers and could be alienated by this move. Shareholders will need to be given the option to continue to receive paper communications in future. So the costs of polling shareholders and the likely numbers who will opt for paperless communication need to be taken into account.

CHAPTER OVERVIEW

- **Ethical values** are assumptions and beliefs about what constitutes 'right' and 'wrong' behaviour. Individuals, families, national cultures and organisation cultures all develop ethical values and norms.

- **Ethical behaviour** is necessary to comply with law and regulation; to protect the public interest; to protect the reputation and standing of a professional body and its members; and to enable people to live and work together in society.

- The **AAT's Code of Professional Ethics** note that: 'the decisions you make in the everyday course of your professional lives can have real ethical implications'.

- **The five fundamental principles** described in the AAT Code are:
  - Integrity
  - Objectivity
  - Professional competence and due care
  - Confidentiality and
  - Professional behaviour

- The AAT's Code sets out a **basic problem solving procedure** for unethical action (the 'conceptual framework'):
  - Identify the threat to the fundamental principles that the action represents
  - Evaluate the threat
  - Apply safeguards to eliminate or reduce the threat
  - If safeguards cannot be applied, decline or discontinue the action

- The IBE sets out simple ethical tests for a business decision:
  - Transparency
  - Effect
  - Fairness

- The concept of **business ethics** suggests that businesses and other corporate entities are morally responsible for their actions.

- Key issues in being an **ethical employee and colleague** include: not undertaking tasks that are beyond your personal experience and expertise; not undermining your professional colleagues; honesty; and ethical relationships.

- Finance professionals have a duty to protect the public interest and promote **sustainability**. They should consider the **economic**, **social** and **environmental aspects** of their work.

- As part of their role, finance professionals have a number of **responsibilities** in relation to upholding the principles of **sustainability**.

- Each sustainability project will have **impacts** as well as **benefits**.

TEST YOUR LEARNING

Respond **to the following by selecting the appropriate option.**

Test 1

Only individuals can have 'ethical values'.

	✓
True	
False	

Test 2

The AAT needs to protect its reputation and standing by maintaining standards of conduct and service among its members in order to be able to:

	✓
Enhance the reputation and standing of its members	
Limit the number of members that it has	
Make sure that its members are able to earn large salaries	

Test 3

A client asks you a technical question about accounting standards which you are not sure you are able to answer correctly. 'You are supposed to be an accountant, aren't you?' says the client. 'I need an answer now.' What should you do first?

	✓
Say that you will get back to him when you have looked up the answer.	
Give him the contact details of a friend in your firm who knows all about accounting standards.	
Clarify the limits of your expertise with the client.	

Test 4

Why are professional standards important?

	✓
It is in the public interest that employees who fail to comply with standards are prosecuted.	
It is in the public interest that services are carried out to professional standards.	

Test 5

Which one of the following statements best describes sustainability?

	✓
Policies aimed at improving efficiency including reducing waste, using less energy and recycling.	
A long-term programme involving a series of sustainable development practices aimed at improving organisational efficiency, stakeholder support and market edge.	
A core part of an organisation's corporate social responsibility comprising efficiency, stakeholder support and market edge.	

ANSWERS TO CHAPTER TASKS

CHAPTER 2   The role of the financial functions

Task 1

The correct answer is:

Information	Required by payroll from other departments	Provided by payroll to other parties
Total wage/salary and overtime costs		✓
Employees' National Insurance details	✓	
Date of commencement of employment	✓	
Information for individual employees about pay and deductions		✓
Statutory returns to external agencies		✓
Standard and overtime hours worked	✓	
Wage/salary and overtime rates	✓	

Task 2

The correct answer is:

EMAIL

To: hskommett@southfield.co.uk

From: yname@southfield.co.uk

Date: | 13/06/12 |

Subject: Cash flow and credit control issues

I'm sure you know how important it is to maintain | positive | cash flow, so
that the organisation has sufficient day-to-day funds to maintain its operations and
pay its | payables | . Recently, however, Southfield has been paying out
money to suppliers | faster | than it has been collecting money from customers.
The Sales department obviously has a key role in this, through its credit control
policies. The Chief Accountant is keen to review this issue with you and the
| Purchasing Manager | .

Kind regards

YN

CHAPTER 3   The organisational framework

Task 1

(a) You report directly to three people: Kellie McDonald, Ron Howard and Jane Chu.

(b) NI contributions are a payroll matter, so the natural person to consult would be Jane Chu, the payroll manager.

(c) The two assistant financial accountants and the payroll manager are on the same level of authority.

(d) This might cause you difficulties because if they make excessive or conflicting work demands on you, it will be difficult to know whose work to prioritise: they all have an equal 'right' to exercise authority over you.

(e) You would need to look further up the chain of command, which leads directly to the Financial Accountant (Jenny Faulkner).

(f) The formal line of communication would be to contact him or her via the production manager.

(g) The finance function only has 'staff' (that is, expert, advisory or policy-making) authority over Logistics in areas to do with finance (such as credit control).

Task 2

(a) The correct answer is:

Action	Correct/Incorrect
Leave the building by the designated route as quickly (but calmly) as possible, not lingering to gather personal belongings	Correct
Use lifts in the event of a fire emergency	Incorrect
Go immediately to the designated Assembly Point and ensure that any visitors are directed and assisted	Correct
Pay particular attention to people with special needs (eg those in wheelchairs or with impaired sight or hearing)	Correct
Stay quiet when your name is called by the Safety Officer who will 'call a roll' of everyone signed in as being in the building	Incorrect
Do not return to the building until instructed to do so by a senior official or the Safety Officer	Correct

(b) It is very important to take part in drills, and to comply with the procedure when doing so. Repeated practice will make employees better at evacuation – contributing to everyone's safety. There is no way of knowing if an alarm is for a drill or 'for real': by failing to take part and follow the procedure, an employee is endangering his/her life and the lives of others. Employees should therefore all be responsible in co-operating with the policy.

Task 3

The correct answer is:

	Yes – Provide Information	No – Personal Information	No – Confidential Information
A customer asks for the address and telephone number of another customer	☐	☐	✓
A colleague asks you for the home address of two other employees	☐	✓	☐
The company's security guard asks for the names of the visitors expected by your department that week	✓	☐	☐

Task 4

You will need to know:

(a) What documents are required (eg appropriate form, attached receipts)

(b) What value of transactions require authorisation, and at what levels

(c) Who the authorising managers or designated signatories are

(e) Deadlines for receipt and authorisation

(f) How transactions should be processed

(g) What you should do if the information is incomplete, incorrectly authorised or otherwise contrary to the policy

CHAPTER 4   Communication skills

Task 1

The correct answer is:

Situation	Medium
New stationery is urgently required from the office goods supplier	Telephone
The managing director wants to give a message to all staff	Notice board/intranet
A member of staff has been absent five times in the past month, and her manager intends to take action	Face to face conversation
You need information quickly from another department	Telephone
You have to explain a complicated procedure to a group of people	Meeting

Task 2

The correct answer is:

Documents can be saved and edited easily ☑

They provide the personal touch ☐

The writer can make corrections and changes which are 'invisible' to the reader ☑

Documents can be tailored to individual circumstances but this takes time – often quicker to write from scratch ☐

Standard or 'template' documents can be created ☑

Task 3

The correct answer is:

Do....	Don't....
Write in full sentences	Use 'text message'-style abbreviations
Use direct (not ambiguous), commonly used (but not clichéd), and factual (less emotional, less 'colourful') language	Use abbreviated forms such as 'There's', 'I'm', 'We've': use the full forms (there is, I am, we have) instead
Remove digressions, rambles and unnecessary words and phrases: keep to the point.	Use colloquial or slang expressions (like 'This sucks': replace with something like 'This is frustrating' or 'This is unsatisfactory'...)
Refer to people by their title and surname, in more formal relationships – or where their expectations about formality are unknown.	Be overly 'familiar' or friendly in tone, or personal in content, unless the other person has expressly invited this.

Task 4

(a) The correct answer is: 20%

If a training programme costs £2,300 out of a total of £11,500:

$$\frac{2,300}{11,500} \times 100 = \frac{230,000}{1,150,000} = \frac{1}{5} = 20\%$$

(b) The correct answer is: 72 degrees

In a pie chart, this would be 20% of a 360° circle:

$$\frac{20}{100} \times 360 = \text{a } 72° \text{ slice of the circle.}$$

(c) The correct answer is:

Amount of discount £345

Net amount payable £1,955

15% discount on £2,300 = $\frac{15}{100} \times £2,300 = £345$

The total net amount payable is £2,300 – £345 = £1,955

Task 5

The correct answer is: £2,499.00

	£
List price	2,450.00
Less discount £2,450.00 × 15/100	(367.50)
	2,082.50
Plus VAT (£2,082.50 × 20/100)	416.50
	£2,499.00

Task 6

(a) The correct answer is:

Provider 1	£400
Provider 2	£376

First, you need to calculate the cost of the Effective Communication courses, so that they fit the rest of the data.

£200 × 3 days = £600   £210 × 2 ½ days = £525

Using the mean:

Provider 1 = (250 + 590 + 260 + 300 + 600) ÷ 5 courses = 2,000 ÷ 5 = £400.

Provider 2 = (340 + 375 + 290 + 350 + 525) ÷ 5 courses = 1,880 ÷ 5 = £376.

(b) The correct answer is:

Provider 1	£300
Provider 2	£350

Using the median:

Provider 1 = 250   260   300   590   600   The median is 300.

Provider 2 = 290   340   350   375   525   The median is 350.

(c) Provider 2 offers the lower average cost based on the mean, however the median value is lower for Provider 1. This discrepancy occurs because, although some of Provider 1's courses are significantly cheaper than any of Provider 2's (providing a lower middle value for Provider 1), the very high cost of the 'payroll' and 'effective communication' courses result in Provider 1's mean value for all courses being 'skewed', and therefore a higher mean cost than for Provider 2. Someone looking to purchase all 5 courses would get better value from Provider 2. However, for 1 to 4 courses only it is possible that Provider 1 may be cheaper, depending on the courses chosen.

Task 7

The correct answer is:

Anne	15.358%
Jaitinder	24.232%
Benjamin	29.352%
Chloe	10.922%
Vimal	20.137%

Workings

	Travel expense £	%
Anne	45/293	15.358
Jaitinder	71/293	24.232
Benjamin	86/293	29.352
Chloe	32/293	10.922
Vimal	59/293	20.137

CHAPTER 5   Presenting information

Task 1

(a)   The correct answer is:

Product	Jan £000	Feb £000	Mar £000	Apr £000	May £000	Jun £000	Total £000
A	800	725	725	400	415	405	3,470
B	210	210	180	150	175	160	1,085
C	25	50	60	95	125	140	495
Total	1,035	985	965	645	715	705	5,050

(b)   We'd recommend a line graph.

(c)   We'd recommend a pie chart.

Product A:

3,470/5,050 × 100 = 68.71% =

approximately 7/10 of the circle

Product B:

1,085/5,050 × 100 = 21.49% =

approximately 1/5 of the circle

Product C:

495/5,050 × 100 = 9.8% =

Approximately 1/10 of the circle

Proportion of six months' sales

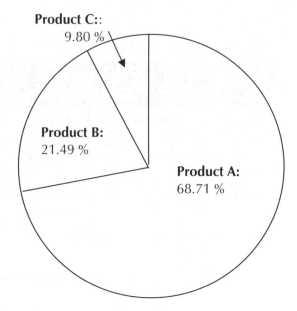

Task 2

The correct answers are:

(a)	Dear Sirs	Yours faithfully,
(b)	Dear Ms Brown	Yours sincerely,
(c)	Dear Mark	Kind regards,
(d)	Dear Sir Joshua	Yours sincerely,

Note that (d) is a special case when it is appropriate to use the person's first name in a formal address. It applies to people with the titles Sir X or Lady Y.

Task 3

(a)   'Following our telephone conversation of [date], I enclose the brochure you requested, which details our services.'

(b)   'I have been asked by my colleague, George Brown, to contact you in regard to your enquiry about career opportunities in the accounts department of our firm.'

(c)   'I look forward to meeting you to discuss the matter in more detail.'

(d)   'If you require any further information, please do not hesitate to telephone me on the number given above.'

Task 4

(a)

SOUTHFIELD ELECTRONICS LTD

MEMORANDUM

To: Jenny Faulkner, Financial Accountant
From: Your Name, Accounts Clerk
Date: 11 September 20X0
Subject   Project re abuse of telephone procedures

I would be very pleased to take on the project of investigating ways to minimise further telephone cost increases. Thank you for the opportunity. I will have to check with Kellie, Ron and Jane, to ensure that there is sufficient flexibility in my workload, but I cannot see that this will be a problem.

My initial thoughts are that we should seek:

(a)   To disconnect handsets that we do not need

(b)   To include telephone usage in the forthcoming briefing on compliance with policy

(c)   To gain some control over staff phone usage, by using a central switchboard or call logging. With your permission, I will start by getting some information about the possibilities from an office equipment provider.

I will keep you informed as the investigation progresses.

YN

(b)

SOUTHFIELD ELECTRONICS LTD

Tomorrow's technology for today's homes

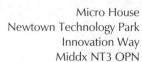

Micro House
Newtown Technology Park
Innovation Way
Middx NT3 OPN

The Sales Manager
TeleComs Ltd
6 Park Way
Brighton
Sussex BN3 4PW

11 September 20X0

Dear Sirs,

Electronic switchboards and call logging devices

I am writing to request information about your models of electronic switchboards and call logging devices, their capabilities and costs.

Southfield Electronics operates a fairly large office, and we are looking to control telephone costs. One of the approaches we will be considering is the monitoring and controlling of outgoing calls. You will no doubt be able to recommend suitable systems for our needs.

In the first instance, please send your information brochure to the office address supplied above. Alternatively, you can send material via email on: yname@southfield.co.uk.

Thank you for your attention. I look forward to hearing from you soon.

Yours faithfully,

Your Name

Your Name

Accounts Clerk

Task 5

	EMAIL
Date:	[inserted automatically]
To:	yourname@southfield.co.uk
From:	alaval@southfield.co.uk
Subject:	RE: Customer analysis
Attach:	customeranalysis.xls

Your name,

I attach an example of a completed customer analysis, as you requested. You will see that it is an Excel file, as I have formatted the analysis as a spreadsheet.

If you need any other help, let me know.

Amy

CHAPTER 6   Working independently

Task 1

The correct answer is:

Routine tasks	Unexpected tasks
Performing the weekly bank reconciliation	Preparing a special report for your manager
Preparing sales invoices daily	Showing a visitor around
Listing cheques received in the post each morning	Dealing with petty cash as the petty cashier is off sick

Task 2

The correct answer is:

Task	Important/urgent
Preparing a credit note listing for your manager due by the end of the month	Important
Producing a staff analysis for the Personnel Director for a meeting this afternoon	Urgent
Producing product costings for the Production manager for a meeting first thing tomorrow morning	Urgent
Checking purchase invoices to goods received notes	Important

Task 3

The correct answer is: Continue printing the sales invoices.

Both tasks are urgent but the sales invoices are more urgent, as they must be sent out today. The report is not needed until 12:00 noon on Monday, so provided that you make sure you can start the print run by 9:00am on Monday, and agree this with your supervisor, this is the best plan of action.

Task 4

THURSDAY tasks	Order of task completion
Generate statement and send to major customer	First task
Respond to customer queries from the day before	Second task
Enter sales invoices/credit notes	Third task
Enter purchase invoices/credit notes	Fourth task
Enter cash receipts and payments	Fifth task
Generate eight customer balances for MD meeting	Sixth task
HR Meeting	Seventh task
Print daily cheque run	Eighth task

Notes and workings

The statement is for a key customer who needs it as soon as possible, therefore this task should have been carried out first.

The assistant did not know about the request by the Managing Director (MD) for customer balances and activities until 2:00pm. Although the data was not needed until the following morning, the assistant would not have any time the next day as the meeting is at 9:00am. In addition as the assistant would only have had 30 minutes of her day left after the compulsory meeting, so would need to complete this task before the meeting in order to get it to the MD in advance of the meeting (since it could take up to an hour and a half.

The remaining tasks are fitted in around the urgent tasks and carried out in order of priority. The only one there will not be time for is the filing of invoices and credit notes.

Assuming everything took the maximum estimated time the order of tasks above would produce a day of tasks as follows:

Task/break	Duration (hrs)	Task order	Time period
Generate statement and send to major customer	0.5	First task	9:00am to 9:30am
Respond to customer queries from the day before	1	Second task	9:30am to 10:30am

Task/break	Duration (hrs)	Task order	Time period
Enter sales invoices/credit notes	0.75	Third task	10:30am to 11:15am
Enter purchase invoices/credit notes	0.75	Fourth task	11:15am to 12:00 noon
Enter cash receipts and payments	1	Fifth task	12:00 noon to 1:00pm
LUNCH	1		1:00pm to 2:00pm
Generate eight customer balances for MD meeting	1.5	Sixth task	2:00pm to 3:30pm
HR Meeting	1	Seventh task	3:30pm to 4:30pm
Print daily cheque run	0.5	Eighth task	4:30pm to 5:00pm

Task 5

The correct answer is:

Table — Ahead of schedule

Shelves — Behind schedule

Kitchen units — Not due to start

Bed — Completed on schedule

The furniture-maker is ahead of schedule in producing the table, having already completed it, even though it was not scheduled for completion until the end of today (Thursday). They are on schedule with the bed, having completed it as planned by the end of Wednesday. However, they are now behind schedule on the shelves, since progress is 'behind' where it should be at the 'time now' line. It may be possible to catch up, since the table-maker has spare time to help out the shelf-maker. The kitchen units aren't due to be started until tomorrow.

Task 6

TIMETABLE					
	Mon 8	Tues 9	Wed 10	Thurs 11	Fri 12
[8.00 – 9.00]	EF2	CD1	AB1	AB2	Train
9.00 – 10.00	EF2	EF1	AB1	AB3	Train
10.00 – 11.00	EF2	EF1	AB1	AB3	Train
11.00 – 12.00	EF2	EF1	AB1	AB3	Train
12.00 – 13.00					
13.00 – 14.00	CD1	EF1	AB1	AB3	Train
14.00 – 15.00	CD1	EF1	AB2	AB3	Train
15.00 – 16.00	CD1	EF1	AB2	AB3	AB4
16.00 – 17.00	CD1	AB1	AB2	AB3	AB4
[17.00 – 18.00]	CD1	AB1	AB2	AB3	AB4

Tasks carried over to week beginning 15 October:

- AB4 (9 hours remaining): Monday 15
- AB5 (2 hours): fit in some time during this week or following

Problem tasks:

- AB2: asked for by end of the day Wednesday, but if I work early overtime, I should be able to complete the task by 9.00am Thursday: check with AB that this is acceptable.

- AB4: asked for by end of the day Monday 15, with nine hours remaining. May not be possible to allocate all nine hours of Monday 15 to this task: need to discuss with AB.

If AB's deadlines are not moveable, I would have to discuss the other tasks with CD and EF to see if there is any flexibility to fit in AB's tasks earlier.

CHAPTER 7 Working as part of a team

Task 1

- The work may have to be transferred to other team members, meaning that their plans and schedules will have to be adjusted, and they will end up bearing a heavier share of the total work load.

- One person's failure to meet a deadline may, if there is little 'slack time' in a schedule, result in others failing to meet their deadlines. This causes them frustration and disruption – and may affect the team's ability to complete the whole task on time.

- Failure to 'pull one's weight' or meet agreed deadlines can have an impact on working relationships within the team. Resentment, frustration, blame and conflict may arise.

Task 2

The correct answer is: Offer to help input the figures on Thursday.

You should not offer to help with analysis on Wednesday, snce you do not have spare time on that day. However, you are likely to have some spare time on Thursday, so you should offer to help your colleague to input the figures to the computer then. The entire project depends upon the figures being ready, and you should offer assistance to ensure that the project team meets this deadline. You might check with your departmental supervisor first, however, to ensure that she agrees this is the best use of your time.

Task 3

You have handled this situation effectively, because you have managed to respect your prior agreements and project deadlines – while still being courteous and co-operative in offering options to Ron Howard.

The key points of the argument are:

- You have made prior commitments, which you wish to respect.

- Breaking your prior commitments, by missing your deadline, will impact on the work of a project team.

- Your prior commitment is to a manager at the same level of authority as Ron, and with the backing of a higher manager (Jenny Faulkner).

- It is not reasonable for Ron to ask you to work long overtime hours so that he can have personal time off: you have a right to say no.

- Ron is still your superior, so you should be calm, respectful and co-operative in your dealings with him.

- You have limited authority to propose alternative options: Ron should settle the matter with Kellie McDonald, since the real problem is between their conflicting demands.

Task 4

The correct answer is: Standing up for your own rights, needs and opinions

Task 5

The correct answer is: Find out why each wants the window desk and look for solutions to meet their needs.

If one team member gets the window desk and the other doesn't it will result in resentment and demotivation of the 'losing' member, so this is a win-lose situation.

If the team members get the window desk on alternate days or weeks, this will result in half-satisfied needs, so both lose out (lose-lose).

The only possibility to create a win-win situation is to establish what each wants the window desk for and to look for solutions to satisfy both employees needs. For example, one may want the view, the other better lighting conditions. This offers options to be explored such as improved lighting being provided for one of the employees.

CHAPTER 8   Developing skills and knowledge

Task 1

EMAIL

From: y.name@reeves.co.uk
To: a.bolt@reeves.co.uk
Cc: g.hoff@reeves.co.uk
Date: *[Today's date]*
Re: RE: Personal Development Plan

Thank you for your email about the cost of PDPs and training requests for the Accounts department. Mrs Hoff has asked me to reply on her behalf.

I am sure you are aware that all professional bodies require their members to keep their technical knowledge up-to-date, as a condition of membership. All members of the Accounts department are therefore bound to complete a certain number of hours of Continuing Professional Development activity, or they will not be able to continue as members of their professional body. This, in turn, would impact on their ability to perform their jobs.

Reeves Ltd will also benefit in many ways from Accounts department CPD activity, in terms of: more competent job performance; less supervision required; increased productivity; reduced risk and cost of errors and non-compliance with regulations/laws; improved staff motivation and morale; and an enhanced ability to recruit and retain professionally qualified staff.

I hope this explains the ambitious PDPs submitted by the department – and also goes some way to justify the cost and time requirements.

I would be happy to give you more information about CPD requirements, if this would be helpful.

YN.

Task 2

The correct answer is:

The │person specification│ for your role sets out what sort of personal qualities the organisation is looking for in your role.

The │ job description │ sets out what a person in your job should be able to do.

Task 3

The correct answer is:

Learning needs	Suitable approach
An accounts clerk wishes to work toward becoming AAT qualified	External training course
A worker is transferred onto a new piece of equipment and needs to learn how to operate it	On-the-job training
A new member of staff is about to join the organisation	Induction training
An organisation decides that its supervisors would benefit from leadership training	Internal training course/External training course*

*The ability to train supervisors internally will depend on the availability of suitably experienced management to provide the necessary training. If this is unavailable the organisation may seek to use an external training company.

CHAPTER 9   Understanding ethical and sustainable values

Task 1

This is personal to you, so that you begin to think about your own assumptions and beliefs about what kinds of behaviour are 'OK' and 'not OK'. Some of these may be in line with the ethical values of the AAT and accounting profession (such as being honest, telling the truth, being fair and working hard) and some may not be (such as using your work position for the benefit of family members, or offering gifts as a smoother of business relationships and negotiations). In a way, these instances – where your values differ from the professional standards – are more useful information: you know where your 'blind spots' are, and where you may have to modify your assumptions and habits.

Task 2

The correct answer is:

	✓
True	
False	✓

Straightforwardness and honesty are related to the fundamental principle of integrity.

Task 3

Continuing professional development (CPD) is important to accountancy professionals as it helps them ⬚ maintain ⬚ competency in their role.

Accountancy professionals attain competence by passing professional exams and gaining relevant experience. It is the maintenance of professional competence that requires continuing awareness and understanding of relevant technical, professional and business developments and is achieved through CPD.

Task 4

The correct answer is:

	✓
If they are asked for during legal proceedings	✓
When your manager tells you to disclose the information	
When writing a report for general circulation within your organisation	

In this case you have a legal duty to disclose the information.

Task 5

The correct answer is:

	✓
Self-interest	
Advocacy	
Intimidation	✓

'Significant pressure' indicates intimidation threat.

Task 6

Your answer will depend on the nature of your job and the type of organisation that you work for. Good answers would include issues relating to economic factors, social factors and the environment.

TEST YOUR LEARNING – ANSWERS

CHAPTER 2   The role of the financial functions

Test 1

The correct answer is:

Human resources	☑
Manufacturing	☐
Stores control	☐
Accounting and finance	☑
Information technology	☑

Test 2

The correct answer is:

Test 3

The correct answer is:

The calculation of gross pay	☑
Purchasing supplies	☐
The calculation of tax, National Insurance and other deductions	☑
Preparing payslips	☑
Bank reconciliations	☐
Paying cash into the bank	☐
Making up wages, or preparing data for direct credit (BACS)	☑
Writing cheques	☐
Distributing payslips to employees	☑

Test 4

The correct answer is:

Providing a service at the least possible cost	☐
Minimum wastage	☑
Paying the minimum wage to employees	☐
Achieving objectives with minimum use of resources	☑

Test 5

The correct answer is:

Health and safety regulation	☑
Pollution emission regulations	☐
HMRC VAT rules	☑
Regulations over the export of goods	☐

CHAPTER 3   The organisational framework

Test 1

The correct answer is:

	Downward	Upward
Instructions	✓	☐
Exception reports	☐	✓
Briefings	✓	☐
Queries and questions	☐	✓
Plans	✓	☐
Routine reports	☐	✓
Decisions	✓	☐

Test 2

The correct answer is: Office manager

Because the relocation is being managed as a cross-functional project by the Office Manager, and this task specifically relates to the project (and not to your everyday work in the accounts department), the person to report to here (in the first instance) will be the Office Manager.

Test 3

The correct answer is: Accounts department where there are rarely any visits from non-employees

In an accounts department where there are rarely any visits from non-employees, the employer may be happy for a degree of personalisation of work areas, eg the display of photographs. (However, these must be acceptable to others in the office, and create a professional appearance and environment.)

In a reception area open to the public or a sales department where there are regular meetings with customers it will be important to give the right impression of the organisation. Therefore, in order to appear professional and efficient, there may be stricter rules regarding the amount of personalisation allowed in these areas.

Test 4

Your supervisor asks you for details of the latest R & D
expenditure on new products.

Y

A telephone caller, saying she is a financial journalist,
asks you for details of your upcoming plans for new products.

N

A customer calls asking for the bank details of one of your
fellow employees, stating that the customer wishes to pay
a cheque into her bank account.

N

One of the senior accounts assistants has asked you
to photocopy the notes for a training course that another
rival company uses. You notice that the course notes
have the copyright © symbol on them.

N

Explanations

The supervisor's request is a legitimate request from someone in a position of authority (provided that the R & D information is not flagged as 'classified', in which case authorisation may be required).

The telephone call request is likely to be sensitive information integral to the organisation's competitive advantage. Even if the caller *is* a journalist (and you have no way of knowing; she may be a competitor's R & D manager...), she has no right to this information, and should be politely refused.

Bank details are personal data (under the Data Protection Act) and should only be used for the purpose of making payments from the payroll. It is also highly personal and confidential information and should not be disclosed to anyone. The customer's request must be denied.

As the training course notes have the copyright symbol on them, they must not be photocopied without written permission from the copyright owner, the rival company. This must be explained to the senior accounts assistant and you should not copy them – unless permission has been obtained.

Test 5

The correct answer is:

Authorisations are points in a procedure at which confirmation or permission to proceed must be obtained from an individual with appropriate authority.

Designated signatories are people who are authorised to sign documents (eg for authorisation purposes) or company cheques.

CHAPTER 4   Communication skills

Test 1

| Feedback | is the response of a person with whom you are communicating, which indicates whether your message has (or has not) been received and understood as you intended.

Feedback is important in enabling you to adjust your message, if necessary, in order to ensure that the message has been received, and that there are no misunderstandings.

Test 2

The correct answer is: £786.23

VAT in May $= \dfrac{20}{120} \times £4,580 = £763.3333333$ (rounded to £763.33)

VAT exclusive price in May = £4,580 – £763.33 = £3,816.67

There is a 3% increase in price for June so the VAT exclusive price in June will be:

£3,816.67 × 103% = £3,816.67 × 1.03 = £3,931.1701 (rounded to £3,931.17)

VAT on June purchase = £3,931.17 × 20% = £786.234 (rounded to £786.23)

Test 3

The correct answer is: 26%

Percentage increase in revenue =

$$\dfrac{\left(£20,916 - £16,600\right)}{£16,600} \times 100 \quad = \quad \dfrac{£4,316}{£16,600} \times 100 = 0.26 \times 100 = 26\%$$

CHAPTER 5   Presenting information

Test 1

The correct answer is:

Situation	Method
Detailing a telephone message left by a supplier for a colleague	Informal note
Informing an employee that his work has not been up to standard recently	Face-to-face discussion*
Requesting a customer's sales ledger account balance from the credit controller	Email
Requesting production details for the last month from the factory manager where the factory is situated five miles away	Email
Sending monthly variances to the sales manager	Email

*A face-to-face discussion is necessary because of the sensitivity of the issue, and the need for interactive question and answer.

Test 2

The correct answer is:

Report section

Content

| Executive summary |
| Main body |
| Introduction |

| Detailed results and findings |
| Summary of key conclusions |
| Purpose and scope of the report |
| Overview of key findings |

BPP
LEARNING MEDIA

Test 3

Your Name
Your Address

Jo Bloggs
3 Market Place
Shepherds Bush
London W12 1AW

[Today's Date]

Dear Jo,

The use of appendices in report writing

In response to your recent request for information about this, I thought you might appreciate the following key points.

The purpose of an appendix (or appendices) to a report is to separate out from the main body of the report any detailed data and supporting documents that might be helpful to the user, but might get in the way of the flow and conciseness of the main report.

In order to be used effectively, appendices should be limited in number, to avoid overloading the user with data. Each appendix should be numbered, and referred to clearly in the body of the report (eg 'see Appendix 1' or 'attached as Appendix 2'), so that the user can easily locate the supporting data if required.

These are very simple points, but I hope they are helpful to you.

If you want any further help with your report writing, just let me know. I'd be happy to help if I can.

Kind regards,

Your Name

CHAPTER 6   Working independently

Test 1

The correct answer is:

Task	Category
Preparing a petty cash summary by the end of next week	Not urgent but important
Packing up out of date files to be archived	Not urgent or important
Preparing a report for a meeting tomorrow	Urgent and important
Replenishing the milk in the kitchen this morning	Urgent but not important

Test 2

The correct answer is:

A | to do list | is a simple short-term planning tool and consists of a checklist listing the tasks that need completing for a particular day.

An | action plan | is a detailed planning tool which can be used for complex longer term projects.

Test 3

The correct answer is:

The latest date on which you could start work on this report is | Friday 10 August |

	August							
	Fri	**Mon**	**Tues**	**Wed**	**Thurs**	**Fri**	**Mon**	**Tues**
	10	*13*	*14*	*15*	*16*	*17*	*20*	*21*
Req. files	X							
Research		X	X	X				
Analysis					X	X		
Typing							X	
Proofing								X

CHAPTER 7   Working as part of a team

Test 1

The correct answer is:

Receivables ledger team	☑
Inventory control section	☐
Human resources team	☐
Payroll section	☑

Test 2

Roles that people might occupy in a team will include:

Leading the team
Generating ideas
Implementing the ideas
Maintaining the relationships between the team members

Test 3

It is highly likely that the tasks that you perform will have an effect on other team members. Information that you provide will be used by others and they may not be able to complete their tasks until you have completed yours. Therefore, schedules and timetables must be set by the team leader to ensure that there is full integration of the work of all team members. It is important that each individual meets their commitments according to the schedules set, in order for the team to achieve its objectives.

Test 4

Synergy is the concept that sometimes two heads are better than one and therefore teams can often accomplish more than the same individuals working alone.

Mutual assistance within teams can help provide synergies when one member of the team, still being able to fulfil his/her other commitments, is able to help another member struggling due to time or other restraints (for example lack of skill/experience in a particular area). This attitude is then reciprocated by the assisted team member when the roles are reversed.

The overall result is that more work is completed on time and its quality is better than it may have otherwise been.

Test 5

The correct answer is: Discuss your concerns with your colleague

You should talk to the accounts assistant initially and explain your concerns. If there is no solution drawn from these discussions (and no improvement in the behaviour towards you), your only action would be to talk to your line manager about the problem.

Test 6

Win-lose: one of you gets the file and the other doesn't. (Result: one party fails to meet their commitments.)

Compromise: one of you gets the file now, and the other gets it later (although this has an element of win-lose, since the other has to work late or take it home).

Win-win: you photocopy the file and *both* take it – or one of you consults his or her boss and gets an extension of the deadline (since getting the job done in time is the real aim – not just getting the file). Result: both deadlines are met, and collaboration has probably enhanced the working relationship between the colleagues.

Test 7

The correct answer is:

Sexual or racial harassment	☑
Unfair treatment or discrimination due to race, gender or disability	☑
Having to share a printer with another department	☐
An argument with a fellow employee over the tidiness of their workspace	☐
An employee being given an unfair workload	☑
An employee being blocked for promotion	☑

CHAPTER 8   Developing skills and knowledge

Test 1

Members of professional bodies are required to complete a certain amount of CPD as a condition of continuing membership. This ensures that their knowledge and skills are always up-to-date and of a good standard – which, in turn, protects the interests of their clients and employers, as well as the standing and credibility of the professional bodies and the accounting profession.

Test 2

The correct answer is:

Enables improved job performance	☑
It saves time in the short term	☐
Potential for increased rewards and recognition	☑
Greater job security	☑
Decreased job satisfaction	☐
Valuable in the external job market	☑

Note that although learning and development will improve performance and save time in the long term, the time taken to undertake proper learning and development will mean the employee has less time to undertake other tasks in the short term.

Test 3

Examples include (only four were required):

Courses	Internal or external educational or training courses
Journals/trade publications	Technical information and updates (and training/educational opportunities)
Books	Technical and educational material
Colleagues	Learning skills, methods and techniques from colleagues on a formal or informal basis
Observation	A method of learning by observing how colleagues or superiors carry out their tasks

Test 4

Popular search engines are often used together with key words to find web pages with details of the laws and regulations you are looking for. However, those websites listed first may not be the most reliable websites if they are not provided by a recognised or reliable source. They may therefore not be up to date or may contain inaccuracies. This can have an impact on the individual using the information as they may rely on, or pass on, this incorrect information in their role as a professional.

In order to make sure the information being learned from is accurate the integrity of the provider should be verified. Sometimes you are able to check the last date the page was updated to ensure it is up to date information and this should be checked wherever possible.

Test 5

You can compare your own progress against your PDP goals on a regular basis. (Have you attained the targets you set?)

Another review method is to get informal feedback from your supervisor or colleagues. (How do they think you have improved – and could improve still further?)

Most organisations plan periodic progress reviews (especially in project work and for new recruits).

There will also probably be annual PERFORMANCE APPRAISAL for all employees.

CHAPTER 9   Understanding ethical and sustainable values

Test 1

The correct answer is:

	✓
True	
False	✓

Group values are very important, eg in families and friendship groups (which is where we get our ideas from), national cultures and organisations (which establish ethical norms and expectations by which we have to operate).

Test 2

The correct answer is:

	✓
Enhance the reputation and standing of its members	✓
Limit the number of members that it has	
Make sure that its members are able to earn large salaries	

The AAT needs to protect its reputation and standing by maintaining standards of conduct and service among its members in order to be able to enhance the reputation and standing of its members (so that, for example, they are able to attract and retain clients).

Test 3

The correct answer is:

	✓
Say that you will get back to him when you have looked up the answer.	
Give him the contact details of a friend in your firm who knows all about accounting standards.	
Clarify the limits of your expertise with the client.	✓

This is an issue of technical competence and due care. You should clarify the limits of your expertise with the client, and *then* seek information or guidance from the relevant source.

Test 4

The correct answer is:

	✓
It is in the public interest that employees who fail to comply with standards are prosecuted.	
It is in the public interest that services are carried out to professional standards.	✓

Test 5

The correct answer is:

	✓
Policies aimed at improving efficiency including reducing waste, using less energy and recycling.	
A long-term programme involving a series of sustainable development practices aimed at improving organisational efficiency, stakeholder support and market edge.	✓
A core part of an organisation's corporate social responsibility comprising efficiency, stakeholder support and market edge.	

Question bank

Chapter 2

Task 2.1

Susan, a manager, has been provided with a payroll report she requested from the payroll function. She wanted the report in order to process the wages payments at the end of the month but she also needed it to assess whether sufficient funds in the business current account were available to ensure the payments went through without incurring bank charges.

Bill, the payroll clerk, knew the manager wanted the report so he took a very long time putting it together making sure all the information needed was included and everything on the report was absolutely correct. However due to his careful approach the report has only just been passed to Susan and there is only one day left before the scheduled date for the wages payments.

Which of the following qualities is the report likely to have?

Complete	☐
Timely	☐
Accurate	☐

Task 2.2

Which of the following information provided by the accounting function can help the organisation maintain its solvency?

Produce a cash budget	☐
Produce a profit statement	☐
Ensure tax bills are paid on time	☐
Ensure inventory is kept at maximum levels	☐
Ensure receivables pay on time	☐
Monitor the cash budget	☐

Chapter 3

Task 3.1

An organisation employs three directors, two managers and four assistants. The managing director is the only director with a personal assistant (PA).

Show who the general ledger assistant, sales manager and payroll assistant would report to by drawing lines between the employee and line manager.

	Finance director
General ledger assistant	Managing director's PA
Sales manager	Managing director
Payroll assistant	Accounting department manager
	Sales director

Task 3.2

Complete the following sentences regarding the security of computerised accounting data by selecting the most appropriate word(s) from the picklist.

Data on computer servers is [▼] daily.

[▼] containing both letters and numbers are required to access accounting systems.

All computers are installed with up to date [▼].

Picklist

filed
access
passwords
programmes
backed up
anti-virus software

....

Chapter 4

Task 4.1

What would be the most appropriate method of communication in each of the following circumstances? Choose from the picklist below.

(a) Explaining to a customer that a cash discount that has been deducted was not valid, as the invoice was not paid within the discount period

(b) Requesting customer balances from a colleague in the sales ledger department

(c) Providing negative feedback to a colleague on the quality of their work

(d) A formal complaint to a supplier regarding the delivery times of goods, which are not as agreed

(e) Information to be provided to the sales director regarding the breakdown of sales geographically for the last two years

Picklist

Email
Telephone
Letter
Face-to-face discussion

Task 4.2

A junior colleague shows you a draft of an email to the Purchasing Director of a company which has recently expressed an interest in your products. He asks you to identify any words or phrases you think are inappropriate. The draft appears as follows.

EMAIL

To: hgwells@retail.com
From: acdoyle@southfield.co.uk
Date: *[Today's date]*
Subject: Your recent enquiry
Attach: Sales brochure.pdf

Hi, Hugh.
Thanks for your msg re our products. Its cool that you were able to come and see our display at the Home Entertainment Trade Fair. More than happy to help with further info.

Our company's one of the best in the field, and our product's have recently one an award as Retail Product of the Year.

I've attached a brochure what details our full product range. it includes prices and terms of trade. Having received it, I will contact you to see if you'd like to place an order.

In the meantime, me and the sales team are availble to answer any questions you may have, it'd be gr8 to hear from you.

Cheers.

Arthur

(a)   Underline any inappropriate words or phrases in the email.

(b)   Re-draft the email and make a note of how you would explain your changes to Arthur, to help him improve his communication skills.

Chapter 5

Task 5.1

The business you work for ordered five laptop computers with a list price of £500 each (order ref NCA124). During a phone conversation on 1 May 20X1 you were promised a 5% bulk discount by an account manager at the supplier (Bell computers) if you purchased five or more laptops. The account manager at the supplier is called Bill Fences.

The laptops arrived today (20 May 20X1) and so did the invoice from the supplier (Invoice number LT241). The invoice shows the total value of the computers to be £2,500 and the 5% discount had not been deducted. You have tried phoning Bill but he is out of the office today.

You are on holiday for the rest of the week and are not going to be able to deal with this so your supervisor Hugh Martin has asked you send him a short memo explaining what happened with any photocopies of related documents attached. He will then contact the supplier to ask for a credit note and a new invoice.

Complete the memo below by selecting the appropriate option from the appropriate picklist, or entering the appropriate reference or number. A dropdown icon indicates there is picklist available and each picklist is numbered. (If there is no dropdown icon you must simply enter the reference/number.)

MEMO

To: (1) [▼]

From: Anne Accountant, Accountant

Date: (2) [▼]

Subject: Bell computers: **(3)** [▼] for laptops.

On **(4)** [▼] an order (reference [ ]) was placed for

five laptop computers which have a list price of **£** [ ] each. On

the same day **(5)** [▼] , an account manager at Bell, agreed we

would receive a 5% bulk discount because the order was for five or more

computers. I enclose my notes from the phone call (including contact details for

the account manager) and a copy of the order for your information.

We received invoice (reference [ ]) for the computers today

which shows the total cost of the laptops to be **£** [ ] . Therefore

the anticipated discount of **£** [ ] has not been applied and we

should request that Bell send us a credit note for the original invoice and re-issue

a new invoice with the discount applied.

Many thanks for dealing with this.

Anne

enc: Copies of the order and invoice
Notes of phone call on 1 May 20X1

Picklists

(1)   Hugh Martin, Accounts supervisor / Bill Fences, Account Manager
(2)   1 May 20X1 / 20 May 20X1 / 31 May 20X1
(3)   Undercharge / Overcharge
(4)   1 May 20X1 / 20 May 20X1 / 31 May 20X1
(5)   Hugh Martin / Bill Fences

Chapter 6

Task 6.1

An accounts assistant works 9:00am to 5:00pm with an hour for lunch at 1:00pm. He has the following routine duties (duration of tasks are in brackets):

- Open the morning post (30 minutes)

- Pass any cheques received to the cashier (30 minutes)

- Enter sales invoices/credit notes daily in batches into computer system by midday (2 hours)

- Match and check purchase invoices to goods received notes daily and pass them all to the accountant for authorisation (6 minutes per invoice) (see related information that follows on the deadline for this)

- File sales invoices/credit notes (between 1 and 2 hours of filing)

Today is Friday 27 September and having already opened the post and passed the cheques to the cashier, you get a telephone call from the accountant to say that one of your colleagues is not coming in today due to sickness. You now also need to enter the weekly purchase invoices into the computer today (which should only take an hour). Another colleague, who is back in the office this afternoon (2:00pm) needs to review a list of these invoices before the end of the day for forecasting purposes. The list is generated from the computer system you are entering the invoices into.

You have 20 purchase invoices that need to be matched to (and checked against) GRNs before the end of the day ready for authorisation first thing on Monday.

Decide on the order you would carry out the tasks included in the picklist.

Order	Task
1st task	▼
2nd task	▼
3rd task	▼
4th task	▼

BPP
LEARNING MEDIA

Picklist

Filing

Match purchase invoices to goods received notes and pass to the accountant for authorisation

Enter weekly purchase invoices into the computer

Enter sales invoices/credit notes into computer system

Task 6.2

You have been asked to prepare a report on the payment patterns of twelve of your organisation's largest customers. The information for the current month will not be available until Tuesday 5 April. However, the information for earlier months is to be collated by a colleague and she thinks that this will take her two days. The report should take you about four days to prepare on your computer around your other tasks. You should be able to work for two days without the current month information. Six copies of the report are required for a Board meeting on Friday 8 March at 2.00 pm. You estimate that it will take three hours to print and collate the copies of the report.

In order to prepare this report what would you do on each of the following days chosen from the picklist that follows.

Day	Action	
Thursday 31 March		▼
Monday 4 April		▼
Tuesday 5 April		▼
Wednesday 6 April		▼
Thursday 7 April		▼
Friday 8 April		▼

Picklist

Print and collate copies of the report

Prepare elements of the report using current information

Request information from colleague

Prepare elements of the report using historic information

Task 6.3

Your name is Justine Spring and you have recently been employed as an accounts assistant by Reeves Ltd, a company which produces and sells a variety of educational children's toys.

The job description below was given to you when you joined the company and was discussed with the HR manager.

JOB DESCRIPTION	
Job title:	Accounts assistant
Summary:	General financial and management accounting duties
Job content:	Enter daily sales invoices into computer
	Enter daily cash/cheque receipts into computer
	Enter daily cash/cheque payments into computer
	Prepare monthly bank reconciliation
	Deal with daily petty cash claims
	Enter petty cash details in computer weekly
	Assist in preparation of weekly payroll
	Other ad hoc financial/management accounting tasks
Reports to:	Accountant – Patrick Fellows
Hours:	9.00am to 5.30pm Monday to Friday
	1 hour for lunch
Training:	Necessary training to be provided
Prepared by:	HR manager

Enter *(CBT: drag and drop)* your daily, weekly and monthly routine tasks using *(into)* the table below.

Daily tasks	
Weekly tasks	
Monthly tasks	

Drag and drop choices:

Assist in preparation of payroll

Deal with petty cash claims

Enter cash/cheque receipts into the computer

Enter sales invoices into the computer

Prepare bank reconciliation

Enter petty cash details into the computer

Enter cash/cheque payments into computer

Other ad hoc accounting tasks

Chapter 7

Task 7.1

| ▼ | is NOT an advantage of working in a team rather than as an individual?

Picklist

Additional resources
Inspiration
Independence
Motivation
Communication

Task 7.2

If you disagree with a decision being made, and wish to influence the decision maker, what style of communication should you use to communicate with him or her?

Aggressive ☐

Passive ☐

Argumentative ☐

Assertive ☐

Task 7.3

Which of the following issues should you try and resolve yourself, and which should you refer to your line manager?

Issue	Resolve yourself	Refer to line manager
You have two tasks with the same deadline and not enough time to complete both. You are unsure which to prioritise and no-one else in your team has the necessary knowledge to help.	☐	☐
Your colleague's noise level on the phone is affecting your ability to concentrate on your work.	☐	☐
A manager from another department has asked you to produce a report they need and have insisted you give the report priority over your regular tasks, despite you informing them you already have deadlines that must be met.	☐	☐
Your colleague has asked you to print out a number of invoices they have been asked to print since they want to concentrate on 'more interesting' jobs.	☐	☐

Chapter 8

Task 8.1

In the context of setting personal development objectives and using the picklist that follows the table below, determine which element of the SMART framework is being described.

Description	Element of SMART	
Objectives must be achievable using available time and other resources		▼
Objectives must be formulated such that the achievement of them can be evaluated		▼
Objectives must be set within a specific time scale		▼
Development objectives must not be general		▼
Must be approved by the appropriate manager		▼

Picklist

Specific
Measurable
Agreed
Realistic
Time-bounded

Task 8.2

Match the following learning needs (on the left) with an appropriate approach (on the right).

Need

An employee wants to ensure that she is aware of the latest rules under the Data Protection Act

An accounts clerk wishes to improve in the use of double-entry bookkeeping and computer spreadsheets

An accounts clerk wishes to improve his participation in team meetings

Approach

Training course

Internet research

Experiential learning

Task 8.3

Which FOUR of the following items would be typically be covered in an appraisal session with a line manager?

Review of work performance since last appraisal ☐

Future holiday plans ☐

Feedback on strengths, weaknesses and improvement/learning needs ☐

Review of progress towards meeting objectives set at last appraisal ☐

Specific problem with this month's bank reconciliation ☐

Setting of new objectives for next period ☐

Chapter 9

Task 9.1

Which of these might (or might be thought to) affect the objectivity of providers of professional accounting services?

	✓
Failure to keep up to date on CPD	
A personal financial interest in the client's affairs	
Being negligent or reckless with the accuracy of the information provided to the client	

Task 9.2

Put the four steps of the problem-solving methodology or 'conceptual framework' for ethical conduct into the correct order:

Apply safeguards to eliminate or reduce the threat to an acceptable level	▼
Evaluate the seriousness of the threat	▼
Discontinue the action or relationship giving rise to the threat	▼
Identify a potential threat to a fundamental ethical principle	▼

Picklist:

1,2,3,4

Answer bank

Answer bank

Chapter 2

Task 2.1

The correct answer is:

Complete	✓
Timely	☐
Accurate	✓

Task 2.2

The correct answer is:

Produce a cash budget	✓
Produce a profit statement	☐
Ensure tax bills are paid on time	☐
Ensure inventory is kept at maximum levels	☐
Ensure receivables pay on time	✓
Monitor the cash budget	✓

Chapter 3

Task 3.1

The correct answer is:

Task 3.2

The correct answer is:

Data on computer servers is | backed up | daily.

| Passwords | containing both letters and numbers are required to access accounting systems.

All computers installed with up to date | anti-virus software |.

Chapter 4

Task 4.1

The correct answers are:

(a) Telephone

(b) Email

(c) Face-to-face discussion

(d) Letter

(e) Email

Task 4.2

(a)

EMAIL

To:	hgwells@retail.com
From:	acdoyle@southfield.co.uk
Date:	[Today's date]
Subject:	Your recent enquiry
Attach:	Sales brochure.pdf

Hi, Hugh.

Thanks for your msg re our products. Its cool that you were able to come and see our display at the Home Entertainment Trade Fair. More than happy to help with further info.

Our company's one of the best in the field, and our product's have recently one an award as Retail Product of the Year.

I've attached a brochure what details our full product range. it includes prices and terms of trade. Having received it, I will contact you to see if you'd like to place an order.

In the meantime, me and the sales team are availble to answer any questions you may have. It'd be gr8 to hear from you.

Cheers.

Arthur

A more appropriate email would be:

EMAIL

To:	hgwells@retail.com
From:	acdoyle@southfield.co.uk
Date:	*[Today's date]*
Subject:	Your recent enquiry
Attach:	Sales brochure.pdf

Dear Mr Wells,

Thank you for your enquiry about our products. I am glad that you were able to come and see our display at the Home Entertainment Trade Fair, and I would be more than happy to help with further information.

Our company is one of the best in the field, and our products have recently won an award as Retail Product of the Year.

I have attached a brochure which details our full product range. It includes prices and terms of trade. Once you have received it, I will contact you to see if you would like to place an order.

In the meantime, the sales team and I are available to answer any questions you may have. We would be glad to hear from you.

Thank you again for your enquiry.

Arthur Doyle

Southfield Electronics

[NB Use the standard signature block for outgoing emails]

(b)   **Note for explaining changes to Arthur**

Arthur, I've just made a few amendments to your draft email, as you requested. For future reference:

- It is better to use a more formal style with senior individuals and new customers. Don't use first name terms unless they've asked you to. Avoid familiar expressions (like 'cheers'), and keep to a more formal written style (eg 'I have' instead of 'I've').

- In business communications, avoid text-message style abbreviations (like 'msg', and 'gr8') and colloquial expressions (like 'cool').

- Remember to check your work for typos (like 'availble') and spelling or grammar related errors (like 'one' instead of 'won').

- You might want to make sure you write in full sentences (which contain a verb and end in a full stop), and look out for errors with clauses and apostrophes.

Chapter 5

Task 5.1

MEMO

To: Hugh Martin, Accounts supervisor

From: Anne Accountant, Accountant

Date: 20 May 20X1

Subject: Bell computers overcharge for laptops.

On 1 May 20X1 an order (reference NCA124) was placed for five laptop computers which have a list price of £ 500 each. On the same day Bill Fences , an account manager at Bell, agreed we would receive a 5% bulk discount because the order was for five or more computers. I enclose my notes from the phone call (including contact details for the account manager) and a copy of the order for your information.

We received invoice (reference LT241) for the computers today which shows the total cost of the laptops to be £ 2,500 . Therefore the anticipated discount of £ 125 has not been applied and we should request that Bell send us a credit note for the original invoice and re-issue a new invoice with the discount applied.

Many thanks for dealing with this.

Anne

enc: Copies of the order and invoice
      Notes of phone call on 1 May 20X1

Chapter 6

Task 6.1

The correct answer is:

Order	Task
1st task (10:00am to 12:00 noon)	Enter sales invoices/credit notes into computer system
2nd task (12:00 noon to 1:00pm)	Enter weekly purchase invoices into the computer
3rd task (2:00pm to 4:00pm) (20 x 6 mins = 120 mins)	Match purchase invoices to goods received notes and pass to the accountant for authorisation
4th task (4:00pm to 5:00pm)	Filing

Task 6.2

The correct answer is:

Day	Action
Thursday 31 March	Request information from colleague
Monday 4 April	Prepare elements of report using historical information
Tuesday 5 April	Prepare elements of report using historic information
Wednesday 6 April	Prepare elements of report using current information
Thursday 7 April	Prepare elements of report using current information
Friday 8 April	Print and collate copies of the report

Task 6.3

The correct answer is:

Daily tasks	Enter sales invoices into the computer
	Enter cash/cheque receipts into the computer
	Enter cash/cheque payments into computer
	Deal with petty cash claims
Weekly tasks	Enter petty cash details into the computer
	Assist in preparation of payroll
Monthly tasks	Prepare bank reconciliation

Unallocated: Other ad hoc accounting tasks.

Chapter 7

Task 7.1

The correct answer is:

| Independence | is NOT an advantage of working in a team rather than as an individual?

∙∙

Task 7.2

The correct answer is: Assertive

If you are trying to influence someone, you will need to communicate assertively (without being aggressive) and put forward your views clearly. You will need to listen, first, to the other person, so that you can argue logically against their reasons, and can tailor your solution to their needs.

∙∙

Task 7.3

The correct answer is:

Issue	Resolve yourself	Refer to line manager
You have two tasks with the same deadline and not enough time to complete both. You are unsure which to prioritise and no-one else in your team has the necessary knowledge to help.	☐	☑
Your colleague's noise level on the phone is affecting your ability to concentrate on your work.	☑	☐
A manager from another department has asked you to produce a report they need and have insisted you give the report priority over your regular tasks, despite you informing them you already have deadlines that must be met.	☐	☑
Your colleague has asked you to print out a number of invoices they have been asked to print since they want to concentrate on 'more interesting' jobs.	☑	☐

Chapter 8

Task 8.1

The correct answer is:

Description	Element of SMART
Objectives must be achievable using available time and other resources	Realistic
Objectives must be formulated such that the achievement of them can be evaluated	Measurable
Objectives must be set within a specific time scale	Time-bounded
Development objectives must not be general	Specific
Must be approved by the appropriate manager	Agreed

· ·

Task 8.2

The correct answer is:

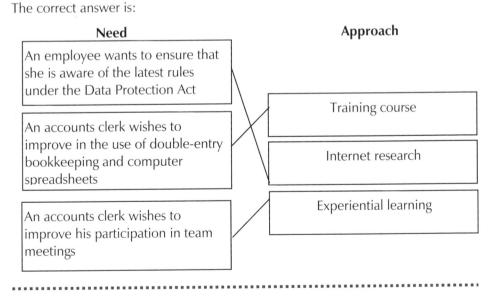

Need	Approach
An employee wants to ensure that she is aware of the latest rules under the Data Protection Act	
	Training course
An accounts clerk wishes to improve in the use of double-entry bookkeeping and computer spreadsheets	
	Internet research
	Experiential learning
An accounts clerk wishes to improve his participation in team meetings	

· ·

Task 8.3

The correct answer is:

Review of work performance since last appraisal	☑
Future holiday plans	☐
Feedback on strengths, weaknesses and improvement/learning needs	☑
Review of progress towards meeting objectives set at last appraisal	☑
Specific problem with this month's bank reconciliation	☐
Setting of new objectives for next period	☑

Chapter 9

Task 9.1

The correct answer is:

	✓
Failure to keep up to date on CPD	
A personal financial interest in the client's affairs	✓
Being negligent or reckless with the accuracy of the information provided to the client	

A personal financial interest in the client's affairs will affect objectivity. Failure to keep up to date on CPD is an issue of professional competence, while providing inaccurate information reflects upon professional integrity.

Task 9.2

The correct answer is:

Apply safeguards to eliminate or reduce the threat to an acceptable level.	3
Evaluate the seriousness of the threat.	2
Discontinue the action or relationship giving rise to the threat.	4
Identify a potential threat to a fundamental ethical principle.	1

AAT SAMPLE ASSESSMENT 1
WORK EFFECTIVELY IN
ACCOUNTING AND FINANCE

Time allowed: 2 hours

AAT SAMPLE
ASSESSMENT 1

Tasks

Task 1

It is important to understand you will be required to follow policies and procedures in the completion of your work and why it is important to adhere to organisational policies and procedures.

(a) Which ONE of the following policies and procedures is most likely to be relevant to those working in an accounting function?

Production quality control policy ☐

Website development procedures ☐

Staff code of behaviour policy ☐

Motor vehicle maintenance policy ☐

(b) Identify which TWO of the following statements are correct:

Organisations, by law, must have at least ten policies and procedures. ☐

It is good practice for organisations to have policies and procedures so all staff work to a consistent standard. ☐

Data protection policy is an example of a policy that would not apply to those staff working in an accounting function. ☐

Organisational procedures always result in staff taking longer to do work tasks. ☐

Ensuring staff adhere to organisational policies and procedures should result in more efficient working practices. ☐

The Health and Safety policy only applies to those working in the production department. ☐

Those working in an accounting function will have to communicate with both internal and external stakeholders.

(c) **Identify which TWO of the following stakeholders a trainee in the accounting function is most likely to communicate with on a regular basis.**

Complete the answer by writing the correct stakeholders in the box provided.

Stakeholders an accounting trainee is most likely to communicate with on a regular basis

Stakeholders:

| Chairperson of the local AAT branch | Government ministers | Trade receivables |
| Trade union representative | HM Revenue & Customs | People living close to the organisation's offices |

....

Task 2

An organisation has five directors. The organisation chart below shows the directors of the organisation and staff working in the finance function.

(a) **Add the correct job titles into the blank spaces to complete this part of the organisation chart.**

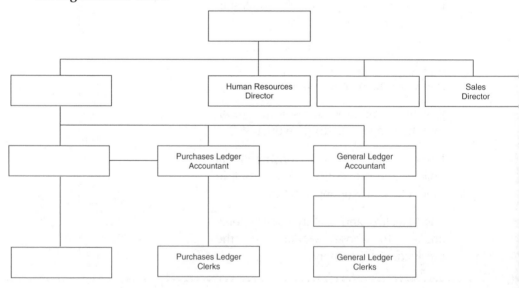

Job roles:

Assistant General Ledger Accountant	Human Resources Manager	Production Supervisor	Auditor	Production Director	IT Consultant
Tax Inspector	Estates Assistant	Finance Director	Sales Ledger Accountant	Managing Director	Sales Ledger Clerks

(b) **Identify which TWO of the following actions will help the solvency of an organisation:**

Action	
Maximise inventory levels	☐
Issue statements to trade receivables on a regular basis	☐
Pay trade payables as soon as invoices are received	☐
Encourage trade receivables to pay the amounts owed on or before the due date	☐
Ensure the organisation has a staff development policy	☐
Issue statements to trade payables on a regular basis	☐

Task 3

The following are the requirements for the accounting function meeting:

Date: 18 August 2013	Time: 10:00am-2.00pm	Tea/coffee required: NO Time: N/A	Lunch IS required Time: 12.00
Purpose: The monthly accounting function review meeting.			
Number of attendees: 25 Plus Finance Director and Managing Director.			
Special requirements: Two members of staff require vegetarian food, no other special dietary requirements.			
Room configuration: Usual, horseshoe style please.			
Other information: We require an overhead projector, white screen and laptop.			
Cost to be charged to: Mr John Brean	Budget Code: ACC3217653		

Your manager (John Brean) has asked you to email the Facilities Manager to advise him of the requirements for the monthly accounting function review meeting.

(a) **Complete the email below to book the meeting with the Facilities Manager Martin Slone (mslone@Mbs.com) by inserting the email address of the recipient and selecting TWO paragraphs that should be inserted into the main body of the email to make all of the arrangements for the meeting.**

From:	AATstudent@Mbs.com
To:	
Subject:	Meeting room booking

Hello Martin

Paragraph 1

Paragraph 2

Regards

AAT Student

	Paragraph 1	Paragraph 2
We require a room for our review meeting on 18 August 2013 between 10:00am and 2:00pm. Tea/coffee is not required but lunch is required at 12:00 noon. Two people require vegetarian food the others have no special dietary requirements.	☐	☐
The room should be arranged in a horseshoe style and an overhead projector, wide screen and laptop will be required for the meeting. The costs associated with the meeting are to be sent for the attention of John Brean. Budget code AC3217653 should be charged.	☐	☐
The accounting function needs a room for its monthly review meeting on 18 August 2013. The meeting is due to start at 10:00am and should finish at 2:00pm. There will be 25 people at the meeting and we shall require lunch at 12:00 noon, two attendees require vegetarian food, nobody else has any special dietary arrangements. There will not be a requirement for tea or coffee.	☐	☐
On behalf of John Brean I write to request a booking for the accounting function's monthly review meeting. There will be 25 staff including the Finance Director and Managing Director attending the meeting and lunch will be required at 12:00 noon. The only special dietary requirements are that two people require vegetarian food. Tea/coffee will not be required.	☐	☐
An overhead projector, white screen and laptop will be required for the meeting. The room should be arranged in our usual style. The costs associated with the meeting are to be sent for the attention of John Brean. Budget code AC3217553 should be charged.	☐	☐
An overhead projector, white screen and laptop will be required for the meeting. The costs associated with the meeting are to be sent for the attention of John Brean. Budget code ACC3217653 should be charged.	☐	☐

	Paragraph 1	Paragraph 2
We will require an overhead projector, white screen and laptop for the meeting. The room should be arranged in our usual horseshoe style. The costs associated with the meeting are to be sent for the attention of John Brean. Budget code ACC3217653 should be charged.	☐	☐
Please arrange for a room to be booked for the accounting function's monthly review meeting. There will be 25 staff plus the Finance Director and Managing Director at the meeting between 10:00am and 2:00pm on 18 August 2013. Tea/coffee will not be required and lunch is requested at 12:00 noon. Two people require vegetarian food; there are no other dietary requirements.	☐	☐

(b) Identify whether the following statements are true or false:

You do not need to proof read emails as this is an informal method of communication. ▢ ▼

Picklist:
True
False

When deciding upon the best method of communication you only need to consider the information you are trying to communicate. ▢ ▼

Picklist:
True
False

Task 4

You are a trainee in the accounting function and you work for both the financial accounting and management accounting functions. You work from 9:00am until 5:00pm and are required to have lunch between 12:00 noon and 1:00pm.

The following tables show your work schedules for the financial and management accounting functions and detail the days when specific jobs have to be completed and the length of time, in hours, each job takes you to complete. The financial accounting function works on a monthly cycle of work whereas the management accounting function works on a weekly cycle of work. For the financial accounting function, work is required by the end of the day identified in the work schedule.

Financial accounting function work schedule					
	Monday	**Tuesday**	**Wednesday**	**Thursday**	**Friday**
Week 1	Bank reconciliation (2 hours)			Bank monies (2 hours)	Trade receivable review (3 hours)
Week 2		Petty cash top up (2 hours)	Supplier payments (3 hours)	Bank monies (2 hours)	
Week 3	Bank reconciliation (2 hours)	Accruals and prepayments (2 hours)		Bank monies (2 hours)	Trade receivable review (3 hours)
Week 4	Wages analysis (3 hours)		Non-current assets (1 hour)	Bank monies (2 hours)	

Management accounting function work schedule			
Task	**Task to be completed by:**		**Task duration**
	Day	**Time**	
Budget run	Friday	09:00	4 hours
Expenses analysis	Tuesday	14:00	2 hours
Departmental reports	Monday	12:00	2 hours
Inventory review	Friday	10:00	1 hour
Variance report	Every day	14:00	1 hour
Departmental charges	Wednesday	12:00	2 hours

In addition to this information the whole accounting function has an hour long meeting at 10:00am on Mondays. Today is Friday in week three of the month.

Complete the To Do List below for next MONDAY by assigning each task to the correct position.

Please note that each task box is one hour in duration, therefore if a task takes more than one hour to complete you will be able to use the task box more than once.

MONDAY To Do List	Time
	09:00 – 10:00
	10:00 – 11:00
	11:00 – 12:00
	12:00 – 13:00
	13:00 – 14:00
	14:00 – 15:00
	15:00 – 16:00
	16:00 – 17:00

Tasks:

Accounting function meeting	Expenses analysis
Accruals and prepayments	Non-current assets
Bank monies	Inventory review
Bank reconciliation	Lunch
Budget run	Petty cash top up
Trade receivables review	Supplier payments
Departmental charges	Variance report
Departmental reports	Wages analysis

Task 5

This is a draft of a letter to be addressed to Mrs Gray, a customer, to advise her of the results of your review of her account. The account information is as follows:

Account number	GR45276091
Credit limit	£5,000.00
Current balance	£4,752.50
Other information	Order placed yesterday, 25.08.13, for £1,750 which cannot be sent due to the customer exceeding their credit limit.

Review the draft letter and identify EIGHT words or collections of letters or digits which are either spelt incorrectly or are technically incorrect.

Acount GR45276091

Dear Mrs Gray,

Please find inclosed a current statement for your account. As you will see from the statement, the current account balance for your organisation is £4,725.50. I have been adviced that you have recently placed an order for goods to the value of £1,750. This order is currently on hold as the extra purchases will result in your credit limit of £5,000 being exceeded.

BPP
LEARNING MEDIA

You are a highly valued customer and I notise that we have not reviewed your credit limit for a number of years. I would therefore suggest that we increase your credit limit to £7,000. If you consider this amount to be insufficient for your current needs please contact me and we can arrange a meeting to review your account.

I would appreciate it if you could make contact as soon as posible so that we can discuss the matter further. I shall be out of the office from next Thursday for a week so if you could contact me before then it would be helpful. I will arrange four the immediate delivery of your outstanding order as soon as I receive your agreement to the revised credit limit.

I look forward to hearing from you.

Yours faithfully

Task 6

(a) **An organisation made total sales of £1.2 million in 2012. These are the figures for sales made by three of the five departments in the year:**

Department	Sales £
1	145,349
2	380,600
3	215,000
4	?
5	?

(i) **What is the total sales figure for departments 4 and 5 for the year?**

£ [   ]

Department 4 made twice as many sales as Department 5.

(ii) **What is the figure for sales made by Department 4 in the year? If applicable, you should round your answer to TWO decimal places, for example 18.494 would become 18.49 and 18.495 would become 18.50.**

£ [   ]

The sales target for all departments was £1.5 million. Department 1 was estimated to contribute 1/8 of the sales target.

(iii) **What is the difference between the sales target and the actual sales made by Department 1?**

£ [   ]

The sales target for Department 2 was £0.5 million.

(iv) **What was the difference between the target and actual sales for Department 2 expressed as a percentage of the sales target? If applicable, you should round your answer to TWO decimal places, for example 18.494 would become 18.49 and 18.495 would become 18.50.**

[   ] %

....

The organisation is about to set its target sales for 2013 and wants to achieve an increase in sales of 10% over the actual sales in 2012. In addition to this there will be a general price increase of 2%.

(b) **What is the total sales target for the organisation for 2013?**

[▼]

Picklist:

£24,000

£120,000

£144,000

£146,000

£1.2 million

£1,224,000

£1,344,000

£1,346,400

Cannot say

....

Task 7

A trainee in the accounting function has been asked to take responsibility for learning about the new computerised accounts system that the organisation will start to use in six months' time. The system is being built by an IT developer specifically for the needs of your organisation. After completing personal development activities the trainee will be expected to provide training and support for staff in the accounting function. According to the timescale for this work, all staff will need to start their training on the new system three months prior to the introduction of the new system.

(a) **Insert the TWO most appropriate development activities for the trainee to complete, in order to prepare for their work associated with this task, into the boxes provided. You should also identify the timescale for the completion of each of these development activities.**

Development activity	Timescale for completion

Development activities and timescales:

Sit with the Finance Director to understand his role	Complete a spreadsheet course at a local college	0-3 months
Complete database training	Attend a one day training course with the developers of the new system	4-6 months
Complete a 'How to provide excellent training' course	Attend an AAT branch meeting	7-12 months
Read AAT magazine	Complete an online word processing course	

(b) **For each of the following statements insert the most appropriate reason into the column to explain why the statement is correct. Note that each reason may only be selected once.**

Statement	Reason
CPD has to be completed by those working in an accounting function because…	
Identifying SMART personal development objectives is important because…	
It is important to discuss personal development with a line manager because…	
An organisation benefits if staff development and CPD activities are completed because…	

Reasons:

they need to know of changes to the organisational structure of their professional body.	it ensures an individual's technical knowledge is up to date.
it looks good to have a large list of CPD activities.	all staff should be SMART.
they may be able to provide a different assessment of your performance and areas for development.	the activities should be clearly identified so that progress and achievement against the objectives can be assessed.
it means that the staff's general standard of work should be improved and should comply with regulatory requirements.	it is good to talk with those who staff report to.

Task 8

(a) Last year the accounting function was restructured ahead of a wider organisational restructuring across all functions. To learn from the implementation of the changes, the finance director sent a questionnaire to all 30 staff within the finance function. The finance director has asked you to review the responses to the five key statements and provide him with conclusions and recommendations which he can present to the other directors so that the rest of the organisation's restructuring goes as smoothly as possible.

Statement	Response		
	Number of staff who agreed	Number of staff who disagreed	Number of staff who did not answer
The company briefing explaining the process and time scales for the restructuring of the finance function helped reduce my concerns about the changes.	27	1	2
My manager kept staff fully informed of developments and changes during the restructuring.	4	24	2
My manager had the time to listen to staff concerns during the restructuring process.	6	16	8
The information provided prior to the restructuring in terms of job roles and responsibilities was helpful in identifying my own role and that of colleagues within the team.	20	7	3
The team building event which took place prior to the restructuring was helpful in getting to know other colleagues within the team.	25	2	3
The new team approach to working has resulted in more efficient working practices.	22	4	4

(i) **Identify from the statements below THREE conclusions and TWO recommendations that the finance director should present to the other directors so that staff stress during restructuring is kept to a minimum.**

	Conclusion	Recommendation
For most staff the company briefing explaining the process and timescales for the restructuring of the finance function helped reduce their concerns and the manager kept most staff fully informed of developments and changes during the restructuring.	☐	☐
Most staff felt that their manager had the time to listen to their concerns during the restructuring process and most staff believe that the new team approach has resulted in increased efficiency of working practices.	☐	☐
For the wider restructuring, managers need to be trained to ensure that they keep staff fully informed and up-to-date and that they have the time to listen to their staff's concerns.	☐	☐
Information about job roles and responsibilities, provided to staff prior to the restructuring, was helpful to staff in positioning both their own and colleagues' roles within their team. However, the team building event prior to restructuring was not considered helpful in enabling staff to get to know colleagues within their team.	☐	☐
Most staff felt that their manager did not keep them fully informed of developments and changes during the restructuring and most staff believe that the new team approach has resulted in increased efficiency of working practices.	☐	☐

	Conclusion	Recommendation
The team building event held before the finance function restructuring should not be implemented across the organisation as finance staff did not consider it to be helpful in getting to know colleagues within their team.	☐	☐
For most staff the company briefing explaining the process and time scales for the restructuring of the finance function helped reduce their concerns and the team building event prior to restructuring was considered helpful in enabling staff to get to know colleagues within their team.	☐	☐
The company briefing explaining the process and time scales for the restructuring of the finance function and the team building event should be features of the wider organisational restructuring as most staff considered they were helpful.	☐	☐
Information about job roles and responsibilities, provided to staff prior to the restructuring, was helpful to staff in identifying both their own and colleagues' roles within their team. However, most felt that their manager did not have the time to listen to their concerns during the restructuring process.	☐	☐

(ii) **Select which of the following would be the most suitable title for this report:**

Results of the questionnaire	☐
A review of the communications strategy	☐
A review of the finance function	☐
A review of restructuring of the finance function	☐
A review of staff perceptions of their manager	☐

(b) **Identify which TWO of the following would occur before the introduction section of a business report:**

Appendices	☐
Recommendations	☐
Main body	☐
Conclusion	☐
Executive summary	☐
Title	☐

Task 9

You have been asked to do an urgent task by your manager which will mean you will not be able to complete the work a senior colleague has already allocated to you to complete by the end of the day.

(a) **Select the most appropriate action to take from the list provided in the table.**

Action	
Complete the additional task as your manager is the most senior person you work for and do whatever other work you can. The colleague will have to wait for their work until you have time to complete it.	☐
Complete the additional task as your manager is the most senior person you work for and do whatever other work you can. You will prioritise the colleague's work for the next day.	☐
Complete the colleague's work as they asked you to do the work first and you will start the manager's work tomorrow.	☐
Discuss your workload with both the manager and the colleague to decide on the work priority and renegotiate deadlines where appropriate.	☐

You have to check supplier statements on a Thursday so that your colleague can receive the necessary information for her to be able to pay appropriate suppliers. A critically important task has been left on your desk by your manager. If you complete this urgent task you will not be able to check all of the supplier statements and provide information to your colleague.

(b) **Identify whether the following statements are true or false in relation to the impact on your colleague or the organisation if you do not supply the information on supplier statements:**

	True	False
There will be no impact. If you can't check supplier statements on Thursday, you can prioritise this work the next day.	☐	☐
Your colleague may be unable to pay suppliers by the due date which may result in problems for the organisation in receiving future supplies.	☐	☐

The area of the accounting function you work in is arranged as a team of four people – a manager and three team members.

(c)   Identify which THREE considerations are important to ensuring the team works effectively.

Team effectiveness

Considerations:

All staff have the same skills, knowledge and experience	Each team member is willing and able to cover the work of other team members if necessary
All team members know only their own job role	Team members work solely within their own job role
All team members have clearly defined objectives and responsibilities	Good communication within the team

Task 10

(a)   Identify which THREE of the following are fundamental ethical principles by writing the appropriate principles in the table.

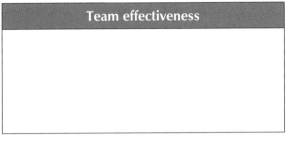

Fundamental ethical principles

Principles:

Subjectivity	Professionalism
Good communication	Control
Objectivity	Honesty
Happiness	Integration

You work for a firm of accountants and your role is to check and calculate information and figures which will be used in the accounts of clients.

(b) State which ONE of the following situations is an example of where a conflict of interest may arise.

You are completing some accounting work at a client's premises but you are the only person on the premises. ☐

Your manager takes the whole department for a meal at lunchtime to celebrate your forthcoming wedding. ☐

You are asked to audit the inventory at a local car dealership which is owned by your uncle. ☐

You are asked to complete the accounts of a national fashion retailer from which you often purchase clothes. ☐

(c) Identify whether the following statements are true or false.

Statement	True	False
Those working within an account environment should act with integrity.	☐	☐
Personal information of a client cannot be given to people unless they are close friends or relatives of the client.	☐	☐
Information about the income generated by the organisation for which you work can be discussed with your friends as at the end of the year the organisation will publish their financial results.	☐	☐
A conflict of interest only has to be declared if the employee feels unhappy about the situation.	☐	☐

Task 11

(a) **Identify which FOUR of the following are sustainability initiatives that a business may implement.**

Arrange virtual rather than face-to-face team meetings. ☐

Have all office lighting linked to motion sensors so they automatically switch off when the office is empty. ☐

Always select the lowest priced suppliers of goods and services. ☐

Ensure all trainee accountants complete CPD. ☐

Do business only with organisations which can demonstrate they follow responsible environmental practices. ☐

Ensure costs and expenses are minimised in every instance. ☐

Arrange monthly management meetings at a central point in the country rather than at head office. ☐

Restrict paper usage to the printing of essential documents only. ☐

(b) Identify whether the following statements are true or false:

Statement	True	False
Sustainability means ensuring the organisation focuses purely on generating the highest profit irrespective of the consequences of the organisation's actions.	☐	☐
When building new premises, trying to ensure the building is carbon neutral even if this results in increased initial costs is an example of a sustainable initiative by the organisation.	☐	☐
Sustainable initiatives do not apply to those in an accounting function but such initiatives do apply to the production function.	☐	☐
Having a policy that office buildings should be well insulated and solar powered may help to reduce the running costs of the organisation and also have a positive effect on the environment.	☐	☐

AAT SAMPLE ASSESSMENT 1
WORK EFFECTIVELY IN
ACCOUNTING AND FINANCE

ANSWERS

Answers to tasks

Task 1

(a) **Which ONE of the following policies and procedures is most likely to be relevant to those working in an accounting function?**

Production quality control policy	☐
Website development procedures	☐
Staff code of behaviour policy	☑
Motor vehicle maintenance policy	☐

(b) **Identify which TWO of the following statements are correct:**

Organisations, by law, must have at least ten policies procedures.	☐
It is good practice for organisations to have policies and procedures so all staff work to a consistent standard	☑
Data protection policy is an example of a policy that would not apply to those staff working in an accounting function	☐
Organisational procedures always result in staff taking longer to do work tasks	☐
Ensuring staff adhere to organisational policies and procedures should result in more efficient working practices	☑
The Health and Safety policy only applies to those working in the production department	☐

(c) Identify which TWO of the following stakeholders a trainee in the accounting function is most likely to communicate with on a regular basis.

Stakeholders an accounting trainee is most likely to communicate with on a regular basis
HM Revenue & Customs
Trade receivables

Task 2

(a) Add the correct job titles into the blank spaces to complete this part of the organisation chart.

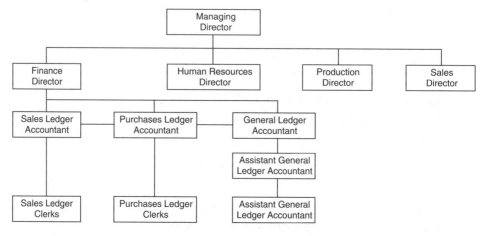

(b) Identify which TWO of the following actions will help the solvency of an organisation:

Action	
Maximise inventory levels	☐
Issue statements to trade receivables on a regular basis	✓
Pay trade payables as soon as invoices are received	☐
Encourage trade receivables to pay the amounts owed on or before the due date	✓
Ensure the organisation has a staff development policy	☐
Issue statements to trade payables on a regular basis	☐

Task 3

(a) Complete the email below to book the meeting with the Facilities Manager Martin Slone (mslone@Mbs.com) by inserting the email address of the recipient and selecting TWO paragraphs that should be inserted into the main body of the email to make all of the arrangements for the meeting.

From:	AATstudents@Mbs.com
To:	mslone@mbs.com
Subject:	Meeting room booking

Hello Martin

Paragraph 1

Paragraph 2

Regards

AAT Student

	Paragraph 1	Paragraph 2
We require a room for our review meeting on 18 August 2013 between 10:00am and 2:00pm. Tea/coffee is not required but lunch is required at 12:00 noon. Two people require vegetarian food the others have no special dietary requirements.	☐	☐
The room should be arranged in a horseshoe style and an overhead projector, wide screen and laptop will be required for the meeting. The costs associated with the meeting are to be sent for the attention of John Brean. Budget code AC3217653 should be charged.	☐	☐
The accounting function needs a room for its monthly review meeting on 18 August 2013. The meeting is due to start at 10:00am and should finish at 2:00pm. There will be 25 people at the meeting and we shall require lunch at 12:00 noon, two attendees require vegetarian food, nobody else has any special dietary arrangements. There will not be a requirement for tea or coffee.	☐	☐

	Paragraph 1	Paragraph 2
On behalf of John Brean I write to request a booking for the accounting's function monthly review meeting. There will be 25 staff including the Finance Director and Managing Director attending the meeting and lunch will be required at 12:00 noon. The only special dietary requirements are that two people require vegetarian food. Tea/coffee will not be required.	☐	☐
An overhead projector, white screen and laptop will be required for the meeting. The room should be arranged in our usual style. The costs associated with the meeting are to be sent for the attention of John Brean. Budget Code AC3217653 should be charged.	☐	☐
An overhead projector, white screen and laptop will be required for the meeting. The costs associated with the meeting are to be sent for the attention of John Brean. Budget Code ACC3217653 should be charged.	☐	☐
We will require an overhead projector, white screen and laptop for the meeting. The room should be arranged in our usual horseshoe style. The costs associated with the meeting are to be sent for the attention of John Brean. Budget Code ACC3217653 should be charged.	☐	✓
Please arrange for a room to be booked for the accounting function's monthly review meeting. There will be 25 staff plus the Finance Director and Managing Director at the meeting between 10:00am and 2:00pm on 18 August 2013. Tea/coffee will not be required and lunch is requested at 12:00 noon. Two people require vegetarian food; there are no dietary requirements.	✓	☐

(b) **Identify whether the following statements are true or false:**

You do not need to proof read emails as this is an informal method of communication. | False ▼ |

When deciding upon the best method of communication you can only need to consider the information you are trying to communicate.
| False ▼ |

Task 4

Complete the To Do List below for next MONDAY by assigning each task to the correct position.

Please note that each task box is one hour in duration, therefore if a task takes more than one hour to complete you will be able to use the task box more than once.

MONDAY To Do List	Time
Department reports	09:00 – 10:00
Accounting function meeting	10:00 – 11:00
Departmental reports	11:00 – 12:00
Lunch	12:00 – 13:00
Variance report	13:00 – 14:00
Wages analysis	14:00 – 15:00
Wages analysis	15:00 – 16:00
Wages analysis	16:00 – 17:00

Task 5

Review the draft letter and identify EIGHT words or collections of letters or digits which are either spelt incorrectly or are technically incorrect.

Acount GR45276091

Dear Mrs Gray,

Please find inclosed a current statement for your account. As you will see from the statement, the current account balance for your organisation is £4,725.50. I have been adviced that you have recently placed for goods to the value of £1,750. This order is currently on hold as the extra purchases will result in your credit limit of £5,000 being exceeded.

You are a highly valued customer and I notise that we have not reviewed your credit limit for a number of years. I would therefore suggest that we increase your credit limit to £7,000. If you consider this amount to be insufficient for your current needs please contact me and we can arrange a meeting to review your account.

BPP
LEARNING MEDIA

I would appreciate it if you could make contact as soon as posible so that we can discuss the matter further. I shall be out of the office from next Thursday for a week so if you could contact me before then it would be helpful. I will arrange four the immediate delivery of your outstanding order as soon as I receive your arrangement to the revised credit limit.

I look forward to hearing from you.

Yours faithfully

Task 6

(a) (i) What is the total sales figure for departments 4 and 5 for the year?

£ | 459051 |

Department 4 made twice as many sales as Department 5.

(ii) What is the figure for sales made by Department 4 in the year? If applicable, you should round your answer to TWO decimal places, for example 18.494 would become 18.49 and 18.495 would become 18.50.

£ | 306034 |

The sales target for all departments was £1.5 million. Department 1 was estimated to contribute 1/8 of the sales target.

(iii) What is the difference between the sales target and the actual sales made by Department 1?

£ | 42151 |

The sales target for Department 2 was half a million pounds.

(iv) What was the difference between the target and actual sales for Department 2 expressed as a percentage of the sales target? If applicable, you should round your answer to TWO decimal places, for example 18.494 would become 18.49 and 18.495 would become 18.50.

| 23.88 | %

The organisation is about to set its target sales for 2013 and wants to achieve an increase in sales of 10% over the actual sales in 2012. In addition to this there will be a general price increase of 2%.

(b) What is the total sales target for the organisation for 2013?

| £1,346,400 ▼ |

Task 7

(a) Insert the TWO most appropriate development activities for the trainee to complete, in order to prepare for their work associated with this task, into the boxes provided. You should also identify the timescale for the completion of each of these development activities.

Development activity	Timescale for completion
Complete a 'How to provide excellent training' course	0 – 3 months
Attend one day training course with the developers of the new system	0 – 3 months

(b) For each of the following statements insert the most appropriate reason into the column to explain why the statement is correct. Note each reason may only be selected once.

Statement	Reason
CPD has to be completed by those working in an accounting function because…	it ensures as individual's technical knowledge is up to date.
Identifying SMART personal development objectives is important because…	the activities should be clearly identified so that progress and achievement against the objectives can be assessed.
It is important to discuss personal development with a line manager because…	they may be able to provide a different assessment of your performance and areas for development.
An organisation benefits if staff development and CPD activities are completed because…	it means that the staff's general standard of work should be improved and should comply with regulatory requirements.

Task 8

(a)   (i)

	Conclusion	Recommendation
For most staff the company briefing explaining the process and time scales for the restructuring of the finance function helped reduce their concerns and the manager kept most staff fully informed of developments and changes during the restructuring.	☐	☐
Most staff felt that their manager had the time to listen to their concerns during the restructuring process and most staff believe that the new team approach has resulted in increased efficiency of working practices.	☐	☐
For the wider restructuring, managers need to be trained to ensure that they keep staff fully informed and up-to-date and that they have the time to listen to their staff's concerns.	☐	✓
Information about job roles and responsibilities, provided to staff prior to the restructuring, was helpful to staff in positioning both their own and colleagues' roles within their team. However, the team building event prior to restructuring was not considered helpful in enabling staff to get to know colleagues within their team.	☐	☐
Most staff felt that their manager did not keep them fully informed of developments and changes during the restructuring and most staff believe that the new team approach has resulted in increased efficiency of working practices.	✓	☐
The team building event held before the finance function restructuring should not be implemented across the organisation as finance staff did not consider it to be helpful in getting to know colleagues within their team.	☐	☐
For most staff the company briefing explaining the process and time scales for the restructuring of the finance function helped reduce their concerns and the team building event prior to restructuring was considered helpful in enabling staff to get to know colleagues within their team.	✓	☐

	Conclusion	Recommendation
The company briefing explaining the process and time scales for the restructuring of the finance function and the team building event should be features of the wider organisational restructuring as most staff considered they were helpful.	☐	✓
Information about job roles and responsibilities, provided to staff prior to the restructuring, was helpful to staff in identifying both their own and colleagues' roles within their team. However, most felt that their manager did not have the time to listen to their concerns during the restructuring process.	✓	☐

(ii) **Select which of the following would be the most suitable title for this report:**

Results of the questionnaire	☐
A review of the communications strategy	☐
A review of the finance function	☐
A review of the restructuring of the finance function	✓
A review of the staff perceptions of their manager	☐

(b) **Identify which TWO of the following would occur before the introduction section of a business report:**

Appendices	☐
Recommendations	☐
Main body	☐
Conclusions	☐
Executive summary	✓
Title	✓

Task 9

(a) **Select the most appropriate action to take from the list provided in the table.**

Action	
Complete the additional task as your manager is the most senior person you work for and do whatever other work you can. The colleague will have to wait for their work until you have time to complete it.	☐
Complete the additional task as your manager is the most senior person you work for and do whatever other work you can. You will prioritise the colleague's work for the next day.	☐
Complete the colleague's work as they asked you to do the work first and you will start the manager's work tomorrow.	☐
Discuss your workload with both the manager and the colleague to decide on the work priority and renegotiate deadlines where appropriate.	✓

(b) **Identify whether the following statements are true or false in relation to the impact on your colleague or the organisation if you do not supply the information on supplier statements.**

Statement	True	False
There will be no impact. If you can't check supplier statements on Thursday, you can prioritise this work the next day.	☐	✓
Your colleague may be unable to pay suppliers by the due date which may result in problems for the organisation in receiving future supplies.	✓	☐

(c) **Identify which THREE considerations are important to ensuring the team works effectively.**

Team effectiveness
All team members have clearly defined objectives and responsibilities
Each team member is willing and able to cover the work of other team members if necessary
Good communication within the team

Task 10

(a)   Identify which THREE of the following are fundamental ethical principles by writing the appropriate principles in the table:

Fundamental ethical principles
Objectivity
Professionalism
Honesty

(b)   State which ONE of the following situations is an example of where a conflict of interest may arise:

You are completing some accounting work at client's premises but you are the only person on the premises.   ☐

Your manager takes the whole department for a meal at lunchtime to celebrate your forthcoming wedding.   ☐

You are asked to audit the inventory at a local car dealership which is owned by your uncle.   ☑

You are asked to complete the accounts of a national fashion retailer from which you often purchase clothes.   ☐

(c)   Identify whether the following statements are true or false:

Statement	True	False
Those working within an accounting environment should act with integrity.	☑	☐
Personal information of a client cannot be given to people unless they are close friends or relatives of the client.	☐	☑
Information about the income generated by the organisation for which you work can be discussed with your friends as at the end of the year the organisation will publish their financial results.	☐	☑
A conflict of interest only has to be declared if the employee feels unhappy about the situation.	☐	☑

Task 11

(a) **Identify which FOUR of the following are sustainability initiatives which a business may implement.**

Arrange virtual rather than face-to-face team meetings ☑

Have all office lighting linked to motion sensors so they automatically switch off when the office is empty ☑

Always select the lowest priced suppliers of goods and services ☐

Ensure all trainee accountants complete CPD ☐

Do business only with organisations which can demonstrate they follow responsible environmental practices ☑

Ensure costs and expenses are minimised in every instance ☐

Arrange monthly management meetings at a central point in the country rather than at head office ☐

Restrict paper usage to the printing of essential documents only ☑

(b) **Identify whether the following statements are true or false:**

Statement	True	False
Sustainability means ensuring the organisation focuses purely on generating the highest profit irrespective of the consequences of the organisation's actions.	☐	☑
When building new premises, trying to ensure the building is carbon neutral even if this results in increased initial costs is an example of a sustainable initiative by the organisation.	☑	☐
Sustainability initiatives do not apply to those in an accounting function but such initiatives do apply to the production function.	☐	☑
Having a policy of office buildings being well insulated and solar powered may help reduce the running costs of the organisation and also have a positive effect on the environment.	☑	☐

AAT SAMPLE ASSESSMENT 2
WORK EFFECTIVELY IN
ACCOUNTING AND FINANCE

Time allowed: 2 hours

AAT SAMPLE
ASSESSMENT 2

Tasks

Task 1

It is important to understand you will be required to follow policies and procedures in the completion of your work. Some policies and procedures will apply solely to those working in a finance function and other policies and procedures will apply to employees across the whole organisation, including those working in the finance function.

(a) Which ONE of the following policies and procedures is most likely to be relevant to those working in an accounting function?

Company vehicle servicing policy	☐
Sales visit procedures	☐
Expenses payment procedures	☐
Production shift handover procedures	☐

(b) Identify which TWO of the following statements are correct:

The accounting function has a legal obligation to review the credit policy every two years.	☐
Organisational procedures prevent staff from suggesting improvements to work processes.	☐
It is good practice for organisations to explain the fire evacuation procedures during staff induction training.	☐
The Staff Development policy only applies to those working in the human resources department.	☐
Many organisational policies and procedures are designed to ensure that working practices comply with legal requirements.	☐
The Data Protection policy is an example of a policy that would not apply to those staff working in an accounting function.	☐

Those working in an accounting and payroll function will have to communicate with, and provide services to, both internal and external stakeholders.

(c) **Identify which TWO of the following services that staff in the accounting and payroll function would be most likely to provide to colleagues in the Production Department.**

Complete the answer by writing the correct services in the box provided.

Services staff in the accounting and payroll function would be most likely to provide to colleagues in the Production Department

Services:

Machine servicing	Conducting job interviews

Budget report analysis	Quality checks on finished goods

Marketing new products

Payment for operator overtime hours

Task 2

The partially completed organisation chart below shows some of the partners of a chartered accountancy practice and their staff.

(a) Add the correct job titles into the blank spaces to complete the organisation chart.

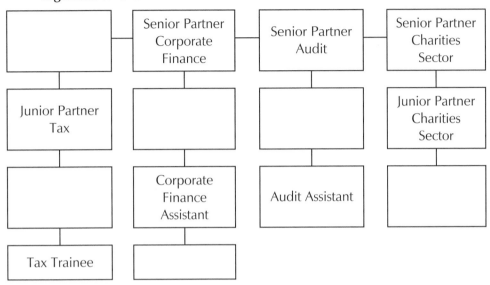

Job roles:

Estates Manager	Practice Manager	Administrative Assistant	Senior Manager Human Resources	Tax Assistant	Health and Safety Consultant
Junior Partner Audit	Senior Partner Tax	Corporate Finance Trainee	Junior Partner Corporate Finance	Chairman	Charities Sector Assistant

(b) Identify whether the following statements are true or false.

Statement	True	False
Ensuring the VAT bill is paid on time will help the organisation meet its legal and regulatory requirements.	☐	☐
Paying supplier invoices as soon as they are received will help the organisation's solvency.	☐	☐

Task 3

The following is a report, file name 'PDBEOct.xls', you have completed detailing expenses for the production department for the month of October.

Expenses	October Budget £	October Actual £
Wages – basic pay	18,000	16,500
Wages – overtime rate	0	3,000
Protective clothing	200	150
Machine oil	500	650
Cleaning materials	300	295
Sundries	1,000	1,050
TOTAL EXPENSES	20,000	21,645

Your manager has asked you to email the production manager, John Uwaifo (j.uwaifo@GCCS.com), to advise him of the differences between budget and actual spend on his expenses for the month of October. You must attach the file you have completed to the email.

(a) **Complete the email below by inserting the email address of the recipient and the filename of any attachments and selecting TWO correct paragraphs that should be inserted into the main body of the email.**

From:	AATstudent@GCCS.com
To:	
Subject:	Production expenses October actual compared to budget
Attached:	

Hello John

> **Paragraph 1**

> **Paragraph 2**

Regards

AAT Student

	Paragraph 1	**Paragraph 2**
Whilst you spent more on wages at the basic rate of pay you spent less than budget on wages at overtime rate. You spent more than budget on your protective clothing, machine oil and cleaning materials. You spent less than budget on sundry expenses. I hope you find this information useful, if you require any further analysis please do not hesitate to contact me.	☐	☐
Following the production of the latest month-end report, see attached, I herewith provide you with an analysis of your expenses paid in the month of October. Overall you spent less than budget on your total expenses by £1,645 but this is made up of different expenses in some of which you exceeded budget and in some of which you spent less than budget	☐	☐
Whilst you spent less on wages at the basic rate of pay you spent more than budget on wages at overtime rate. You spent less than budget on your protective clothing and cleaning materials. You spent more than budget on machine oil and sundry expenses. I hope you find this information useful, if you require any further analysis please do not hesitate to contact me.	☐	☐
Following the production of the latest month-end report, see attached, I herewith provide you with an analysis of your expenses paid in the month of October. Overall you spent more than budget on your total expenses by £1,465 but this is made up of different expenses in some of which you exceeded budget and in some of which you spent less than budget.	☐	☐

	Paragraph 1	Paragraph 2
Whilst you spent less on wages at the basic rate of pay you spent less than budget on wages at overtime rate. You spent more than budget on your protective clothing, machine oil and cleaning materials. You spent less than budget on sundry expenses. I hope you find this information useful, if you require any further analysis please do not hesitate to contact me.	☐	☐
Following the production of the latest month-end report, see attached, I herewith provide you with an analysis of your expenses paid in the month of October. Overall you spent more than budget on your total expenses by £1,645 but this is made up of different expenses in some of which you exceeded budget and in some of which you spent less than budget.	☐	☐

(b) Identify whether the following statements are true or false.

It is not necessary to proofread emails if they are sent to people within your organisation but external emails must always be proofread.

▼

The main problem with sending information in an email is that irrespective of the file size only one file may be attached to an email.

▼

Picklist:

True
False

Task 4

You are a trainee in the accounting function and you work for both the financial accounting and management accounting functions. You work from 9:00am until 1:00pm daily.

The following table shows your work schedule for the financial accounting function which details the days in the month when specific jobs have to be completed and the length of time, in hours, each job takes you to complete. The financial accounting function works on a monthly cycle of work and the work required for the end of the day is identified in the work schedule.

You also work for Sue Baines, the Management Accountant, but this work allocation is less structured. Sue usually allocates work by leaving you notes explaining the work she needs to be completed, the expected duration of the work and when it has to be completed by.

Financial accounting function work schedule					
	Monday	Tuesday	Wednesday	Thursday	Friday
Week 1	Bank reconciliation (2 hours)			Bank monies (2 hours)	Debtor review (3 hours)
Week 2	Wages analysis (1 hour)	Petty cash top up (1 hour)	Supplier payments (3 hours)	Bank monies (2 hours)	
Week 3	Bank reconciliation (2 hours)			Bank monies (2 hours)	
Week 4	Accruals and prepayments (2 hours)		Fixed assets (1 hour)	Bank monies (2 hours)	Debtor review (3 hours)

Note from Sue
WEEK 2

Hi

I have some jobs for you to complete this week. I have a meeting with the Sales Director on Tuesday afternoon and I need an analysis of expenses for Region 6 to take to that meeting. I shall leave the office at 12:00pm on Tuesday. I know that there are some expenses waiting to be processed and I have been advised these will be completed by close of business on Monday so it is important that you do not start the analysis before these expenses are processed. I expect the analysis to take you about two hours.

On Monday I need to complete an exercise on stock analysis and so I need a breakdown of closing stock by month for each of the months in the current financial year. I think this is about a two hour job but I need the information by 11:00am. Could you also complete the usual regional reconciliation by 12:00pm on Monday, this usually takes you an hour.

Thanks

Sue

In addition to the above information, the whole accounting function has an hour long meeting at 9:00am on Tuesdays. Today is Monday of week 2 of the month and you are required to identify, using the To Do lists below, what jobs you will do for today and tomorrow and when you will do them.

Complete the To Do List below for MONDAY and TUESDAY of week 2 by assigning each task to the correct position.

Please note that each task box is one hour in duration, therefore if a task takes more than one hour to complete you will be able to use the task box more than once.

MONDAY To Do List	TUESDAY To Do List	Time
		09:00 - 10:00
		10:00 - 11:00
		11:00 - 12:00
		12:00 - 13:00

Tasks:

Accounting function meeting	Closing stock breakdown	Regional reconciliation
Accruals and prepayments	Debtor review	Region 6 expenses analysis
Bank monies	Fixed assets	Supplier payments
Bank reconciliation	Petty cash top up	Wages analysis

Task 5

This is a draft of a letter to be addressed to Mrs Oboh, a supplier, to advise her of the results of your reconciliation of the statement of account you received from her. The differences are as follows:

Transaction date	Amount	Comment
12.10.13	£794.35	The invoice for this entry has been located however the invoice total is £749.35.
26.10.13	£375.29	We have no record of ever ordering or receiving goods to this value from Mrs Oboh.

Review the draft letter and identify EIGHT words or collections of letters or digits which are either spelt incorrectly, are inappropriate or are technically incorrect.

October Statment Reconciliation

Dear Mrs Oboh,

Many thanks for providing the October statement which we have now reviewed and compared to our records of amounts owing by you. We would like too highlight two discrepancies:

1.   Your entry for £794.35 on 12.01.13 does not corespond with the invoice we have for that date. The invoice shows an amount of £749.35 for these goods.

2.   Your entry for £375.29 on 26.10.13 is not known to us. We have no record of ever ordering or sending this amount of goods on this date.

Please investigate these differences as we want to be sure our records agree before we setle our account with you. If you would prefer to contact me by telephone to discuss this matter please do so as we would like to resolve these differences as soon as posible.

Yours sincerely

Task 6

(a)   The annual production quantities of finished goods in numbers of units for an organisation are set out in the table below. The figures in the table are a mixture of actual values, fractions of total finished goods and percentages of total finished goods:

Product	Finished goods
A	79,872
B	11%
C	1/5
D	85,488
E	3/8
F	5%
TOTAL FINISHED GOODS (UNITS)	624,000

(i)   What is the total number of units of finished goods for product B for the year?

(ii)   What is the total number of units of finished goods for product C for the year?

(iii)   What is the total number of units of finished goods for product E for the year?

(iv)   What is the total number of units of finished goods for product F for the year?

(v)   Which TWO products equate to 26.5% of the total number of units of finished goods for the organisation for the year?

 ▼

Picklist:

Products A and B / Products A and C / Products A and D / Products A and E / Products A and F / Products B and C / Products B and D / Products B and E / Products B and F / Products C and D / Products C and E / Products C and F / Products D and E / Products D and F / Products E and F

(b)   The total number of units of finished goods of 624,000 showed a 4% increase over the budget for the year.

Calculate the total budget for numbers of units of finished goods for the year. If applicable, you should round your answer to TWO decimal places, for example 18.494 would become 18.49 and 18.495 would become 18.50.

Task 7

An accounting trainee who is studying for an AAT Level 2 qualification is about to start a new role working in the management accounts function. The priority in the first three months will be for the trainee to take over responsibility for the production and distribution of the monthly budget reports from a colleague. It is critical that this work is addressed without delay as the colleague is moving to another work location very shortly. In the following three-month period, the trainee will then be supporting the assistant management accountant who has been given the task of introducing standard costing methods into the production department.

(a) **Insert the TWO most appropriate development activities that the trainee should undertake in the first six months of taking up the new role in the management accounts function. The order in which you place the activities is important, and you should place the activity with the highest importance first in the table.**

Accounting trainee's development activities

Development activities:

Sit with a colleague when the monthly budget reports are produced	Attend a seminar on auditing
Set up a study group with fellow AAT students	Attend a communicating with suppliers course
Read a book on standard costing in a production environment	Complete an online training module on credit management
Complete a buyer's course	Complete training on the purchases ledger computer system

(b) Identity TWO of the following statements which are consequences to the organisation and/or the individual of NOT maintaining appropriate and sufficient CPD activities. Insert the appropriate statements into the table provided. The order in which you place the items is not important.

Consequences of NOT maintaining CPD activities

Reasons:

Work performance will improve.	If knowledge is not up to date then staff could give incorrect professional advice.
Development activities will take account of future needs of the job role.	New skills will be acquired and career prospects enhanced.
A chartered accountant may be prevented from continuing as a member of their professional body.	It will be easier to cover colleagues' job roles when they are on holiday.

(c) Identify whether the following statements are true or false in relation to the completion of CPD activity.

Statement	True	False
Conducting research in the library at the local college as part of your AAT studies is one type of CPD activity.	☐	☐
Making sure that an accounting trainee has completed sufficient CPD activities is the sole responsibility of the organisation's Human Resources department.	☐	☐

Task 8

(a) The following is an income and expenditure statement for the Faculty of Business and Finance at a local college for the first half of the financial year. The Finance Director has asked you to analyse the results shown in the statement and provide him with conclusions and recommendations which he can present to the College Principal.

Income and Expenditure Statement	Actual £	Budget £	% Variance */-	Comments
INCOME				
Full-time course fees	301,000	350,000	-14%	Lower numbers of students than expected registered for full-time courses.
Part-time course fees	58,125	46,500	+25%	The number of students registering for the new AAT part-time study programme exceeds budget.
One day course fees	7,800	13,000	-40%	A reduction in marketing activity led to insufficient numbers of students to enable the planned practical bookkeeping course and revision courses to be run.
TOTAL INCOME	**366,835**	**409,350**		
EXPENDITURE				
Basic salaries – Full-time staff	89,250	105,000	-15%	Saving is a result of covering one vacant full-time post with part-time hours for the whole period.
Basic salaries – Part-time staff	37,440	31,200	+20%	Overspend is a result of covering the full-time vacancy with additional part-time hours.

Income and Expenditure Statement	Actual £	Budget £	% Variance */-	Comments
Student registration fees	22,500	25,000	-10%	Lower numbers of students for full-time and one day courses.
Student exam fees	28,620	27,000	+6%	Lower numbers of full-time registrations compensated for by increases in part-time registrations.
Teaching materials	9,500	10,000	-5%	Lower numbers of full-time students.
Books	15,000	20,000	-25%	Obtained a bulk ordering discount on new accounting text books.
TOTAL EXPENDITURE	**202,310**	**218,200**		

(i) **Identify, from the statements below, THREE conclusions and TWO recommendations that the Finance Director should present to the College Principal.**

Statement	Conclusion	Recommendation
The reduction in actual full-time course fee income when compared to the budget is fully offset by the amount that the actual part-time course fee income exceeds budget.	☐	☐
The new AAT study programme has been successful in increasing actual part-time course fee income and exceeding the budget, but the actual one day course fee income is less than the budget.	☐	☐

Statement	Conclusion	Recommendation
The faculty has been successful in reducing the actual cost of books by 25% when compared to the budget, but has overspent on the cost of teaching materials by 5% when compared to the budget.	☐	☐
The reduction in actual full-time course fee income when compared to the budget is only partially offset by the amount that the actual part-time course fee income exceeds budget.	☐	☐
The faculty should continue to cover the full-time vacancy with part-time staff as the savings made from the full-time salaries budget are more than twice the additional amount spent in part-time salaries.	☐	☐
Total actual income is less than the total budgeted income, but total actual expenditure is greater than the total budgeted expenditure.	☐	☐
The faculty should investigate why the numbers of students registering for part-time courses was less than expected.	☐	☐
The faculty should increase marketing activity to promote higher numbers of students registering for the one day practical bookkeeping course and the revision courses.	☐	☐
The reduced numbers of students registering for full-time and one day courses has led to a reduction in expenditure on registration fees.	☐	☐

(ii) **Select which of the following would be the most suitable title for this report:**

Business and finance budget ☐

Faculty income and expenditure performance review ☐

Faculty income and expenditure results ☐

Review of business and finance faculty income and expenditure against budget ☐

Review of business and finance ☐

(b) **Identify which ONE of the following describes the contents of the 'main body' section of a business report.**

Provides suggested actions to overcome the problems identified ☐

Provides an analysis of the results of the research ☐

Summarises the main points of the research and analysis ☐

Provides suggested actions to be taken in the future ☐

(c) **Complete the following statement by selecting the most appropriate answer from the list.**

When considering the order of a formal business report, which section will usually appear between the executive summary and the main body?

▼

Picklist:

Appendices
Conclusions
Introduction
Title

Task 9

You have been promoted from Finance Trainee to Assistant Sales Ledger Manager within the finance team of your organisation. A new Finance Trainee is due to start work today however the Financial Accountant has been called out of the office for the morning and he has asked you to look after the new Finance Trainee until he returns in the afternoon when he will do the trainee's induction. You have two tasks to finish this morning: a budget analysis for the production department and to check attendance by members of the finance function at a conference.

(a) **From the actions below select the THREE things you will do, during the morning, to help the trainee settle into their new role within your team but also to meet your work commitments to colleagues.**

Action	
Tell the Finance Trainee to go home and return after lunch when the Financial Accountant is in the office.	☐
Meet the Finance Trainee and introduce yourself and explain about the Financial Accountant not being available until lunchtime.	☐
Contact the production department to advise them of the situation and request an extension to the deadline for the budget analysis information.	☐
Tell the trainee to sit at a desk and occupy themselves by looking at some leisure magazines whilst you complete your work.	☐
Ask the trainee to think of what training courses they want to attend.	☐
Take the trainee with you as you visit members of the department to confirm attendance at the conference, introducing the new team member at the same time.	☐

(b) **Identify whether the following would or would not necessarily have a positive effect on the team performance of the finance function.**

	Would usually have a positive effect	Would not necessarily have a positive effect
Having a leader who does not encourage communication with other team members.	☐	☐
Ensuring there are at least four members in the team.	☐	☐
Selecting team members that have complementary experiences and skills.	☐	☐

Task 10

It is important that those who work within an accounting function uphold fundamental ethical principles.

The table below details four situations which may arise in business.

(a) **From the options provided select the fundamental ethical principle that applies in each situation. Note each option may be used more than once.**

Situation	Fundamental ethical principle applicable
You are asked by a colleague to provide the contact details of a client as they were at school together.	
You have been asked to complete a VAT return which is a subject you have not yet studied at college and about which you have little knowledge.	
Your organisation has a Disciplinary and Grievance policy which applies to all staff in the organisation from the most senior partner down.	
A new accountant asks you to check an advertisement which is to be placed in the local newspaper. In this he states 'We are the best accountants in the area and half the price of Jones and Co'.	

Options:

Professional Compliance	Confidentiality	Objectivity	Subjectivity
Professional Behaviour	Integration	Equality	Professional Competence

Conflicts of interest may arise during your work as an accountant and it is important you act correctly when they occur.

(b) Review each of the following situations and select the most appropriate course of action from the options provided.

(i) Whilst conducting a year-end audit at a client's business the client offers to take you on an all expenses paid holiday to her villa in Spain once you have finished the year-end work.

Politely decline the offer and do not tell anyone about it. ☐

Politely accept the offer but ask the client not to mention the holiday to any other members of the audit team. ☐

Politely accept the offer and work extremely hard to finish the year-end work. ☐

Politely decline the offer and discuss the situation with your manager. ☐

(ii) You have been asked to act as an interviewer to help assess and select prospective new trainees for your organisation. Your niece has been selected for one of the interviews.

Complete the work as interviewer but treat each interviewee fairly and don't tell anyone about your connection with one of the applicants. ☐

Complete the work as interviewer and ensure you are able to help your niece through to the next stage of the recruitment process. ☐

Refuse to be involved in any aspect of the assessment and selection of prospective trainees but do not explain to your manager why. ☐

Discuss the situation with your manager to see if you could complete the work but abstain from being involved in the assessment of your niece. ☐

(iii) You have been asked by a family friend to advise them of the names of current bidders and details of their offers regarding a contract that they wish to tender for.

Provide them with the requested details of current bidders and their offers. ☐

Provide them with the requested details of the names of the bidders but not the details of their offers. ☐

Politely decline to provide any details explaining you are not allowed to disclose such information. ☐

Provide them with incorrect details of the other bidders' offers. ☐

(c) **When can information about a client be disclosed to their spouse?**

[▼]

Picklist:

Always, they are spouses so you can disclose information.
Never, in no circumstances can you ever disclose information to a spouse.
Sometimes, but only if you have the permission of the client.

Task 11

Organisations have a moral obligation to implement sustainability initiatives which promote the long term maintenance and well-being of the environment, the economy and society as a whole.

(a) Identify which FOUR of the following are sustainability initiatives that a business may implement.

Introduce a waste recycling scheme. ☐

Recruit only fully trained staff. ☐

Use video conferencing to save staff having to travel to team meetings. ☐

Increase prices every time costs go up. ☐

Obtain goods and services from the cheapest supplier. ☐

Give all staff a pay rise every year. ☐

Introduce procedures to ensure that all electrical equipment is fully switched off each day when the office is vacated. ☐

Encourage staff not to print emails unless absolutely necessary. ☐

(b) Identify whether the following statements are true or false.

Statement	True	False
Sustainability means ensuring the organisation focuses purely on economic growth at all costs.	☐	☐
Encouraging suppliers to send electronic invoices can be part of an organisation's sustainability agenda.	☐	☐
When sourcing goods and services an organisation should check that potential suppliers have good environmental policies.	☐	☐
Planning the routes of delivery vehicles to minimise distance travelled may reduce the running costs of the organisation and also have a positive effect on the environment.	☐	☐

AAT SAMPLE ASSESSMENT 2
WORK EFFECTIVELY IN
ACCOUNTING AND FINANCE

ANSWERS

Answers to tasks

Task 1

(a) **Which ONE of the following policies and procedures is most likely to be relevant to those working in an accounting function?**

Company vehicle servicing policy ☐

Sales visit procedures ☐

Expenses payment procedures ☑

Production shift handover procedures ☐

(b) **Identify which TWO of the following statements are correct:**

The accounting function has a legal obligation to review the credit policy every two years. ☐

Organisational procedures prevent staff from suggesting improvements to work processes. ☐

It is good practice for organisations to explain the fire evacuation procedures during staff induction training. ☑

The Staff Development policy only applies to those working in the human resources department. ☐

Many organisational policies and procedures are designed to ensure that working practices comply with legal requirements. ☑

The Data Protection policy is an example of a policy that would not apply to those staff working in an accounting function. ☐

(c) Identify which TWO of the following services that staff in the accounting and payroll function would be most likely to provide to colleagues in the Production Department.

Complete the answer by writing the correct services in the box provided.

Services staff in the accounting and payroll function would be most likely to provide to colleagues in the Production Department
Budget report analysis
Payment for operator overtime hours

Task 2

(a) Add the correct job titles into the blank spaces to complete the organisation chart.

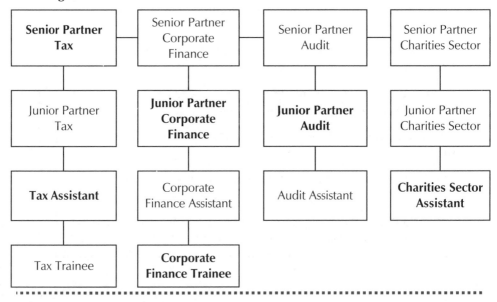

(b) Identify whether the following statements are true or false.

Statement	True	False
Ensuring the VAT bill is paid on time will help the organisation meet its legal and regulatory requirements.	✓	☐
Paying supplier invoices as soon as they are received will help the organisation's solvency.	☐	✓

Task 3

(a) **Complete the email below by inserting the email address of the recipient and the filename of any attachments and selecting TWO correct paragraphs that should be inserted into the main body of the email.**

From:	AATstudent@GCCS.com
To:	j.uwaifo@GCCS.com
Subject:	Production expenses October actual compared to budget
Attached:	PDBEOct.xls

Hello John

Paragraph 1

Paragraph 2

Regards
AAT Student

	Paragraph 1	Paragraph 2
Whilst you spent more on wages at the basic rate of pay you spent less than budget on wages at overtime rate. You spent more than budget on your protective clothing, machine oil and cleaning materials. You spent less than budget on sundry expenses. I hope you find this information useful, if you require any further analysis please do not hesitate to contact me.	☐	☐
Following the production of the latest month-end report, see attached, I herewith provide you with an analysis of your expenses paid in the month of October. Overall you spent less than budget on your total expenses by £1,645 but this is made up of different expenses in some of which you exceeded budget and in some of which you spent less than budget	☐	☐

	Paragraph 1	Paragraph 2
Whilst you spent less on wages at the basic rate of pay you spent more than budget on wages at overtime rate. You spent less than budget on your protective clothing and cleaning materials. You spent more than budget on machine oil and sundry expenses. I hope you find this information useful, if you require any further analysis please do not hesitate to contact me.	☐	✓
Following the production of the latest month-end report, see attached, I herewith provide you with an analysis of your expenses paid in the month of October. Overall you spent more than budget on your total expenses by £1,465 but this is made up of different expenses in some of which you exceeded budget and in some of which you spent less than budget.	☐	☐
Whilst you spent less on wages at the basic rate of pay you spent less than budget on wages at overtime rate. You spent more than budget on your protective clothing, machine oil and cleaning materials. You spent less than budget on sundry expenses. I hope you find this information useful, if you require any further analysis please do not hesitate to contact me.	☐	☐
Following the production of the latest month-end report, see attached, I herewith provide you with an analysis of your expenses paid in the month of October. Overall you spent more than budget on your total expenses by £1,645 but this is made up of different expenses in some of which you exceeded budget and in some of which you spent less than budget.	✓	☐

(b) Identify whether the following statements are true or false.

It is not necessary to proofread emails if they are sent to people within your organisation but external emails must always be proof read.

| False | |

The main problem with sending information in an email is that irrespective of the file size only one file may be attached to an email.

| False | |

Task 4

Complete the To Do List below for MONDAY and TUESDAY of week 2 by assigning each task to the correct position.

Please note that each task box is one hour in duration, therefore if a task takes more than one hour to complete you will be able to use the task box more than once.

MONDAY To Do List	TUESDAY To Do List	Time
Closing stock breakdown	Accounting function meeting	09:00 - 10:00
Closing stock breakdown	Region 6 expenses analysis	10:00 - 11:00
Regional reconciliation	Region 6 expenses analysis	11:00 - 12:00
Wages analysis	Petty cash top up	12:00 - 13:00

Task 5

Review the draft letter and identify EIGHT words or collections of letters or digits which are either spelt incorrectly, are inappropriate or are technically incorrect.

October Statment Reconciliation

Dear Mrs Oboh,

Many thanks for providing the October statement which we have now reviewed and compared to our records of amounts owing by you. We would like too highlight two discrepancies:

1. Your entry for £794.35 on 12.01.13 does not corespond with the invoice we have for that date. The invoice shows an amount of £749.35 for these goods.

2. Your entry for £375.29 on 26.10.13 is not known to us. We have no record of ever ordering or sending this amount of goods on this date.

Please investigate these differences as we want to be sure our records agree before we setle our account with you. If you would prefer to contact me by telephone to discuss this matter please do so as we would like to resolve these differences as soon as posible.

Yours sincerely

Task 6

(a) The annual production quantities of finished goods in numbers of units for an organisation are set out in the table below. The figures in the table are a mixture of actual values, fractions of total finished goods and percentages of total finished goods:

Product	Finished goods
A	79,872
B	11%
C	1/5
D	85,488
E	3/8
F	5%
TOTAL FINISHED GOODS (UNITS)	624,000

(i) What is the total number of units of finished goods for product B for the year?

68,640

(ii) What is the total number of units of finished goods for product C for the year?

124,800

(iii) What is the total number of units of finished goods for product E for the year?

234,000

(iv) What is the total number of units of finished goods for product F for the year?

31,200

(v) Which TWO products equate to 26.5% of the total number of units of finished goods for the organisation for the year?

Products A and D	▼

(b) The total number of units of finished goods of 624,000 showed a 4% increase over the budget for the year.

Calculate the total budget for numbers of units of finished goods for the year. If applicable, you should round your answer to TWO decimal places, for example 18.494 would become 18.49 and 18.495 would become 18.50.

600,000

Task 7

(a) **Insert the TWO most appropriate development activities that the trainee should undertake in the first six months of taking up the new role in the management accounts function. The order in which you place the activities is important, and you should place the activity with the highest importance first in the table.**

Accounting trainee's development activities
Sit with a colleague when the monthly budget reports are produced
Read a book on standard costing in a production environment

(b) **Identity TWO of the following statements which are consequences to the organisation and/or the individual of NOT maintaining appropriate and sufficient CPD activities. Drag the appropriate statements into the table provided. The order in which you place the items is not important.**

Consequences of NOT maintaining CPD activities
If knowledge is not up to date then staff could give incorrect professional advice.
A chartered accountant may be prevented from continuing as a member of their professional body.

(c) **Identify whether the following statements are true or false in relation to the completion of CPD activity.**

Statement	True	False
Conducting research in the library at the local college as part of your AAT studies is one type of CPD activity.	✓	☐
Making sure that an accounting trainee has completed sufficient CPD activities is the sole responsibility of the organisation's Human Resources department.	☐	✓

Task 8

(a) **(i)** **Identify, from the statements below. THREE conclusions and TWO recommendations that the Finance Director should present to the College Principal.**

Statement	Conclusion	Recommendation
The reduction in actual full-time course fee income when compared to the budget is fully offset by the amount that the actual part-time course fee income exceeds budget.	☐	☐
The new AAT study programme has been successful in increasing actual part-time course fee income and exceeding the budget, but the actual one day course fee income is less than the budget.	✓	☐
The faculty has been successful in reducing the actual cost of books by 25% when compared to the budget, but has overspent on the cost of teaching materials by 5% when compared to the budget.	☐	☐
The reduction in actual full-time course fee income when compared to the budget is only partially offset by the amount that the actual part-time course fee income exceeds budget.	✓	☐

Statement	Conclusion	Recommendation
The faculty should continue to cover the full-time vacancy with part-time staff as the savings made from the full-time salaries budget are more than twice the additional amount spent in part-time salaries.	☐	☑
Total actual income is less than the total budgeted income, but total actual expenditure is greater than the total budgeted expenditure.	☐	☐
The faculty should investigate why the numbers of students registering for part-time courses was less than expected.	☐	☐
The faculty should increase marketing activity to promote higher numbers of students registering for the one day practical bookkeeping course and the revision courses.	☐	☑
The reduced numbers of students registering for full-time and one day courses has led to a reduction in expenditure on registration fees.	☑	☐

(ii) **Select which of the following would be the most suitable title for this report:**

Business and finance budget ☐

Faculty income and expenditure performance review ☐

Faculty income and expenditure results ☐

Review of business and finance faculty income and expenditure against budget ☑

Review of business and finance ☐

(b) **Identify which ONE of the following describes the contents of the 'main body' section of a business report.**

Provides suggested actions to overcome the problems identified ☐

Provides an analysis of the results of the research ☑

Summarises the main points of the research and analysis ☐

Provides suggested actions to be taken in the future ☐

(c) **Complete the following statement by selecting the most appropriate answer from the list.**

When considering the order of a formal business report, which section will usually appear between the executive summary and the main body?

| Introduction ▼ |

Task 9

(a) **From the actions below select the THREE things you will do, during the morning, to help the trainee settle into their new role within your team but also to meet your work commitments to colleagues.**

Action	
Tell the Finance Trainee to go home and return after lunch when the Financial Accountant is in the office.	☐
Meet the Finance Trainee and introduce yourself and explain about the Financial Accountant not being available until lunchtime.	☑
Contact the production department to advise them of the situation and request an extension to the deadline for the budget analysis information.	☑
Tell the trainee to sit at a desk and occupy themselves by looking at some leisure magazines whilst you complete your work.	☐
Ask the trainee to think of what training courses they want to attend.	☐
Take the trainee with you as you visit members of the department to confirm attendance at the conference, introducing the new team member at the same time.	☑

(b) **Identify whether the following would or would not necessarily have a positive effect on the team performance of the finance function.**

	Would usually have a positive effect	Would not necessarily have a positive effect
Having a leader who does not encourage communication with other team members.	☐	✓
Ensuring there are at least four members in the team.	☐	✓
Selecting team members that have complementary experiences and skills.	✓	☐

Task 10

It is important that those who work within an accounting function uphold fundamental ethical principles.

The table below details four situations which may arise in business.

(a) **From the options provided select the fundamental ethical principle that applies in each situation. Note each option may be used more than once.**

Situation	Fundamental ethical principle applicable
You are asked by a colleague to provide the contact details of a client as they were at school together.	Confidentiality
You have been asked to complete a VAT return which is a subject you have not yet studied at college and about which you have little knowledge.	Professional Compliance
Your organisation has a Disciplinary and Grievance policy which applies to all staff in the organisation from the most senior partner down.	Equality
A new accountant asks you to check an advertisement which is to be placed in the local newspaper. In this he states 'We are the best accountants in the area and half the price of Jones and Co'.	Professional Behaviour

(b) **Review each of the following situations and select the most appropriate course of action from the options provided.**

(i) Whilst conducting a year-end audit at a client's business the client offers to take you on an all expenses paid holiday to her villa in Spain once you have finished the year-end work.

Politely decline the offer and do not tell anyone about it. ☐

Politely accept the offer but ask the client not to mention the holiday to any other members of the audit team. ☐

Politely accept the offer and work extremely hard to finish the year-end work. ☐

Politely decline the offer and discuss the situation with your manager. ☑

(ii) You have been asked to act as an interviewer to help assess and select prospective new trainees for your organisation. Your niece has been selected for one of the interviews.

Complete the work as interviewer but treat each interviewee fairly and don't tell anyone about your connection with one of the applicants. ☐

Complete the work as interviewer and ensure you are able to help your niece through to the next stage of the recruitment process. ☐

Refuse to be involved in any aspect of the assessment and selection of prospective trainees but do not explain to your manager why. ☐

Discuss the situation with your manager to see if you could complete the work but abstain from being involved in the assessment of your niece. ☑

(iii) You have been asked by a family friend to advise them of the names of current bidders and details of their offers regarding a contract that they wish to tender for.

Provide them with the requested details of current bidders and their offers. ☐

Provide them with the requested details of the names of the bidders but not the details of their offers. ☐

Politely decline to provide any details explaining you are not allowed to disclose such information. ☑

Provide them with incorrect details of the other bidders' offers. ☐

(c) **When can information about a client be disclosed to their spouse?**

> Sometimes, but only if you have the permission of the client. ▼

Task 11

(a) **Identify which FOUR of the following are sustainability initiatives that a business may implement.**

Introduce a waste recycling scheme. ☑

Recruit only fully trained staff. ☐

Use video conferencing to save staff having to travel to team meetings. ☑

Increase prices every time costs go up. ☐

Obtain goods and services from the cheapest supplier. ☐

Give all staff a pay rise every year. ☐

Introduce procedures to ensure that all electrical equipment is fully switched off each day when the office is vacated. ☑

Encourage staff not to print emails unless absolutely necessary. ☑

(b) **Identify whether the following statements are true or false.**

Statement	True	False
Sustainability means ensuring the organisation focuses purely on economic growth at all costs.	☐	☑
Encouraging suppliers to send electronic invoices can be part of an organisation's sustainability agenda.	☑	☐
When sourcing goods and services an organisation should check that potential suppliers have good environmental policies.	☑	☐
Planning the routes of delivery vehicles to minimise distance travelled may reduce the running costs of the organisation and also have a positive effect on the environment.	☑	☐

BPP PRACTICE ASSESSMENT
WORK EFFECTIVELY IN
ACCOUNTING AND FINANCE

Time allowed: 2 hours

PRACTICE ASSESSMENT

Tasks

Task 1.1

You work for a company in the accounts department. You have been passed a company 'information' policy that your manager says is relevant to you when carrying out your daily tasks.

An extract from the policy is given below:

INFORMATION POLICY
■ Personal data must be accurate.
■ Personal data must only be kept for as long as necessary.
■ Personal data must be kept securely.
■ No information about customers or employees must be revealed to other customers or employees

(a) Complete the following sentence by selecting the appropriate option from the picklist.

This policy has been compiled to aid compliance with

Picklist

Employee Protection Legislation
Data Protection Legislation
Confidentiality of Information Legislation

The accounting department will provide information to other departments within the business.

(b) **Select ONE type of information that will be provided by the accounting department to EACH of the departments shown below.**

Draw lines between the left hand side and right hand side boxes to indicate your selections. *(CBT instruction: Select your answer by clicking on the left hand box and then on the right hand box. You can remove a line by clicking on it.)*

Department the accounting department will provide information to	**Information**
Sales Department	Analysis of cash payments and receipts
Purchasing Department	Analysis of sales revenue by region compared to budget
	Details of employee costs
	Discrepancies between supplier invoices and purchase orders

Task 1.2

For each of the following actions, indicate whether they primarily contribute to:

- Compliance with applicable laws and regulations
- The management of working capital and solvency
- The smooth running of the business

Action	Contributes to:	
Reduce customer credit terms so they pay their debts earlier		▼
Ensure IT support is in place in case staff encounter computer problems		▼
Produce a Health and Safety policy to be circulated to all staff		▼
Ensure all staff are paid at least the minimum wage		▼
Ensure staff recruited for each job have the relevant experience and skills		▼
Avoid the build up of surplus inventories		▼

Picklist

Compliance with applicable laws and regulations

The management of working capital and solvency

The smooth running of the business

Task 1.3

You work in the accounts department and have been asked by your Manager, Nigel Allen, to send a memo to David Wright, a manager in the sales department. You know David well as you often provide him with financial analysis. Nigel wants you to let David know that the accounting department needs to receive all sales department expense claims relating to expenses in May 20X2 by 10 June 20X2. This is so that all sales department staff can be reimbursed for their May expenses before the end of June 20X2. Today's date is 1 June 20X2.

Complete the memo below. Select the appropriate items from the picklists.

MEMO

From: AAT student

To: (1) [▼]

Date: (2) [▼]

Subject: (3) [▼]

(4) [▼] , accounts department manager, has asked me to inform you that this month, all sales department expense claims relating to

(5) [▼] expenses must be passed to the accounting department by

(6) [▼] at the latest.

This is so that we can ensure all (7) [▼] employees are reimbursed before the end of (8) [▼] .

Thanks

AAT Student

Picklists

(1)   David Write / Nigel Allen / David Right / Nigel Alan / David Wright
(2)   31 May 20X2 / 1 June 20X2 / 10 June 20X2 / 30 June 20X2
(3)   Providing financial analysis / Expense claim deadline / Meeting notification
(4)   David Write / Nigel Allen / David Right / Nigel Alan / David Wright
(5)   May 20X2 / June 20X2 / July 20X2
(6)   31 May 20X2 / 1 June 20X2 / 10 June 20X2 / 30 June 20X2
(7)   sales department / accounting department
(8)   May 20X2 / June 20X2 / July 20X2

Task 1.4

(a) It is Friday morning. A colleague usually banks the weekly cash on a Friday morning. As the colleague is on holiday, she has left a note asking you to do it. Your line manager has also asked you to complete some project work which you think will take all of Friday. You are not sure that you will have time to do both tasks and you know that the business is suffering from cash flow problems.

Which TWO of the following are possible consequences of you NOT banking the money on Friday?

The business may have insufficient funds available to pay a debt becoming payable next week ☐

You will not be able to complete the work for your line manager ☐

You will be able to complete the work for your line manager ☐

The money will not have to be banked by someone else ☐

(b) **Complete the following sentence.**

The most appropriate action to take is:

▼

.

Picklist

Bank the money and then move on to the project work

Explain the situation to your manager and try and find a solution

Complete the project work and bank the money next week

Throw away the note from your colleague and claim you did not receive it

Your weekly workload (excluding completed tasks) is shown in the table below. You need to carry out all these tasks, but you also have to respond to business needs as required. Your working day is 9:30am to 5:30pm. Your lunch break is an hour long (12:30pm to 1:30pm). It is 9:30am on Wednesday and you have completed your routine tasks on time so far this week.

Your remaining tasks for the week are as follows:

Task	Task to be completed by:		Task duration
	Day	Time	
Receivables reconciliation	Thursday	09:30	45 minutes
Supplier statement reconciliations	Thursday	10:15	1 hour
Calculate depreciation and process the related journals	Wednesday	11:30	1.5 hours
Collect and distribute post	Every day	10:00	30 minutes
Enter cash payments and receipts	Every day	17:00	3 hours
Prepare payroll listing	Friday	15:00	1 hour
Bank reconciliation	Friday	13:00	2 hours

On arriving at your desk, you pick up an email informing you that the Managing Director has called a meeting to brief all employees on a proposed project to relocate the business to another nearby premises. All employees must attend the briefing at 11:30am which will last for 1 hour.

(c) **Complete the To Do list below for WEDNESDAY by selecting the appropriate tasks from the Picklist provided.**

WEDNESDAY To Do List		Order of task completion
	▼	First task
	▼	Second task
	▼	Third task
	▼	Fourth task
	▼	Fifth task
	▼	Sixth task

Picklist

Receivables reconciliation

Supplier statement reconciliations

Calculate depreciation and process the related journals

Collect and distribute post

Enter cash payments and receipts

Prepare payroll listing

Briefing from Managing Director

Bank reconciliation

Task 1.5

This is a draft of a letter to be addressed to Mrs Baxter, a supplier, querying an invoice because the goods she supplied were damaged when they arrived.

Review the draft letter and Identify FIVE words which are spelled incorrectly, or are inappropriate. *(CBT instructions: Click on a word to select it and click on the word again if you want to remove your selection.)*

Hello Ms Baxter

I am writing to query an invoice with reference AB123. The invoice is for goods we received from you on 1 July 2012. A copy of invoice AB123 is inclosed.

Staff at our warehouse inspected the goods when they arrived and found that they had been damaged in transit. In accordance with the contract we have in place with you, the goods are being returned to you and I would be greatful if you could issue a credit note for the full amount shown on invoice AB123.

We look forward to hearing from you.

Yours hopefully

Task 1.6

You have been looking at a presentation which the assistant management accountant is preparing. The pie chart below looks fine but it would be helpful if there were some numbers. These appear to have been missed off.

(a) Using the percentages from the pie chart, fill in the sales figures below.

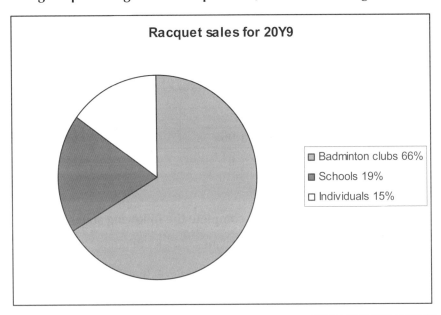

	Sales £
Badminton clubs	
Schools	
Individuals	
Total	**5,912,000**

You have recently been working in the payroll section and have a schedule to complete.

(b) Calculate the missing figures on the spreadsheet extract (given below). Give your answers to the nearest whole number.

	A	B	C
1	Employee name	Qualifying salary	NI at 12%
2	A Lot	3,600	
3	B Good	1,210	
4	C Clearly	1,550	
5	D Light	999	
6	E Bygum	2,566	
7	F Blinding	1,961	
8	G Wizz	817	

(c) Using the information above, complete the following statement

The sum of the qualifying salaries of F Blinding and D Light is

[▼] the amount arrived at if the qualifying salary of G Wizz is subtracted from the qualifying salary of A Lot.

Picklist

the same as

less than

greater than

Task 1.7

There are many benefits of employees undergoing Continuous Professional Development (CPD). The ongoing development of relevant skills and knowledge can be beneficial to both the individual and the organisation.

(a) **Indicate whether the following statements in relation to CPD, training and development are true or false.**

Statement	True/False
Employers who invest in the ongoing training and development of employees will need to increase supervision of those employees in the long term.	▼
Employers are solely responsible for ensuring employees meet their CPD requirements.	▼
CPD requirements usually only apply to full members rather than student members of professional accountancy bodies.	▼
Although accountancy bodies require their members to undertake CPD, members are not required to keep a record of their CPD activity.	▼

Picklist

True

False

You work as an accounts assistant reporting to the accounting department manager. No staff report to you.

A recent appraisal with your manager highlighted that despite your many strengths (including being proficient in the use of spreadsheets and computerised accounting packages) you have two weaknesses that have become apparent over the last six months. These are preventing you from completing your tasks as efficiently as you could do.

The weaknesses are:

- You are too willing to take on extra work when you already have a full workload.

- Your word processing skills are poor and this means it takes you a long time to complete routine correspondence.

(b) Indicate which TWO of the following development opportunities could address these weaknesses.

Attend a leadership course aimed at improving management skills.	☐
Attend a training course aimed at improving assertiveness.	☐
Study the quickstart guide that accompanies the computerised accounting package you use.	☐
Complete an online course which takes you through the key features of word processing packages and how to use them.	☐
Complete an online course which takes you through the key features of spreadsheet packages and how to use them.	☐

Task 1.8

You are helping to prepare a report to present the findings of a recent project commissioned to establish how effectively key internal controls are operating within the business and within individual departments. Internal controls are processes that help to make sure the organisation or an area of the business meets its objectives, so it is important they are working properly (operating effectively). The findings from the project have been summarised below:

Department	Number of key controls identified	Number of key controls tested	No. of key controls found to be operating effectively
Accounting	20	18	10
Personnel	12	10	6
Purchasing	14	12	7
Sales	16	10	7

(a) **In which section of the report is the table above most likely to appear?**

Executive Summary ☐

Introduction ☐

Appendix ☐

Recommendations Section ☐

(b) **Which THREE of the following are valid conclusions for the report?**

The majority of the key controls tested are operating effectively. ☐

The majority of the key controls identified are operating effectively. ☐

The majority of the key controls identified were tested. ☐

Based on the key controls tested, the sales department had the highest percentage of key controls operating effectively. ☐

Based on the key controls identified, the purchasing department had the highest percentage of its key controls tested. ☐

The same number of key controls were tested in the purchasing department as in the sales department. ☐

(c) **Complete the following sentence to give a valid recommendation for inclusion in the report.**

There should be an investigation into

▼

Picklist

how the ineffective key controls can be modified to ensure they operate effectively

why the accounting department has more key controls than each of the other departments

why only a minority of controls were tested

Task 1.9

(a) Complete the following sentence.

A(n) [_____ ▼] is used to show the structure of an organisation or function.

Picklist

Job description
Person specification
Organisation chart
Personnel chart

An accounting department, headed up by the finance director (James Smith) also has:

- A financial accountant (Jill Jones)
- A management accountant (Bill Williams)
- A management accounts assistant (Emily Brooks)
- A financial accounts assistant (Nicky Rivers)

(b) Which TWO of the following statements are true?

Jill reports to Bill	☐
James reports to Jill	☐
Nicky reports to Bill	☐
Nicky reports to Jill	☐
Bill reports to James	☐
Emily reports to Jill	☐

When there are conflicts in the workplace then you could try to resolve some issues yourself but others will have to be referred to your line manager.

(c) **Which of the following issues would you try to resolve yourself and which would you refer to your line manager?**

Issue	Resolve myself	Refer to line manager
Your line manager has asked you to complete a calculation of wage deductions. However, having started to look at the calculation, it is more complex than you thought and you do not feel you have not had enough training to be able to perform it.	☐	☐
You suspect a colleague has been setting up fictitious employees on the payroll in order to commit fraud.	☐	☐
Your colleague has asked you to swap your work for the afternoon with her work, as yours looks more 'exciting'. However you do not know how to carry out her tasks.	☐	☐
Your feel you are being bullied by a colleague.	☐	☐

....

Task 1.10

(a) **Identify which THREE of the following are fundamental ethical principles by writing (CBT drag and drop) the appropriate principles into the table:**

Fundamental ethical principles

Picklist

Materiality

Control

Peace of mind

Professional competence

Confidentiality

Due care

(b) **State which ONE of the following situations is an example of where a conflict of interest may arise:**

You regularly complete accounting work at a client's premises. ☐

Your manager takes the whole department for a meal at lunchtime to celebrate the year's financial results. ☐

You are asked to audit the accounts of your aunt's business when you have been writing up the books for the past year. ☐

You are asked to complete the accounts of a local car retailer from which your family often purchase their cars. ☐

(c) **Identify whether the following statements are true or false:**

Statement	True	False
Those working within an accounting environment do not need to act with integrity.	☐	☐
Personal information of a client cannot be given to other people unless the client authorises it.	☐	☐
Information about the income generated by a client listed on the Stock Exchange can be discussed with your friends as at the end of the year the organisation will publish its financial results.	☐	☐
A conflict of interest never has to be declared if the employee feels happy about the situation.	☐	☐

Task 1.11

(a) **Identify which THREE of the following are sustainability initiatives which a business may implement:**

Hold all meetings face-to face rather than virtually. ☐

Have all corridor, hall, and passage lighting linked to motion sensors so they automatically switch off when no one is using them. ☐

Always select the most competitively priced suppliers of goods and services. ☐

Ensure all qualified accountants complete CPD. ☐

Do business with any organisations regardless of their environmental practices. ☐

Ensure costs and expenses are minimised in every instance. ☐

Arrange monthly management meetings virtually rather than at head office. ☐

Encourage employees not to print out emails.

(b) **Identify whether the following statements are true or false:**

Statement	True	False
Sustainability means ensuring the organisation focuses purely on generating the highest profit possible after taking into account the consequences of the organisation's actions.	☐	☐
When installing a new heating system, trying to ensure the work is carbon neutral even if this results in increased initial costs is an example of a sustainable initiative by the organisation.	☐	☐
Sustainability initiatives apply to all functions within an organisation.	☐	☐
Having a policy of office buildings being heated at the lowest possible cost will have a positive effect on the environment.	☐	☐

BPP PRACTICE ASSESSMENT WORK EFFECTIVELY IN ACCOUNTING AND FINANCE

ANSWERS

Answers to tasks

Task 1.1

(a) The correct answer is:

This policy has been compiled to aid compliance with

Data Protection Legislation

(b) The correct answer is:

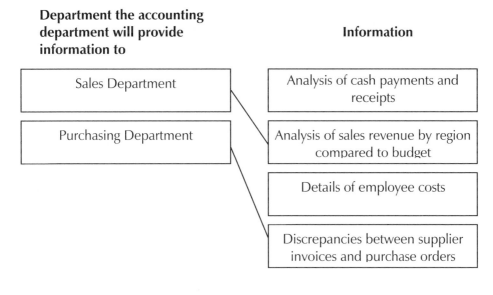

Department the accounting department will provide information to	**Information**
Sales Department	Analysis of cash payments and receipts
Purchasing Department	Analysis of sales revenue by region compared to budget
	Details of employee costs
	Discrepancies between supplier invoices and purchase orders

Task 1.2

The correct answer is:

Action	Contributes to:
Reduce customer credit terms so they pay their debts earlier	The management of working capital and solvency
Ensure IT support is in place in case staff encounter computer problems	The smooth running of the business
Produce a Health and Safety policy to be circulated to all staff	Compliance with applicable laws and regulations
Ensure all staff are paid at least the minimum wage	Compliance with applicable laws and regulations
Ensure staff recruited for each job have the relevant experience and skills	The smooth running of the business
Avoid the build up of surplus inventories	The management of working capital and solvency

Task 1.3

MEMO

From: AAT student

To: **(1)** David Wright

Date: **(2)** 1 June 20X2

Subject: **(3)** Expense claim deadline

(4) Nigel Allen , accounts department manager, has asked me to inform you that this month, all sales department expense claims relating to **(5)** May 20X2 expenses must be passed to the accounting department by **(6)** 10 June 20X2 at the latest.

This is so that we can ensure all **(7)** sales department employees are reimbursed before the end of **(8)** June 20X2 .

Thanks

AAT Student

Task 1.4

(a) The correct answer is:

The business may have insufficient funds available to pay a debt becoming payable next week ✓

You will not be able to complete the work for your line manager ☐

You will be able to complete the work for your line manager ✓

The money will not have to be banked by someone else ☐

(b) The correct answer is:

The most appropriate action to take is:

Explain the situation to your manager and try and find a solution.

(c) The correct answer is:

WEDNESDAY To Do List	Order of task completion
Collect and distribute post	First task
Calculate depreciation and process the related journals	Second task
Briefing from Managing Director	Third task
Enter cash payments and receipts	Fourth task
Receivables reconciliation	Fifth task
Supplier statement reconciliations	Sixth task

This results in the following timetable and ensures all tasks are completed on time:

Task/break	Duration (hrs)	Task order	Time period
Collect and distribute post	0.5	First task	09:30 to 10:00
Calculate depreciation and process the related journals	1.5	Second task	10:00 to 11:30
Briefing from Managing Director	1	Third task	11:30 to 12:30
LUNCH	1		12:30 to 13:30
Enter cash payments and receipts	3	Fourth task	13:30 to 16:30
Receivables reconciliation	0.75	Fifth task	16:30 to 17:15
Supplier statement reconciliations	0.25 (of 1)	Sixth task	17:15 to 17:30*

*Starting this task will mean it can be completed before the deadline on Thursday since there will only be 45 more minutes worth of work to do on Thursday morning.

Task 1.5

The incorrect/inappropriate words are underlined and in bold.

<u>Hello</u> <u>Ms</u> Baxter

I am writing to query an invoice with reference AB123. The invoice is for goods we received from you on 1 July 2012. A copy of invoice AB123 is **<u>inclosed</u>**.

Staff at our warehouse inspected the goods when they arrived and found that they had been damaged in transit. In accordance with the contract we have in place with you, the goods are being returned to you and I would be **<u>greatful</u>** if you could issue a credit note for the full amount shown on invoice AB123.

We look forward to hearing from you.

Yours **<u>hopefully</u>**

Tutorial note:

The corrected letter would look like this:

<u>Dear</u> <u>Mrs</u> Baxter

I am writing to query an invoice with reference AB123. The invoice is for goods we received from you on 1 July 2012. A copy of invoice AB123 is **<u>enclosed</u>**.

Staff at our warehouse inspected the goods when they arrived and found that they had been damaged in transit. In accordance with the contract we have in place with you, the goods are being returned to you and I would be **<u>grateful</u>** if you could issue a credit note for the full amount shown on invoice AB123.

We look forward to hearing from you.

Yours **<u>sincerely</u>**

Task 1.6

(a) The correct answer is:

		Sales £
Badminton clubs	(5,912,000/100) x 66	3,901,920
Schools	(5,912,000/100) x 19	1,123,280
Individuals	(5,912,000/100) x 15	886,800
Total		**5,912,000**

(b) The correct answer is:

	A	B	C
1	Employee name	Qualifying salary	NI at 12%
2	A Lot	3,600	432
3	B Good	1,210	145
4	C Clearly	1,550	186
5	D Light	999	120
6	E Bygum	2,566	308
7	F Blinding	1,961	235
8	G Wizz	817	98

(c) The correct answer is:

The sum of the qualifying salaries of F Blinding and D Light is ⟨ greater than ⟩ the amount arrived at if the qualifying salary of G Wizz is subtracted from the qualifying salary of A Lot.

Workings

F Blinding plus D Light = £1,961 + £999 = £2,960

A Lot less G Wizz = £3,600 – £817 = £2,783

Task 1.7

(a) The correct answer is:

Statement	True/False
Employers who invest in the ongoing training and development of employees will need to increase supervision of those employees in the long term.	False
Employers are solely responsible for ensuring employees meet their CPD requirements.	False
CPD requirements usually only apply to full members rather than student members of professional accountancy bodies.	False
Although accountancy bodies require their members to undertake CPD, members are not required to keep a record of their CPD activity.	False

Reasoning:

Employers who invest in the ongoing training and development of employees should be able to **decrease** supervision of those employees in the long term as they become more skilled.

Employees are responsible for their CPD and should work with their employee to undertake suitable learning and development.

CPD requirements **apply to both full members and student members** of professional accountancy bodies

CPD activity should be recorded.

(b) The correct answer is:

Attend a leadership course aimed at improving management skills.	☐
Attend a training course aimed at improving assertiveness.	☑
Study the quickstart guide that accompanies the computerised accounting package you use.	☐
Complete an online course which takes you through the key features of word processing packages and how to use them.	☑
Complete an online course which takes you through the key features of spreadsheet packages and how to use them.	☐

Task 1.8

(a) The correct answer is:

Executive Summary ☑

Introduction ☐

Appendix ☐

Recommendations Section ☐

The table is essentially a summary of the key findings so should appear in the executive summary.

(b) The correct answer is:

The majority of the key controls tested are operating effectively. ☑

The majority of the key controls identified are operating effectively. ☐

The majority of the key controls identified were tested. ☑

Based on the key controls tested, the sales department had the highest percentage of key controls operating effectively. ☑

Based on the key controls identified, the purchasing department had the highest percentage of its key controls tested. ☐

The same number of key controls were tested in the purchasing department as in the sales department. ☐

The first conclusion is valid as more than half of the controls **that were tested** were found to be operating effectively in each department. Therefore the majority of those tested are operating effectively.

The second conclusion is not valid. In total only 30 of the 62 key controls **identified** were found to be operating effectively (since the rest were not operating effectively or were not tested). Therefore it is not possible to conclude the majority of all the key controls are definitely operating effectively (although to say 'based on those tested it is likely they are' is a more reasonable conclusion).

The third conclusion is valid, since 50 of the 62 key controls identified were tested.

The fourth conclusion is also valid. Of the key controls tested in the sales department, 70% (7/10) were found to be operating effectively. This compares to 56% in accounting, 60% in personnel and 58% in purchasing.

The fifth conclusion is not valid, as purchasing only had 86% (12/14) of its identified controls tested. Accounting had 90% (18/20) of its identified controls tested.

The final conclusion is also invalid. 12 key controls were tested in purchasing, only 10 were tested in sales.

(c) **Complete the following sentence to give a valid recommendation for inclusion in the report.**

There should be an investigation into

how the ineffective key controls can be modified to ensure they operate effectively

It is important to the business that the controls are operating effectively (as stated in the task information). Therefore the business should seek to make sure any controls that were found not to be working properly are modified so that they do.

Task 1.9

(a) The correct answer is:

An | Organisation chart | is used to show the structure of an organisation or function.

(b) The correct answer is:

Jill reports to Bill ☐

James reports to Jill ☐

Nicky reports to Bill ☐

Nicky reports to Jill ☑

Bill reports to James ☑

Emily reports to Jill ☐

(c) The correct answer is:

Issue	Resolve myself	Refer to line manager
Your line manager has asked you to complete a calculation of wage deductions. However, having started to look at the calculation, it is more complex than you thought and you do not feel you have not had enough training to be able to perform it.	☐	☑
You suspect a colleague has been setting up fictitious employees on the payroll in order to commit fraud.	☐	☑
Your colleague has asked you to swap your work for the afternoon with her work, as yours looks more 'exciting'. However you do not know how to carry out her tasks.	☑	☐
Your feel you are being bullied by a colleague.	☐	☑

Task 1.10

(a) Identify which THREE of the following are fundamental ethical principles by writing (CBT drag and drop) the appropriate principles into the table:

Fundamental ethical principles
Professional competence
Confidentiality
Due care

(b) State which ONE of the following situations is an example of where a conflict of interest may arise:

You regularly complete accounting work at a client's premises. ☐

Your manager takes the whole department for a meal at lunchtime to celebrate the year's financial results. ☐

You are asked to audit the accounts of your aunt's business when you have been writing up the books for the past year ☑

You are asked to complete the accounts of a local car retailer from which your family often purchase their cars. ☐

(c) Identify whether the following statements are true or false:

Statement	True	False
Those working within an accounting environment do not need to act with integrity	☐	☑
Personal information of a client cannot be given to other people unless the client authorises it	☑	☐
Information about the income generated by a client listed on the Stock Exchange can be discussed with your friends as at the end of the year the organisation will publish its financial results	☐	☑
A conflict of interest never has to be declared if the employee feels happy about the situation	☐	☑

Task 1.11

(a)   Identify which THREE of the following are sustainability initiatives which a business may implement:

Hold all meetings face-to face rather than virtually. ☐

Have all corridor, hall, and passage lighting linked to motion sensors so they automatically switch off when no one is using them. ☑

Always select the most competitively priced suppliers of goods and services. ☐

Ensure all qualified accountants complete CPD. ☐

Do business with any organisations regardless of their environmental practices. ☐

Ensure costs and expenses are minimised in every instance. ☐

Arrange monthly management meetings virtually rather than at head office. ☑

Encourage employees not to print out emails. ☑

(b)   **Identify whether the following statements are true or false:**

Statement	True	False
Sustainability means ensuring the organisation focuses purely on generating the highest profit possible after taking into account the consequences of the organisation's actions.	☑	☐
When installing a new heating system, trying to ensure the work is carbon neutral even if this results in increased initial costs is an example of a sustainable initiative by the organisation.	☑	☐
Sustainability initiatives apply to all functions within an organisation.	☑	☐
Having a policy of office buildings being heated at the lowest possible cost will have a positive effect on the environment.	☐	☑

INDEX

Notes

REVIEW FORM

How have you used this Combined Text and Question Bank?
(Tick one box only)

☐ Home study

☐ On a course_____

☐ Other _____

Why did you decide to purchase this Combined Text and Question Bank?
(Tick one box only)

☐ Have used BPP Texts in the past

☐ Recommendation by friend/colleague

☐ Recommendation by a college lecturer

☐ Saw advertising

☐ Other _____

During the past six months do you recall seeing/receiving either of the following?
(Tick as many boxes as are relevant)

☐ Our advertisement in Accounting Technician

☐ Our Publishing Catalogue

Which (if any) aspects of our advertising do you think are useful?
(Tick as many boxes as are relevant)

☐ Prices and publication dates of new editions

☐ Information on Text content

☐ Details of our free online offering

☐ None of the above

Your ratings, comments and suggestions would be appreciated on the following areas of this Text.

	Very useful	Useful	Not useful
Introductory section	☐	☐	☐
Quality of explanations	☐	☐	☐
How it works	☐	☐	☐
Chapter tasks	☐	☐	☐
Chapter overviews	☐	☐	☐
Question and answer bank	☐	☐	☐
Assessments	☐	☐	☐
Test your learning	☐	☐	☐
Index	☐	☐	☐

	Excellent	Good	Adequate	Poor
Overall opinion of this publication	☐	☐	☐	☐

Do you intend to continue using BPP Products? ☐ Yes ☐ No

Please note any further comments and suggestions/errors on the reverse of this page. The Head of Programme of this edition can be emailed at: nisarahmed@bpp.com

Please return to: Nisar Ahmed, AAT Head of Programme, BPP Learning Media Ltd, FREEPOST, London, W12 8AA.

REVIEW FORM (continued)

TELL US WHAT YOU THINK

Please note any further comments and suggestions/errors below